CHOICES

CHANGES

Joni Eareckson Tada

ZONDERVAN BOOKS 🎵 GRAND RAPIDS, MICHIGAN

CHOICES . . . CHANGES
Copyright © 1986 by Joni Eareckson Tada

Zondervan Books are published by the Zondervan Publishing House
1415 Lake Drive S.E., Grand Rapids, Michigan 49506

Library of Congress Cataloging in Publication Data

Tada, Joni Eareckson.
Choices, changes.

Bibliography: p.
1. Tada, Joni Eareckson. 2. Christian biography —
United States. I. Title.
BR1725.T2A3   1986   209'.2'4   [B]   86-18947
ISBN 0-310-24010-7

The following songs have been quoted in this book: "Joni's Waltz" by
Nancy Honeytree, 1979, copyright © 1981 by Word Music (a division of
Word, Inc.). All rights reserved. International copyright secured. Used by
permission. "When Pretty Things Get Broken" by Joni Eareckson Tada.
Copyright © 1982 by Word Music. All rights reserved. International
copyright secured. Used by permission. "Journey's End" by Rob
Tregenza. Copyright © 1982 by World Wide Pictures. From the motion
picture *Joni*. Used by permission.

Unless otherwise specified in the Notes, Scripture references are from the
New International Version (North American Edition), copyright © 1973,
1978, 1984, by the International Bible Society. Used by permission of
Zondervan Bible Publishers.

Designed and edited by Judith E. Markham

Printed in the United States of America

86 87 88 89 90 91 / 10 9 8 7 6 5 4 3 2 1

To Ken

CONTENTS

ACKNOWLEDGMENTS

Special thanks to World Wide Pictures for taking a bold step with the movie Joni. Their film gave shape to my conviction of how the power of Christ can slice through the anger or indifference of someone with a severe disability. And much gratitude to the Billy Graham Evangelistic Association for their encouragement and support in the launching of Joni and Friends, our ministry that brings together Christians and disabled people throughout the world.

Dr. John MacArthur and the Special Ministries Department of Grace Community Church have lent time and staff in helping Joni and Friends design and implement its materials and workshops.

Dr. Sam Britten and the Center of Achievement for the Physically Disabled have also provided their expertise and advice on understanding and meeting the needs of those with disabilities.

I am grateful for the understanding Joni and Friends staff and volunteers who quietly passed by my closed office door as I shut myself away to write this book. Also my appreciation to Judy Butler for telling me, "You can do it!" She along with Bev Singleton, Francie Lorey, and Joe Davis were my sounding boards as well as my hands in pulling together the manuscript.

Thank you, Judith Markham, my editor, for teaching me more about the craft of writing.

And thank you, Steve Estes, for helping me find "my style."

In my third episode, several ideas were borrowed from Mike Mason's *The Mystery of Marriage*. He put into remarkable words what my husband and I are experiencing each day.

Also, Ken and I have enjoyed using Chuck Swindoll's

devotional *Seasons of Life,* and I have echoed his essay on "Risking Liberty" at the close of my first episode.

Liv Ullman's autobiography, *Changing,* touched me deeply, and I often read her chapters for stylistic inspiration.

But God's Word and its constant admonition to "speak the truth in love" remained the plumb line of my content.

He changes times and seasons.
—Daniel 2:21

*All of us, then, reflect the glory of the Lord with
uncovered faces; and that same glory, coming
from the Lord . . . transforms us into His
likeness in an ever greater degree of glory.*
—2 Corinthians 3:18 (GOOD NEWS BIBLE)

INTRODUCTION

Here I sit in the middle of eternity, asking God to transform me into His shining likeness. That, to me, is an exhilarating prospect, even if a bit frightening. But that's not all. He expects me to uncover my face — a thought more frightening than exhilarating.

There is danger in doing that. A risk. My books *Joni* and *A Step Further* were a risky uncovering of my life. But there have been so many choices and changes since then. Sometimes I have cowered behind a carefully constructed façade. Other times I have been too much the bold spiritual exhibitionist, wearing my faith on my sleeve.

But mostly I have lived life between the two extremes.

So I've prayed — really prayed — about opening my life in this book. It's not *Joni.* Twenty years have passed since I broke my neck in that diving accident. Nor is it a walk through theology like *A Step Further.*

Instead, you hold in your hands my journal in which I write about sin and its subtlety to deceive and manipulate my heart. About a choice to grow, changing from a young girl into a mature woman. And about the risk of opening my life to one man, the man I believe in with all my heart.

Why do I put these things in a book? Obviously, I hope to play a small part in building up your faith in Christ. And for those who remain skeptical about God and the Bible, I believe I offer some reasons why life in Christ makes real sense.

But there's more. And it has a lot to do with "sitting in the middle of eternity." This wheelchair has helped me sit still. I've observed with curiosity the way we Christians grasp for the future, as if the present didn't quite satisfy. How we, in spiritual fits and starts, scrape and scratch our way along, often missing the best of life while looking the other way, preoccupied with shaping our future.

In my least consistent moments I too try to wrest the future out of His hands. Or worse, I sink back into the past and rest on long-ago laurels. But God is most concerned with the choices I make now. I know — truly know — what God expects of me. An uncovering. An unmasking. He expects me to change.

And what sort of change, may I ask so gently, does God expect in you? Are you impatient about sitting in the middle? Do you feel you must grab ground for your future, a future in which you hope God won't mind going along with your plans and dreams?

God, standing silently and invisibly and presently with us in the middle of eternity, is interested in a certain kind of change. And as Oswald Chambers has mused, "If we have a further end in view, we do not pay sufficient attention to the immediate present: if we realize that obedience is the end, then each moment as it comes is precious."

For this reason I write *Choices . . . Changes* in the first person present. Because it is happening now — right now. I do not know how the Spirit of Christ performs it, but He brings us choices through which we never-endingly change, fresh and new, into His likeness.

Uncover your face with me. It's a risk. But the journey is full of surprises.

The Movie

Surely you desire truth in the inner parts.
—Psalm 51:6

Tanned hands grasp the edge of the raft, and in one graceful motion she lifts her body out of the water. She reaches up and smooths her blond hair back, wringing it in a tiny knot at the base of her neck. She tugs at the elastic of her royal blue bathing suit and shakes the water from each leg. In another fluid movement, knees bend, arms swing, and she pitches forward in a dive. Her body slices the surface of the water. She is under.

"Cut! That's a print!" the director, Jim Collier, yells from a rubber raft floating nearby.

I am jarred back to the present. The actress, tall and brown with a blond wig, could easily be mistaken for me. Except that I sit at the water's edge. In my wheelchair.

They will film me next. Taking over where the actress left off, I am to float face down in the water. Another actress, playing the part of my sister Kathy, will rescue me.

I wait while the crew members position lights and reflectors, anchor the movie camera to the crane, and float the sound equipment out by the raft. Sound men and cameramen bustle about quietly.

They eye me politely, and I sense a tension in them. Either they are apprehensive because this scene is being shot without rehearsals or because they think I'm nervous. I'm not. The past is far behind me. I can't be touched by memories of my accident so many years ago. God is in control of my life now. I have His grace. I am content.

I eye the crew politely in return, feeling my own form of hesitancy. I wonder what they think of my faith. I'd like to help these men and women know Jesus. Maybe they'll see Him in my life or hear about Him in the script. The producer has given them each a copy of my book *Joni*. I hope they read it.

A sound man carries a boom mike on his shoulder and smiles as he passes. I return his smile and imagine his thoughts: "Handicapped people need religion."

The girl in the blue bathing suit is back on shore now. She flings a terry towel over her shoulders and presses a corner of it to her face, smiling and chatting with another crew member.

My mind replays her short scene. The velvet way she slipped out of the water, hands slicking the wetness from her hair and suit. The hot sun glazing the natural tawny glow of her skin. She waves at me. Embarrassed to be caught staring at her, I quickly acknowledge her greeting and then look down.

I sit slouched. I watch a breeze lift the towel off my lap, exposing my legbag and catheter. My bulky corset is buckled on the outside of my suit so I can breathe while I sit and wait. The strap of my bathing suit — my blue bathing suit — has slipped off my shoulder.

"Okay, we're ready for Joni. Let's get her out here!"

Two paramedics lay me on a rubber raft, take off my corset, and float me out into the shallow bay.

"Way to go, kid." The assistant cameraman waves from the crane above.

"Not to worry. You'll do fine," the property master calls from the shore.

Miss Blue Bathing Suit wades knee deep into the water, watching intently. I'm touched that she cares. I should have told her — should have told all of them — that I float in pools all the time. I'm not afraid of the water. Really.

Shivering a bit, I float on my back and wait for the cast and crew to get in position. Everyone is quiet. I take a deep breath, and Jim Collier signals the paramedics to flip me over, face down, in the water.

Above water, the camera begins rolling. In the curious underwater acoustics I hear Jim yell, "Action!" I strain to hear "Kathy" splash through the water and call my name. I hear her voice, muffled. Seconds tick by. The bay is cold and dark. My lungs are hungry for air.

I am going to shake my head — a prearranged signal to warn the paramedics that I need help. Suddenly, hands grab my shoulders. As "Kathy" lifts me from the water, I sputter and gasp for breath.

It's real. But . . . oh, yes, I am supposed to act. "Kathy. Butch. I can't move. I . . . I can't feel," I manage to splutter as they carry me to the shore. A crane follows. Cameras whir. People take notes. Gaffers tilt reflectors.

"Cut! It's a print!"

I breathe deeply with relief. A pat on the back and smiles break the tension. The scene has come and gone so quickly. The reality we just filmed is now at a distance, recorded neatly on a strip of celluloid encased in a can. The cooks from the catering truck set out snacks and everyone gravitates toward donuts and coffee.

The pretty girl in the blue bathing suit has taken off her wet wig and donned a fresh white sweat shirt. She approaches and we greet one another warmly. I feel the camaraderie. We are a team.

Yet something is troubling me. I glance at the raft still anchored off shore. It looks bleak and lonely, no longer surrounded by the crew and their trappings. I look toward the catering truck where everyone is chatting and laughing. I glance again at the raft, rocking slowly on gentle swells.

The gnawing stops. I know what it is. It has been a long time since I've listened to its whispers, felt its icy fingers around my heart. Pity, an old enemy, is trying to move in on old territory.

Me? . . . Pity?

How can that be? I've learned not to compare myself with others. I've written chapters in books about it. I speak about it to audiences all the time. God knows, I wouldn't be doing this movie if all those old matters weren't settled.

19

But what is happening? Have so many years passed since that July day in 1967 that I've become too comfortable? Has the camera lens focused too sharply today on those old details? This July day in 1978? I marshal fragments of faith. Something about contentment. Something about grace. A simple Scripture verse floats to the surface of my mind and turns to face me: "Therefore let him who thinks he stands take heed lest he fall."[1]

"Lest he fall . . ." That's fair warning. Especially since I've never done anything like this before. Playing the lead in a movie about my life. Re-creating my own experiences before the cameras. What do I know about acting? Oh, sure, I sold toothpaste to my bathroom mirror when I was a kid, but that's about the extent of my dramatic experience.

But I'm up to it. I talked it over thoroughly with my family and friends, with Bill Brown, executive producer at World Wide Pictures, and with Billy Graham. With absolutely no pressure from anyone, I was the one who decided to play my own part. I figured if the real person could say the real thing to a lot of people with problems, then the film would have an even greater impact. And wouldn't it be wonderful to create something lasting, something permanent? It couldn't be that much different from writing a book or painting a picture.

"Let him who thinks he stands take heed . . ." *Lest he fall,* I ponder again. If anyone were to fall, I suppose it could easily happen in Los Angeles, the City of the Angels. Fallen angels. And Hollywood, the film capital of the world, is a long way from my desk at the farm in Maryland or from the art easel in my study.

But World Wide Pictures wants the movie *Joni* to be a top-notch production that can hold its own against other movies shown in local theaters. Here in Hollywood they can assemble some of the most talented sound engineers, set designers, gaffers, and grips in the industry.

Being fresh off the Maryland farm, what do I know about these people and their cosmopolitan ways? Yet here, for six months, I'll be living and working with them, rubbing shoulders with their world every day. I tingle at the thought, at what kind of witness this could be.

No. I won't fall. And I should, at least, be a match for the glittery, empty trappings of Hollywood.

Hollywood. It brings to mind a dark and foreboding verse out of Ephesians: "So I tell you this, and insist on it in the Lord, that you must no longer live as the Gentiles do, in the futility of their thinking. They are darkened in their understanding and separated from the life of God because of the ignorance that is in them due to the hardening of their hearts. Having lost all sensitivity, they have given themselves over to sensuality."[2]

Hmm. Heavy words. In these surroundings — by this bay, on this beautiful beach — they seem stuffy, strait-laced, even out of place. The crew, the cast, even the girl in the bathing suit — they're genuinely nice people. No, this world won't touch me. I'll touch it for Christ!

So why all the fuss? Everything is under control. Dr. Graham himself has cautioned me that this filming will be difficult. I understand about reliving hospital experiences, complaining before a camera that I long to be healed, rehashing old relationships — some successful, some splintered.

World Wide Pictures has bent over backwards, rallying people to pray daily for me and the crew. They've made arrangements for my sister Jay to stay with me, along with a nice English lady named Judy Butler from the Billy Graham office. They've even rented a little house nearby for us on a quiet tree-lined street.

But as urgent as everyone is to calm me, I am equally insistent on calming them. Hollywood may be "way out," but it's still on planet earth. And my diving accident was many years ago. Those painful memories of my early days of paralysis are all but clouded over. I proved that today in the water. I wasn't nearly as unnerved as everyone else.

No, it wasn't the scene in the water that bothered me.

It was what went on behind the scene.

I am discovering that people in movies wear masks. They substitute one kind of reality for another. It seems all the more confusing since my lines aren't, in fact, voiced from my heart as they were years ago. They are read from a script. The mask of a hospitalized seventeen-year-old girl doesn't quite fit me any more. They have to re-create "me" with pasty, pale foundation, dark make-up under my eyes, a matted blond wig, and a wrinkled hospital gown.

Today I lay face down on a Stryker frame — a narrow canvas bed. With my chin and forehead resting on cushioned strips of cloth, I can follow everyone's steps. I memorize the shoes of the cast and crew. The sound man with the boom mike stands over my head. A strip of adhesive tape on one of his shoes reads, "Hi," and on the other, "Joni."

Minutes tick by. Camera rehearsals take time. I wish they would hurry, though. My chin and forehead are beginning to ache from the pressure. This mask is real.

I must concentrate. The director and the cameraman are almost ready. Footsteps across the sound-stage floor become attendants and nurses. The director flips through a script much like a doctor making notes on my chart. Cameras and lights become giant X-ray machines positioned around my body.

"Let's make a movie, children." Jim Collier claps his hands for positions. "Remember, Joni, you're dazed. Disoriented."

"Yes," I say obediently. I am, in fact, dazed and a little disoriented.

Filming begins as Cooper, the actor who wears the mask of my boyfriend, smuggles a puppy up nine flights of hospital steps, makes his way past a nurses' station on hands and knees, and into my room. He pulls the panting puppy from under his jacket and lifts him to my cheek. "Here, pup. Lick Jon's face."

"Oh, he's so cute," I mumble. Under the heat of the stage lights the puppy droops and whines to be let loose.

"Cut! Change the slate for another take!" The crew takes a break, stretching and talking idly as the camera is repositioned.

We begin again, but the pup ignores his lines.

We try a third take. A fourth. They bring in a second puppy.

Offstage, the dog wrangler tries to tease his pups into a playful mood. Onstage, my mood sours. My chin and forehead are hot and sore. Yet I apologize to the director. Perhaps my frightful wig and pallid features put the puppies off?

We try the scene again. I strain to reach the pup with my cheek. *Oh, please lick my cheek!* By now, the crew members chuckle every time a new puppy goes into his "I'm not interested" routine. I realize I'm not smiling and weakly join the laughter.

Four puppies and fifteen takes later, I lamely give permission for the wrangler to smear liver-flavored baby food on the side of my cheek away from the camera. I apologize again. It must be my fault.

"Action!"

The puppy wriggles and squirms in Cooper's hands. He catches a whiff of the liver and furiously licks my cheek. The camera catches this precious bit of action, everyone cheers, and Jim finally calls a wrap.

It takes just minutes to pack the camera, clear the set, dim the lights, and say good night. It takes longer to flip me face up on the Stryker. Oh, the relief!

Jay and Judy lift me in their familiar and friendly embrace into my wheelchair. They push me to the dressing room. It will take even longer to remove the pasty make-up, wig, and gown. Before they begin, the girls walk back to the sound stage to gather up our sweaters and other belongings.

Alone in front of the brightly lit make-up mirror I look into a pale, drawn face. The hair is askew. The hospital gown is oversized and obliterates the body underneath. The girl is alive only from her shoulders up, just like in the hospital. Even the dry, crusty food on her cheek is a reminder of those first sorry attempts at feeding herself. She is exhausted and humiliated. Cowing before dogs and directors, she has allowed herself to be intimidated. Just like in the hospital.

Tired and hurting, I feel so sorry for the girl in the mirror. The past overpowers me. It eats away like acid. I look at my paralyzed legs and a feeling of claustrophobia envelopes me — I can't move. Hot tears well in my eyes. Who am I crying for? The girl in the mirror or the woman in the chair? Is it the past I grieve for . . . or the present?

Ashamed and embarrassed by these thoughts darting beneath the surface, I lean my head back and let the tears drain behind my eyes. I press my nose against the sleeve of the white gown, dabbing at the wetness as though painstakingly retouching the flaws on a mask. The smile I hastily assume as Jay and Judy return from the sound stage is just that — a mask.

I stare straight ahead as they wipe away the thick make-up with cotton balls and astringent. A steaming-hot washcloth brings quick color to my cheeks. The make-up man inches the wig from my scalp. The wrinkled gown is folded away. My hair is brushed, my sweater buttoned, and refreshing drops are put in my eyes. I like what I see in the mirror now.

But I don't like who I am. My self-image has been slammed back into the wheelchair. How clever I've been at learning the art of masking the "handicap" part of my disability, whether with an attractive hairstyle, a fashionable outfit, or a streamlined wheel-chair with color-coordinated leather. But strip away all those props and stick me in a hospital gown with messy hair and a lifeless complexion, and my grip on life — even paralyzed life — seems lost.

Perhaps I am not so content after all.

"Time for rushes!"

"Time for what?" I power my wheelchair toward Rob Tregenza, the assistant to the director, who is flipping through sheets of dialogue.

"Rushes. Dailies. Every afternoon the lab sends back footage shot the day before." He tucks the sheets under his arm and helps maneuver my bulky chair through the narrow door to the screening room.

Only a handful of people are gathered in the dimly lit room. The cameraman is here to check his angles, while his assistant examines the focus and the gaffer makes notes about the lighting.

The director, who is here to oversee the general look of the film, waves his arm as the lights dim. "Okay, roll it."

It is like watching home movies as the unedited footage of the day before begins. Still it's a little fantastic to think of me on such a big screen. Huge out-of-focus hands holding a slate suddenly appear. Loud beeps begin the sound track. The image on the screen sharpens into focus and the slate claps, marking the first print of puppy number one who whines to be let loose. As the film continues to roll, Rob huddles close to my chair to give me information. He explains that the clapping of the slate helps the lab synchronize the sound track with the screen images.

The next slate marker claps and a second print begins. Another puppy fails. I glance at Jim Collier who is shaking his head and penciling notes. The screen goes dark. More beeps tell us another print is coming on the roll.

"Get ready." Jim leans forward in his chair. "This is the one."

The slate appears on the screen. A voice off-camera drones, "Sound."

"Speed," says another voice.

"Camera?"

"Rolling," comes the reply.

"Mark it. Scene 29, take 14." The slate claps, and I hear the director's voice whisper for action.

DICK: "Hi, gorgeous."

Seconds pass.

JONI: "People die here, Dickie."

The camera dollies smoothly, following Cooper as he crawls underneath the Stryker frame. The focus remains sharp as he lifts the puppy from his jacket. There is plenty of underlighting. The audience will be able to see the actors' expressions. The microphones pick up the nuzzly sounds of the pup licking the girl's face.

Rob is still kneeling by my side, making comments about the acting. I am not listening. My attention is not on the finer points of film making — the lighting, directing, sound, or focus. My attention is riveted on the pale, lifeless expression of that seventeen-year-old girl on the screen. She is paralyzed. She is helpless. She is . . . me.

In the darkened screening room before an image that looms larger than life, I neglect the grace which God offers me.

"So what is it like — starring as yourself in your own film?" The interviewer, his glasses propped on his balding head, leans back on the couch and taps the point of his pencil on his steno pad. His khaki safari jacket, properly crumpled and oversized, gives the impression that he has been published in the *New Yorker* or the *Atlantic Monthly.* We are alone in the small press room. I wish Jay or Judy were here, but they have gone to get our lunch while I do the interview.

"I . . . I don't feel very comfortable with that word. I mean, it's not like I'm a star or anything," I reply. In an effort to make my role more comfortable, I suggest that it is more like "playing my own part" or "re-creating my life story."

The man writes for a daily paper. We don't speak the same language. I sense he is looking for a dirty angle to tarnish the Christian purpose behind our movie. "The Billy Graham people are just great . . . the movie crew is helpful and very nice . . . World Wide is even providing an art instructor to give me painting lessons," I ramble, hoping he'll pick up on the good points.

I willingly tell him my own weaknesses, ladle out how really ordinary I am, hoping all the while I will charm the socks off him.

I relate a funny story about a policeman pulling me over as I wheeled across the street near NBC studios.

"Were you going too fast?" the reporter asks with a hint of a smile.

"Oh, no. I was jaywalk . . . er, jaywheeling, I guess you could say." My story falls a little flat.

Hiking his collar, he settles again into a serious vein. He sips black coffee and occasionally jots certain of my comments on his pad in shorthand. When I want him to record a point, I speak more slowly, giving him plenty of time to quote me accurately. It's a game, and we both know it.

"How do you think starring . . . er, portraying yourself will change your plans for the future?"

"Do you mean if I want to act in more movies or something?" I ask.

He shrugs his shoulders and waves his hand. "Whatever."

"No. No, I have no designs on doing *Joni: Part Two,* or, ah, *Son of Joni,*" I laugh. He loosens a bit. "Seriously. After it's over, I think I will just go back to the farm in Maryland and continue to paint and maybe write some more. Whatever," I say, mirroring his gesture. "I love the farm, my sisters, our horses. It's pretty this time of year. . . ." My voice trails off. I have not thought much lately about the barns or horses or the fact that the folks at home must be cutting and baling hay right now. Admit it or not, this movie is beginning to consume my thoughts.

I am relieved when the grilling is over. But I have a cramped uneasiness that I have been far too aware of my own actions, as though I were auditioning for the approval of the reporter. A mask, it seems, can be worn even behind the scenes.

I am glad when Jay, Judy, and I break out through the swinging glass doors at the end of the day. The sun has dropped behind the Hollywood Hills, flattening them to a one-dimensional shade of maroon. The bottoms of the clouds are underlit in pink and mauve, an effect the gaffer would love.

"Cut. That's a print!" Jay points to the sunset.

"Put it in the can," adds Judy. Laughing at the lingo which has become a part of us, we head for the car.

We resolve to leave work behind and visit a nearby shopping center. Light relief from the heavy pressure of the shooting schedule. Something ordinary and everyday to get us back in the real world. Yet as we wheel and walk through the mall, we jabber about the film. People we like on the crew, amateur criticism of wardrobe and set design, reviews of the latest rushes. We find it difficult to leave the movie world behind. And who could blame us? We are a secretary and two farm girls come to town.

"Let's choose a salad place for dinner," I suggest. Jim Collier has asked that I lose a few pounds for the remaining hospital scenes. "No dessert for me."

"Hey! I've got an idea," Jay says. "We just passed a T-shirt place. You know, where they print anything you want on the front?" She waves for us to follow and then disappears into the store.

I stop at the front window to look at the shirt styles, colors, and slogans. In a short while Jay comes out and announces, "You now have the perfect answer for those guys on the crew who keep stuffing donuts in your mouth." She holds up a T-shirt that reads DON'T FEED ME!

"And you're not the only one who needs to lose weight," she adds, whipping another T-shirt out of the bag. It reads OR ME. Judy stands behind her displaying a big grin and one more shirt that says NOR ME.

We giggle our way through supper on leftover movie adrenaline, guessing the crew's reaction to our silly shirts.

Behind the smile, however, I calculate calories: a salad, no dressing; no cream in real coffee. No breakfast tomorrow. No donuts at the studio. Maybe a light lunch and no dinner tomorrow evening.

I am not hungry anyway. I live on energy.

I am becoming obsessed with myself.

I listen eagerly to every direction Jim Collier gives for each scene. He wrote the screenplay and directed the movie *The Hiding Place,* and I know I can learn a lot from him.

"You're angry at this point. Angry at God. Angry at your friends." His voice is quiet but intense as he strokes the page of script with his fingers. I appreciate his suggestions, but I wish he'd give me more technical cues.

He leans back and adjusts his glasses. "It's important that you come across as natural as possible," he says, as if guessing my thoughts. "We've talked about it. Just relax and let it happen."

He rises and walks with Rob toward the cameraman, I suppose to discuss important technical things. Jim folds his arms, rubs his chin, and listens to the cameraman. With outstretched arms they peer through their hands to frame the shot. Jim examines the set through the eyepiece of the camera. They motion the gaffer over and point to several stage lights above.

I watch and wonder about Jim's work on *The Hiding Place,* the movie about the life of Corrie ten Boom. I read her book several years ago and was impressed with the film version of her years with her family in Holland, hiding Jews in their attic during the war, her ironclad faith during her internment in the Nazi concentration camps. The movie was stirring. Jim did a good job.

But it was Corrie's life. I wonder how she felt about watching her experiences come back to life on screen. How did she react to seeing others play the parts of family or friends? What did she feel when they portrayed those awful scenes in the death camps? Were the memories too painful? Here on the edge of the sound stage I have a hard time imagining her, like me, watching Jim Collier and his crew translate pain, horror, and even faith through actors and a script.

Jim has told me that Corrie ten Boom is now praying for this movie. She's praying for me too. I picture her in a wheelchair by the fireplace in her home, sipping tea, gently turning the thin pages of an opened Bible on her lap. She is in her eighties, limited in her traveling and speaking. But now she ministers through her powerful and effective prayers.

I smile, remembering a recent convention where she was honored and presented with a large bouquet of yellow roses. As the crowd stood to applaud her, she lifted the bouquet heavenward, and I knew she was saying, "Lord Jesus, this is Yours."

And picturing her by the fireplace in my thoughts, I decide, *No, Corrie would not have gotten caught up in any movie. Certainly not to the point of worrying.*

But here I am — uptight, stomach in knots, biting my nails as I wait on the edge of the sound stage.

I force my eyes to make contact with the young boy sitting rigid and upright in a body cast. A metal halo bolts into his skull, keeping his neck stabilized as it heals. The fluorescent light of the occupational-therapy department washes any color from his skin. I angle my chair closer to his side. Still, with his head fixed forward, he must strain to see me from the corners of his eyes. He smiles and weakly lifts his thin arm in a greeting.

"They tell me you're filming here today." His voice cracks.

"Yes, I am. I mean, we are. They're making a movie about my diving accident and rehabilitation and stuff." I try to sound casual, to include him, to make myself "one of the guys."

I notice his arms and hands are supported by an overhead sling attached to the back of his wheelchair. He must feel so bulky, I think to myself, like some sort of mechanical contraption. I back up my chair so he can see me better.

"You're moving your arms. That's a good sign," I offer.

"Yeah, they've got me in O.T. to do some work." He points to a painted ashtray with the brush a therapist has taped to his armsplint. The table beside us is strewn with newspapers splattered with red and yellow. A Mason jar holds colored pencils and brushes. Several other chalky ashtrays and candy dishes are organized neatly, waiting for the kiln.

I look around the table and smile at the other young guys working on projects. Some look up and grin. A few study me suspiciously. Others seem not to notice me, their lifeless eyes and tired expressions fixed on weaving a potholder or painting a dish.

"You were here at Rancho, huh?" one paraplegic asks as he wheels away from the table to get another jar of paint.

"Yes. About ten years ago, though." I try to spot a familiar face among the therapists. "Lots of things have changed."

I am uncomfortable. All our movie paraphernalia and personnel seem an intrusion into the private lives and pain of these patients at Rancho Los Amigos Hospital. The fellows know they are about to be filmed. Some are interested, while others shrug their weak shoulders indifferently. I want to put everyone — them and me — at ease. I explain that this film will help others understand the everyday difficulties people like us face.

By now the sound technicians, the grips, and their helpers are pulling in large electric cables, carts with tape recorders, and lighting stands. The occupational-therapy department is beginning to look like the sound stage of a movie studio. Nurses and therapists are grouped in the corner, watching. I hope the production people will be careful.

The gaffer begins to anchor lights on tall stands above an art easel. I am to be filmed against the backdrop of the fellows at the table. Along with them, I am to "learn" how to do as much as I can with what little I have left. An actress playing the part of a therapist is to teach me how to write with a pen between my teeth.

I'm glad that they do my make-up and wardrobe in the dressing-room trailer in the hospital parking lot. I don't want to be made-up in front of the young boy in the halo cast.

A knock on the trailer door tells us that filming is about to begin. I power my wheelchair back over the cables into the O.T. room and take my place at the easel. The young black actress who plays the part of my therapist resembles the real woman from my past. But then every prop and person in this film is reminding me of too much already.

Slab of clay is thrown down to table by Joni's easel.

JONI: "You gonna throw that at me?"

THERAPIST: "I want you to draw something on it."

JONI: "You gotta be kidding."

Therapist has two sticks in her hand.

THERAPIST: "Draw something you like. Use these."

JONI: "It won't work. I used to do a lot of sketching in charcoal. My father's sort of an artist. But that was when I had my hands."

THERAPIST: "The skill, the talent, comes from up here." (*Points to her head.*) "With a little practice you can do as well with your mouth as your hands."

The lens focuses tightly on me as I take the stick in my mouth and press it into the soft clay. I carve a line that wiggles and worms its way across the surface, and I try hard to control the shaking. The frightening part is I'm not acting. Every tense muscle in my neck, every raw nerve communicates directly through the stick onto the clay. I want to relax. I'm afraid that others will know I am not pretending to be a novice with the mouthstick. Thankfully, I hear someone say, "Cut."

"Is that real enough?" I ask the director.

I shake my head to clear the scene from my mind, then slowly turn my neck, tilting it back and forth to relax the tightness. This is another bit of filming I am relieved to see finished. Too many real things caught up in movie things.

During break I wheel outside to the therapy courtyard. Some brawny fellows in wheelchairs are playing a fast game of basketball. I watch them for a few moments and then wheel over to a group of girls in wheelchairs. They are smiling and chatting under the shade of some palms. The group looks friendly and inviting. I want to get over these stupid feelings of uneasiness and awkwardness. I battle to come up with a conversation opener.

"You're Debbie Stone, aren't you?" I say to a smiling girl whose wheelchair is stickered with a plastic "Because He is God, Jesus Lives Yesterday, Today and Forever."

"Yes, and you're Joni," she says, reminding me that we met earlier. World Wide has asked Debbie to round up people in wheelchairs for several movie scenes. I had forgotten that her permanent place of work is here at Rancho, collecting information and preparing patients for the outside world.

Debbie's disability is obvious — polio at a young age. She sits upright with her brown hair cascading down her small bent body. She smiles her way through an incredible story of abandonment, adoption, rejection, hospitals, and rules and regulations. Debbie is the first disabled person I've ever met with such an upfront testimony in the midst of an irreligious environment. I can tell that she tries to spread good news around this cold and impersonal institution. She is an oddity in this place, but everyone likes her.

"You met the guys in O.T.?" she asks, turning the conversation away from herself.

"Yes." I nod and then add, "Things in occupational therapy haven't changed much ... potholders and paints and stuff. But those guys seem to have a good attitude about it."

Debbie's smile fades. "Well, not all of them. Did you meet the boy with the halo cast?"

I nod again.

"His parents don't want anything to do with him. He broke his neck in a motorcycle accident, driving when he was drunk. They figure he got himself into this mess, so he can get himself out." She sighs and shakes her head.

I wince and look toward the window of the therapy room. I wish I had said more to him.

"And the good-looking paraplegic? His wife just filed for divorce. I've tried talking to him about God, but he just won't listen. He's losing himself ... in pity. In drugs."

I stare at the therapy room windows. The stories she relates are strikingly similar to many I heard when I was at Rancho as a patient years ago. But they didn't touch me then as they do now.

Debbie picks up on my mood. "Joni, you wouldn't believe the problems most handicapped people face. Spiritual struggles, yes. But down-to-earth, practical problems too."

Debbie is doing what I would like to do. In a real world, in a real way, she is helping people see Christ. No masks here.

"Hey, get a load of this!" Jay is reclining on the couch, crunching an apple while flipping through my script for the following week. "They've got a kissing scene in here, and guess whose name is on the call sheet." She rises to show me the page, her Cheshire-cat grin shining.

The script describes the scene in less than half a page. I have a line or two. Cooper, the actor playing my boyfriend, has even less to say. The rest is action.

Only a half page for all those memories. The real scene held all the drama. When my boyfriend Dick came to the hospital, there was no place he could wheel me so we could be alone. The solarium was filled with visitors, and the auditorium was off-limits. The only place we could hide and escape my six-bed ward was the elevator. We'd catch an empty one, press the third-floor button, and then flip the "stop" switch between floors. There we had plenty of privacy . . . until a nursing supervisor tracked us down one evening.

"I'm glad they've included that in the script. It'll add a fun moment to all those other drab hospital scenes," I reason.

"Yeah, and you'll have all the fun." Jay tousles my hair on her way back to the couch.

But will it really be fun to do a kissing scene in front of a movie crew with an actor I hardly even know? Cooper is very nice and very handsome, but what I know about him goes no further than his 8 x 10 glossy tacked to my dressing-room wall along with other cast members. Taking no chances, I decide to prepare. That night when I'm alone I practice the best kisses I can remember — on my wrist.

In the following days Cooper and I are thrown together frequently as we act our way through other scenes. Always, I wonder what he is thinking. Has he read ahead in the script? Does he have the same silly thoughts about the elevator scene as I do? Probably not. He's a Hollywood actor. He probably kisses leading ladies all the time.

The day arrives, and we go on location at a local hospital. An elevator is rigged with stage lights, microphones, and electric cables. The large camera is anchored on a tripod in the corner.

Cooper walks up behind me. "Think we'll fit in there?" He grins, popping a breath mint in his mouth. I envy his nonchalance.

When all is ready, I'm pushed into one corner of the elevator, and Jim pulls Cooper next to me, briefing us on our few lines. "The rest," he says, smiling, "will come naturally."

Then Jim shoulders up to the cameraman to discuss the mood he wants to capture. Cooper carefully sits on my lap, taking cues on how close to me he appears through the lens. The script lady, armed with her clipboard, pulls up a stool and sits within feet of us. She is ready to record every word and movement for the editors who will piece the film into one smooth scene.

"You'll do fine," Cooper whispers as he pats my shoulder. I admire his confidence.

"Action!"

Cooper turns toward me, brushes my cheek with his hand, and tilts my chin. His lips touch mine. Electricity. The foreign feel of lips on mine melts in an instant. I forget the lights and camera.

The director asks for a cut. Cooper breaks off his embrace, leaving me in mid-emotion. The lady on the stool fans us with her script. It is getting warm under the lights.

"Boy, you kiss good," Cooper laughs, patting my hand.

"Okay, let's do another." Jim scribbles a few notes and motions to begin.

Again Cooper leans toward me, only this time I am quicker to respond. I am surprised how easily I relax into his kiss. We linger a bit longer past the "Cut."

"We don't need another take, you two," Jim breaks in. Everyone laughs. I glance at the cameraman and the script lady and laugh nervously. Do they know it wasn't all acting?

I purse my lips. They feel hot. My heart rushes with passion — another foreign feeling. I'm hit with guilt and the rush instantly vaporizes. I smile, still a little shaky. After all, God knows I haven't kissed anyone in a decade. The thought of never kissing anyone for another decade registers and my smile quickly fades.

A new day of filming other scenes with other actors helps me put — or try to put — that silly kiss out of my mind. Late in the afternoon they call for rushes, and we head for the screening room. I smother — or try to smother — my excitement about reviewing the footage of yesterday's kissing scene.

As the rough prints roll by, I gaze like some heart-struck moviegoer. The screen sizzles. But the scene is short, and as quickly as the footage begins, it is completed. Jim Collier and the rest of his crew scrawl a few notes and comment on the color intensity, then leave.

"Wow, that sure looked real," Jay says as we wheel into the blast of air conditioning in the hallway.

I feel humiliated. Silly, foolish, and even a little angry. That kiss was nothing but celluloid, to be clipped, cut, and edited.

This movie thing mustn't take control of my life. Why do the script, the cast, the crew, and even the way I look on film mean so much to me? Why can't I just go back to our little rented house at the end of a day and put it all out of my mind?

I take deep breaths and try to relax in front of the large art easel. I have many paintings to complete for scenes in the movie, and time is slipping by. James Sewell, the art director, coaches me on the various brushes and paints I should use, but the harder I try to pay attention and concentrate, the further my mind wanders away.

"Joni . . . are you listening?" James asks. "Which shade of pink do you believe would work against this cool color?" He fans several tubes of paint in his hands for my inspection.

"Wh–what?" I say, startled. "I'm sorry, James. I guess my mind is elsewhere. I have such a difficult time concentrating these days."

James lays the paints on the table, folds his hands, and leans on the corner of the canvas. He takes the brush out of my mouth, wipes it with a damp cloth, and sets it next to the other brushes.

Between scenes, this kind and fatherly, yet exacting professional has worked hard to instruct me about my artwork. I hate to disappoint him. After a long moment, he leans down and gives me a warm hug. "It's near lunch. Why don't we break early?" he says as he straightens.

I nod sheepishly.

"I'll push you out to the courtyard. You look like you need some fresh air." He smiles and tweaks my cheek.

The cement courtyard on the third floor of the studios is a nice place to escape movie commitments for the moment. Today a breeze has swept away the heavy smog, and the California sun shines bright and hot. Here, there is time to think.

Jim Collier warned that once this movie began we'd be on a greased slide — movie lingo for "no stopping." He was right. These first weeks of filming have been a wild initiation. There's hardly been time to think about the unexpected: the girl in the blue bathing suit, that ridiculous dog, the unnerving visit to Rancho Hospital — and that kiss.

It is all so perplexing. Like déjà vu. I've been here before. I look at the script on my lap, opened to a new page of dialogue. I didn't write these lines, but they are mine. And somehow, I'm acting . . . but I'm not. Feeling inferior, even ugly next to an attractive girl in a blue bathing suit. Feeling the pain of rejection from a mere dog. Fighting off intimidation. And that kiss. Old desires bubbling to the surface of my heart.

I catch my reflection in the large glass panel that separates the courtyard from the studio. The wheelchair takes up three-quarters of the space that makes up "me." I look like a bulky movie prop.

This movie image is too real. The script is about my life ten years ago, but the scenes are much too close for comfort. I am actually reliving the same old problems — from self-image to singleness!

Suddenly the sun is too hot. My skin prickles with anxiety. The shade of a small potted tree in the middle of the courtyard and a light breeze offer little relief from the heat of my thoughts.

I retrace my steps one by one. *How did I get myself into this predicament?* Prayer should have prevented this from happening.

Prayer. I have been praying, concentrating on the crew, the actors, the believers who will be inspired by the film, the unbelievers who will be brought into the Kingdom, the folks who are supporting the movie. But prayer for myself? No, I have assumed that my past, neatly shelved, is so far behind that it cannot touch me. Now I'm not so sure. Must I learn the same old lessons? In a new way? I don't think I can ... I'm so tired.

And my Bible. For the past two weeks I've barely opened it. Oh, I've rehearsed a few familiar verses on my way to work each morning, verses memorized some time back. But nothing new. Nothing fresh. Just cruising on the top of a wave of God's grace.

One of those verses comes to mind now: "Do not think of yourself more highly than you ought, but rather think of yourself with sober judgment."[3]

Lots of things are beginning to slip on the greased slide. I've gotten my back against the wall spiritually. I'm growing tired. I'm failing. I feel like I'm letting people down. What if they knew?

I throw my head back and open my mouth in a silent scream. *How can I act out my love for God in a film when I can't get my act together for real?*

"Joni, got a minute?" Rob Tregenza jolts me out of my thoughts.

I erase the panic from my face and switch gears too easily from meditation to movie making.

Rob motions me into the screening room and spreads sheets of music on the carpeted floor. A girl sits at the piano and begins toying with a melody while Rob sings the words.

> Father, set my soul sailing like a cloud upon the wind,
> Free and strong to carry on until the journey's end.
> Each mile I put between the past and the future in your
>   hand
> I learn more of your providence and find out who I am.

"What do you think of it as a song for the close?" Rob holds the second page of music for me.

"I like it ... keep singing." I close my eyes.

> I want to thank you for the gift of your Son
> and for the mystery of prayer
> And for the faith to doubt, and yet believe,
> that you're really there.[4]

Rob gathers the music sheets and taps them together on the piano lid. "Jim wanted me to run this song by you. Get your input."

"Well, the words are great. Especially the part about putting miles between the past and the future. You know, seeing it all as in His hand," I say. "But I don't get that line about having faith to doubt and yet believe."

He smiles knowingly, nodding his head as he closes the lid on the piano. "We all have doubts, Jon," he says. "Don't you think the faith God gives us is large enough to handle even them?" He speaks with a hint of challenge in his voice, as though his own faith has been stretched at some point.

I want to mouth a stock answer to his rhetorical question, like a recording on replay. But I don't. This conversation seems isolated for a special reason, as though I am the one who has something to learn. I can't counter with a quick reply.

I know I have the faith to doubt and yet believe. The miles between my past and future are in His hand. But I'm beginning to wonder — do I know who I am?

My chair jostles up the gravel driveway, and I wheel into the shade of a spreading coast oak. The dusty, sweet aroma of a barn with hay. A green pasture bordered with rusting barbed wire. A corral with horses. It's not the farm in Maryland, but the movie people have found a convincing counterpart here behind the hills of Santa Barbara.

We have traded the smog of Los Angeles for the dust of a country road near Solvang. The cast and crew have swapped their Porsches for pickups and cowboy hats. There's an air of freedom and fun. No more hospital scenes for me.

It's easy to act these outdoor scenes. Being in Solvang is as exciting as my first real break from the hospital. It's easy to relax with the cast and crew. This morning one of the guys presented me with a cowboy hat of my own. The cameraman gave me a ride on his crane. During a break, I talked horses and saddles with several grips down by the corral. These people are so friendly. They have so much to say. Nobody here sounds like that verse from Ephesians — having a darkened or hardened heart.

I sit in the shade of this oak, reveling in the new freedom. It's not only a change in scenery and scenes; it is my brand-new power wheelchair. My arm straightens against the joystick and the chair inches forward. No more being pushed everywhere. Pride combines with independence as I choose to move or not move. I can turn my chair to chime in on a conversation. Or I can turn away.

Jim Collier introduces me to the young actor who will play the part of Steve Estes, the dear friend who was instrumental in getting my feet on the ground spiritually.

"I'm Richard," the boy says with a broad smile and seats himself on the stump of a log beside me. He resembles Steve at sixteen — tall, lanky, a little shy at first. "I've read all about Steve," he begins as he gestures with a *Joni* book. "He had a big impact on your life, didn't he?"

The make-up artist approaches and sets his bag on the gravel. "Mind if I start on you two?" He wets his brush and begins to line Richard's eyes for the camera.

"Yeah . . . uh, yes," I say absently as I return my attention from the actor's eyes to his question. "I mean . . . yes, Steve had a big impact on me."

Richard cracks open the book to show paragraphs he has highlighted in yellow. "I was hoping I could learn more about him from you."

The make-up artist wipes his brush and begins on my eyes.

"Well, I was barely out of the hospital when I met Steve . . . he was a teenager like me . . . but he was so enthusiastic about the Bible. He taught me how God had control over my accident and — "

"Okay," Richard interrupts, "but I guess I need to know more about his mannerisms. You know, how he would gesture and stuff."

"Oh. I see." I quickly switch gears and push away enthusiasm for Steve and those wonderful old truths. I concentrate instead on the importance of the moment — the art, the drama. The mask this actor needs to wear.

The assistant director calls the crew together over his megaphone. We are ready to start the next segment of filming. "Steve" and I are to exchange a few lines down by the barn.

While they fasten the camera to the huge crane, I practice wheeling my chair up and down the dirt path that parallels the barn. I'll have to drive straight while I deliver lines and look up at "Steve" sitting on the barn roof. After practice runs and rehearsals with the crane, we are ready.

"Action!"

As instructed, I drive slowly up the path, watching for the crane to rise above the backside of the barn roof. I look up at "Steve" as the camera slowly swings into position behind him.

"Whatcha reading?" I say my first line.

He looks up from the open book on his knee. "The Bible. 'They that wait upon the Lord shall renew their strength; they shall mount up with wings as eagles; they shall run, and not be weary; and they shall walk, and not faint.'"[5]

The words seem distant. From the past. Rather than inspired Scripture, I am hearing just lines from a script.

I shake my head on cue and say dryly, "That's very poetic." The dryness comes too easily. Too naturally.

Upon direction, I continue to power my brand-new wheelchair, leaving "Steve" behind on the roof.

The summer sun above the Solvang farm is already high and hot, but the script calls for the cool days of fall. Autumn scenes need to be shot around the barn. I sit at a distance and watch the crew spray-paint the green summer leaves of an oak tree with tints of gold and red. The movie company goes to incredible lengths to re-create reality.

While I wait, I occasionally glance down at the open book on my lap. I'm attempting to catch up on my reading with a book by an English pastor about Jesus' sermon on the mount.[6] Each sentence is a stumbling block, the language weighty with old and stiffened words. But I ought to work through at least several pages.

The author is speaking about the verse, "Blessed are they that mourn."

"Let us, then, try to define this man who mourns. What sort of man is he? He is a sorrowful man . . . he is a serious man . . . he is a sober-minded man . . . he is a grave man."

I only scan these words from the book. My attention is easily diverted to the spray-painting of the leaves. I observe with an artist's eye how they choose the colors for different branches. I return to the page.

"The true Christian is never a man who has to put on an appearance of either sadness or joviality. No, no; he is a man who looks at life seriously; he contemplates it spiritually, and he sees in it sin and its effects."

Something about this paragraph nettles me. Perhaps I should read more closely.

"That is the man who mourns; that is the Christian. That is the type of Christian seen in the Church in ages past, when the doctrine of sin was preached and emphasized . . . a deep doctrine of sin, a high doctrine of joy, and the two together produced this blessed, happy man who mourns, and who at the same time is comforted."

The words sour as I reread the paragraph. I check the cover. Is this the same book I started reading months ago? Back then it was a favorite. Now the pastor seems to be writing for stuffy English saints from years ago. His words don't apply. Especially now.

I forget the book and wheel over to the director and "Steve" to rehearse my lines for the day.

Much later I drop into bed, exhausted after another emotionally charged day of filming and of too much caffeine on an empty stomach. My body is weary, but my mind does instant replays of the afternoon. The laughter. The chatter with the cameraman. The pats on the back.

In the middle of my thoughts, other words stick out like a sore thumb. *"The Christian is a man who looks at life seriously . . . contemplates it spiritually . . . sees in it sin and its effects."*

I lie alert for a moment, letting the two worlds play against each other. Like pieces of a puzzle. I make a half-hearted attempt at fitting them together. But oddly, they don't.

I sigh, turning my head and nestling into the pillow. I can't ponder such weighty matters at this hour. Tomorrow is another busy day.

The morning sun rises and crests the mountains, exploding like a diadem into the sky. Jay and I are being driven from our Solvang hotel to the movie farm. In high spirits, we sing Linda Ronstadt style. I look at my sister. Hair, long and blond, just as she wore it in her twenties. Granny glasses. Faded blue jeans. I am glad she is here. She brings a touch of stability and reality to this movie mania.

But even Jay is not above change. Rob Tregenza, who has researched so many details for the film, has spent a good bit of time researching my sister. I noticed him admiring the way she handled the horses for one of the scenes. I've watched them sit and talk much during breaks.

Our driver turns onto the dirt road leading to "our farm." The shaded lawn and tranquil house are overrun with cables and light stands, movie trucks and cranes. Everywhere there are people putting up props, hammering, and sawing. The excitement draws us in.

I wheel into the house over power cables and through a maze of trunks and boxes. The interior is to resemble the living room back at our Maryland farm. The old farm is difficult to picture with all this film-making paraphernalia. But in the middle of the set stands my art easel. A familiar touch. My heart warms, and I smile, remembering those first sketchy attempts to paint with a brush between my teeth — an experience I must soon re-create on film.

Jim Collier rallies the crew. Jay finds my place in the script. I am to be filmed painting a beautiful butterfly making its journey from caterpillar to cocoon to winged flight.

I watch the kind elderly prop man ready his jar of caterpillars. Through the network of this crazy industry, he has located a supply house for bugs and insects. He has ten or fifteen, in case any die, crawl away, or fail their screen test. (Memories of the puppy linger.) We tease him about being a caterpillar wrangler. He responds with mock dignity. Why, he has trained these caterpillars to crawl, on cue, across the window sill of the set. I laugh. All this for the movie to suggest that I am the one coming out of the cocoon.

For the camera to film my painting and then switch focus to capture the tiny creature on the window sill, the gaffer is asked to brighten the set with extra lights. I sit on the sidelines watching him converse with Jim and the cameraman. Their comments become as heated as the room from the glare of lights.

"It's too much light," says the gaffer. "We've got to think of Joni under all this heat." My ears catch his defensive tone. It's nice to be the object of such consideration.

"But we need the depth of field to have the foreground and the background in focus. Look at those shadows by the window!"

As a compromise, they decide to cut the glare with flags and nets. But as I move into position under my easel, I still feel the intense heat of the stage lights above me. My advocate approaches with a solid flag, a rectangular frame covered with black cloth. He stands and shields me from the dazzling lights as the camera readies.

"Please, I'll be okay."

"Not to worry." The gaffer smiles.

I hardly know this man. He is merely a name on my prayer list for the movie crew. But I've observed his friendly manner with everybody. He's even-tempered and flexible. He's also strong, I register, thinking back on his discussion with the cameraman and Jim.

"This is helping," I add, groping for something to say. "I don't handle heat very well. It's my, uh . . . handicap."

Our exchange is cut short as Jim calls for action. Despite the heat, the caterpillar and I perform on cue. We applaud the prop man for his excellent coaching, and we break for coffee.

As I wheel off the set, I glance toward the gaffer and his helpers dismantling the heavy lights. Jay has difficulty clearing cables from my path. The gaffer quickly comes to help, as though assisting me is far more important than juggling thousand-dollar stage lights.

"Sometimes . . . this wheelchair . . . ," I half apologize for interrupting him.

"You don't seem handicapped at all to me." He smiles and returns to his work.

"Wrap" comes early. A small group clusters to make dinner plans. The camera assistant and the gaffer want to join us.

Our movie making is finished for the day, yet I freshen my face to prepare for my next "scene." The location will be a little Scandinavian restaurant that has received rave reviews. I plan the dialogue carefully—the sorts of questions I want to ask, the direction I want the conversation to take. The meal is incidental. Plates are props. I will make the gaffer center stage.

Our dinner conversation is spirited. I am delighted that my new friend is sitting next to me. As on the set, he doesn't seem to mind helping—cutting my meat or lifting a glass of water to my mouth. Without prompting, he dabs my mouth with a napkin at the end of the meal.

Our little group chatters idly as we meander up the street outside the restaurant, stopping now and then to peer through shop windows. Rob reaches for Jay's hand as they walk.

It's a warm Southern California night and a clear, starry dome twinkles above us. Crickets court in the woods beyond the little town and the air is sweet with gardenia. Under the street lamps, I discover my own sense of backlighting.

I'm not above change either, I decide.

I push the joy stick of my new wheelchair, powering ahead. With sly pleasure I choose to leave my sister and the rest behind and wheel beside the gaffer.

We are back in Los Angeles, away from the camera. The gaffer — handsome, wealthy, kind — has asked me to dinner. I wonder what to wear. A simple blouse with matching bow? No. An elegant V-neck sweater? Perhaps. Yes.

"You don't seem handicapped at all to me." I recall his words and his smile. I picture the hills of Santa Barbara. The quiet California night. The blanket of stars above us. Back there I didn't feel handicapped — for a change.

Waiting by the window, I watch the shiny red Porsche pull up outside our house. It is familiar on the studio lot, but parked in our driveway it moves out of the professional world and into the personal. I am ready.

"Are you sure it'll fit?" I cringe. I don't want my clunky push wheelchair to damage the leather of the tiny back seat.

"Not to worry." My gaffer friend struggles to angle the chair behind his seat. "There!" The chair is lodged into place. Thank God. Who would have guessed a wheelchair would fit into a Porsche?

I am surprised at how much we have to talk about. There is no awkwardness. Our working together every day for many weeks now has not drained ideas for conversation. I don't feel uncomfortable trying to bridge the gap between our worlds.

"So this movie's a lot like your real life?" he says soon after we're on our way.

"Yes." I lean back into the cushiony headrest and sigh. "It's pretty much the way it happened."

"You know, what I said the other day is true," he interjects. "None of us on the crew even notice your wheelchair."

I am flattered by his attempt to put me at ease, but I am also uneasy with this talk about me. Surely he is tired of hearing about "Joni" stuff. I am.

"I bet you've filmed other things a lot more exciting," I say in an effort to turn the conversation back on him.

He shakes his head. "I wouldn't exactly call Pepsi commercials exciting."

"That's because you own stock in Hawaiian Punch. I've seen you drinking cans of that stuff on the set. Come on, where's your Pepsi spirit?"

"In my garage. They gave us cartons of the stuff after the shoot." His eyes and smile meet mine for an instant, warmed in the glow from his dash lights. I snap a mental photo.

We speed up the on-ramp of the Ventura Freeway, the lights of the Hollywood Hills twinkling like stars. He is right. Tonight this handicap is not going to get in the way.

I plan not to drink any water so my legbag will not need to be emptied. I have lost a great deal of weight during this movie, so I know I'll be easy to lift. I think about what I'll order for dinner — something easy to eat so that no food will fall off my special spoon. I glance at my feet. It's early in the evening, and thankfully, my ankles aren't swollen and unsightly.

I listen to the click of the turn signal as we shift into the fast lane and watch the people in the cars we speed past. An elegant blonde with her hair in a sophisticated chignon drives a black Mercedes — it's night, but she wears dark glasses, hiding any trace of an expression. A rowdy group of teenagers out for a good time — the windows of their Pontiac Firebird are shut, but I can see them lip-syncing to a rock beat on their radio. A man in a station wagon, eyes straight ahead and hands clutching the wheel in driver's ed. form — he ignores his wife who leans into the back seat to slap their child's knees.

The freeway is a drama with its own players and plot, a teeming world rushing this way and that. I feel a part of its pulse, its beat. With my wheelchair tucked out of sight behind the seat, the people in the cars we zoom by would never think I am handicapped.

We pull up sharply in front of an exotic oriental restaurant. The Porsche idles while my friend walks toward the valet, slips him a folded bill, and explains our need for special parking. The boy smiles and runs ahead to escort us.

Within minutes my wheelchair is unfolded and ready for me. I hope my shoes don't fall off while he's lifting me. And I hope I don't hurt his back!

There are steps, but my friend handles my chair with confidence. He has obviously studied my sister's technique. I breathe a sigh of relief. My legs fit underneath the table. I order a dish I can handle easily with my special spoon in my armsplint.

"Okay, so how would you light your glass if you were doing a wine commercial?" I ask, wanting to show my interest in his work.

He thinks for a moment, lifting his glass to the light, letting the wine swirl. He sets it down and runs his finger around the rim. "I'd place the wine here." He gestures toward the glass, leaning back. He pulls an empty chair closer to him. "Then I'd sit a beautiful woman here." He pats the arm of the chair. "A dark brunette. Full mouth. High cheekbones. Long neck. Lots of skin."

My smile stiffens.

"Then I'd put a nine light or an H.M.I. here and a couple of twinnes for back light and a lee filter to soften things up." He uses the language of his profession. "In other words I'd light the wine to outshine the girl. Who needs the beautiful woman?" He smiles as he sips his drink.

I laugh. I'm still in the fast lane. I fantasize that my hands can gesture . . . long graceful fingers, polished nails, stirring coffee as I talk.

During the drive home, the Cinderella magic begins to wear off. My legbag needs emptying. (Is that a faint whiff of urine?) My sweater has pulled out of my slacks from all the lifting. My corset has ridden up, digging into my skin and making it harder to breathe. I'm getting "sweats," which tells me something is wrong somewhere. My reflection in the mirrored visor tells me my make-up needs repairing, but there is nothing I can do about it. I look closer. My face has that same pale, lifeless expression I once saw in the movie mirror.

I'm glad Jay is home when we arrive. I feel heavier as they lift me into my wheelchair. My friend senses I am uncomfortable so our good-bys are quick. I am happy to get out of the sweater, unstrap the corset, take off the legbag, and be in bed where I don't feel quite as paralyzed.

I think back on the evening — the light, the sound, the action. I have edged closer to a world I've known little of in the last decade. I wonder how close I can get without it weakening me.

Tomorrow is another day of filming. More scenes about adjusting to a wheelchair. More about being handicapped. More about coping. I am getting tired of hearing about "those days." I am getting tired of hearing about "Joni" and how she has it all together.

But I almost had it all together tonight. The thin mask very nearly, but not completely, stayed intact.

"Jay! Judy!" My voice is urgent. I have been awakened in the middle of the night by a pounding headache. My heart is racing. It is not with fear. Something is desperately wrong with my body.

"Jay!" I wait for an answer or for someone to flick on a light in the adjoining room.

Jay stumbles into the room. "What is it?" She reads the panic in my eyes. "Oh, Joni, you're sweating buckets!"

"I think it's my catheter. It must be blocked or kinked or something." I breathe deeply, trying to control my heart rate. "Do something, please, quick."

Jay goes into high gear and throws back my covers. She turns me on my side and discovers that I've been leaking around the catheter. "The bed is soaked. Your bladder must be bursting!"

I think of the two quarts of water I drank before bed, a necessary part of my nighttime routine. I haven't gotten rid of any of that fluid. I'm in dysreflexia — a dangerous reaction in spinal-cord injured people that can result in a cerebral hemorrhage.

"I'm going to change it. We don't have time to fool around." Jay scrambles urgently through the dresser for a new catheter, syringe, sterile solution, and scissors.

My head is hammering. I know my blood pressure is shooting up rapidly, uncontrollably. I try not to think about a brain hemorrhage.

Within minutes, a new catheter is inserted. "Come on . . . drain bladder, drain," Jay whispers nervously as she looks for a flush of fluid in the clear urological tubing.

I cannot tolerate the pain. "What's happening? Why isn't it working?" I cry.

"I don't know. I don't know! I've checked everything. It must be a faulty catheter."

I read panic in my sister's face. She knows as well as I how dangerous this is. Doctors have warned us. We've read about it in books. But this is the first time it has happened.

A tight band squeezes my head. "Oh, God, forgive me. Forgive me for knowing what to do one minute, then forgetting the next," I mumble. "Please . . . if this happens . . ."

Jay fumbles for the phone and calls the transportation captain of the movie. "Get the paramedics for Joni. Quick!"

"Praise the Lord . . . praise the Lord," I say as deliberately as my breathing and the pain allow. I wait — either for the paramedics to arrive or for the rising pressure to stop or for my brain to snap. I wait and fight off the panic with praise.

As I am rushed to the hospital, some of the pain in my head subsides. My bladder must be draining. I breathe deeply with relief. I know I am soaking the sheets and stretcher. But who cares? I'm alive!

In the emergency room I am fitted with a new catheter. They monitor my blood pressure and pulse for an hour, waiting to make sure everything is stabilized. It is 2:30 in the morning by the time we head back to the hotel. I joke about looking bright-eyed and bushy-tailed in just a few hours for the morning's film schedule.

"You can't be serious." Jay looks stunned. "Don't you think you ought to take the day off? The production can wait. Nobody will mind."

I consider her concern. Yet I know I will feel better if I don't lie around worrying and wondering about what could have happened. "Okay, let's compromise. We'll sleep in and ask Jim if we can start filming at noon."

Back in bed, where just hours ago I panicked, I remember my praises to God. I'm relieved I had enough sense to rush to Him when I needed Him. But now I only rush a quick prayer of thanks to heaven. After all, I need to get to sleep for tomorrow's schedule. I fight off guilt. God will understand.

Later that day when we arrive on the set, the crew is unusually quiet. No "How ya doin' there, kid!" Obviously, they have heard about my middle-of-the-night emergency. I suppose I look tired. Judy floods my eyes with Visine to cover the redness.

Since it is after noon and time is short, we quickly enter the first thing on the schedule: Scene 648.

JONI: "I'm okay. I can still feel."

Cut to Jay.

JONI: (*continuing*) "And I guess I'm alive. I just wanna be alone for a while."

After the scene is shot, I curtly dismiss Judy's suggestion that I take a nap or an early break. She and Jay just don't understand. I've got a job to do. I can't let Jim and the cast and crew down. I must make sacrifices. I can handle the pressure.

And I really do just want to be alone.

The various movie scenes are slowly linking together, forming a strong message about the hope that can be found in Christ. But I'm growing weaker — physically, emotionally, and spiritually.

I sit on the sidelines of the sound stage and watch. But I don't want to just watch; I should be doing something. *Like praying.* I sense the faint suggestion from God's Spirit. I remember the clogged catheter and the answered pleas, so I push myself into an obligatory prayer.

The camera assistant looks tired. *Lord, help him find rest in You.* I wonder if the prop man understands the message behind this film yet. *Lord, may he find You to be the answer to his deepest longings.* That actor I kissed . . . *Lord, he's not needed in the filming schedule any more. Whatever he's into now, bring Yourself often to his memory.*

I watch the gaffer. He wears a red plaid flannel shirt. His jeans, though faded, are nicely creased. He raises a can of Hawaiian Punch in my direction, smiling his broad, easy grin. I cannot, will not, pull my eyes away.

Prayers for him? Yes, I pray. Although I wonder about my motives. I seem to be more concerned about my heart than his soul. And he has no idea.

But I have ideas. Some of the cast and crew will be flying back East to Maryland to capture the fall colors. We will shoot beautiful scenes among real trees this time — fiery red maples and tall yellow oaks. Everyone will see the real farm, meet my real family and friends. I'll show the crew — including the gaffer, of course — other horse farms in Maryland, parks up in the mountains, and maybe even Washington, D.C. Maryland in the fall. They'll love it.

In the scenes to be shot there even the script is beautiful . . .

Shot of wheel of Joni's chair moving through leaves.

STEVE: "'And just as there are different kinds of seeds and plants . . .'"

Steve and Joni moving through woods.

STEVE: (*continuing*) "'so also there are different kinds of flesh. . . . The angels in heaven have bodies far different from ours, and the beauty and glory of their bodies is different from the beauty and glory of ours. . . . But all who become Christ's will have the same kind of body as His.'"

Pan from leaves to Joni and Steve moving away down path. Music starts. Steve reading out in front of Joni as they move up hill.

STEVE: "'I tell you this, my brothers —'"

Joni gets stuck and Steve goes back and pushes her up hill.

STEVE: (*continuing*) "'an earthly body made of flesh and blood cannot get into God's Kingdom. These perishable bodies of ours are not the right kind to live forever.'"[7]

All who become Christ's . . . Oh, how I wish these words would get through to all the crew — the prop man, the script lady, both cameramen, and, yes, the gaffer. I sit on the sidelines, this time on the edge of a field in Maryland, and watch them film footage of the trees.

The Californians look like foreigners in their down jackets next to Marylanders who need no coats against the nippy air. Betsy and Diana, close companions of mine since high school, seem comfortable with only sweaters. They have come on location near the Sykesville farm to watch. I am glad my Maryland friends show an interest in the movie making.

"So what's this thing do?" Diana points to a large white sheet of styrofoam.

"It's a fill card," my gaffer friend begins. "Like when a face is too dark on one side? You'd bounce light onto the cheek with a tilt of this white card." He angles the reflector to focus the sun's rays toward Diana.

"So *that's* what I'm missing." Diana poofs her hair in Marilyn Monroe fashion. "I just need to walk around with a fan in front of me for the windblown look, and a fill card to get the sunken cheeks." She flattens her hands against her face. "Then a spot behind me for backlighting. Au naturel."

"That's right." The gaffer laughs and points. "That's right. We do that to Joni every day. But you know . . ." He grows serious. "No matter what light I use, it's hard to make her look bad."

I should be studying the script on my lap, but all I can do is stare at this man. His compliment is sincere and innocent. And my heart is probably making far more of it than he intends. But I don't care. Diana sees the silly moon-struck look on my face and shoots a glance to Betsy.

After the break my friends join me behind the set to watch more filming. The big camera silently records the sight and sound of wind in trees. For several minutes we look on with no words between us.

"It's neat watching them, isn't it?" I whisper and motion toward the crew and equipment. A gust of wind tousles the crisp skirts of the trees. We gather closer for warmth.

Betsy leans over from behind my chair and wraps her arms around me. "Just so you're okay, Jon." She pats my arms and straightens up.

Her comment annoys me. "What's your problem?" I snap. "There's nothing wrong."

Betsy backs away slightly. "Oh. I was just thinking how thin you've gotten. You know, and tired." She looks puzzled. "I love you. The pressures of this movie and all . . . I'm just worried about you."

Her soothing words are convicting. "Look, I'm okay, you guys." I paste on a smile. "There's nothing to worry about." My rehearsed line is a trowel, smoothing out their concerns like bumps and unsightly pebbles until the surface appears glossy and flat.

I must not let them know that I truthfully don't prefer their company . . . that I hardly read my Bible now . . . that I'm nearly anorexic — I cannot eat . . . that my prayers are lifeless, even self-centered . . . that I want to date anybody . . . and that I don't like this wheelchair.

All who become Christ's . . . I think of the crew. Yet I stubbornly push away any meaning the thought may hold for me. People in movies wear masks, substituting one kind of reality for another.

The change of Maryland seasons sweeps in with the north wind which blows across the farm fields and roars through the trees. The colorful leaves are drying to a dull brown and falling off the branches. The few remaining scenes must be shot quickly.

In a shaven cornfield across the river from the farm, "Steve" and I fly a kite for the camera. The fickle fall wind lifts and drops the kite far out of the frame of the camera. We have to do many retakes.

> *Steve, flying a kite high, looks at Joni.*
> JONI: "My life is like that, full of ups and downs."

I say the phrase almost shamelessly and am pricked that nearly every line in this movie reads too close for comfort. But so what, I rationalize. Everybody has ups and downs, and I'm no exception. So I've had a few struggles lately.

Ups and downs. Jay seems to be the only one whose life is on an even keel these days. Although she and Rob have known one another only a short time, those weeks have been filled with hours of long, heart-to-heart talks — more conversation than Jay has ever shared with anyone before.

Frankly, I haven't paid much attention until recently. I did notice them during coffee breaks between scenes when they would sit in directors' chairs by the edge of the sound stage, discussing the lifelikeness in the set design. And in Solvang I did think it curious that they spent so much time together after each day's shoot. But now I see the change coming. And it is not simply the season.

In fact, being home in Maryland — surrounded by family and friends — has pushed something new to the surface. Marriage. It doesn't surprise me. I've often wondered why some white knight hasn't galloped up sooner. When Jay sits in her rocking chair, her Scandinavian blond hair shining and swaying, no one could be more beautiful. She tends her garden with the care of a mother for her children. Her home on the farm exudes warmth and welcome. She has shown total commitment in all the years I've lived with her and her daughter Kay.

Though Jay and Rob will marry, they assure me that life as we've known it on the farm will continue. But now I must look at Jay's life and mine from a clinical distance. An incredible change — not a movie scene but a real one — is about to upheave my life and hers. What do I feel?

I don't feel anxious or even envious. I don't even consider myself adrift because of this great new direction in my sister's life. Oddly, I don't feel anything. It occurs to me that I'm simply numb. My sister is about to be married, yet I am pleasantly numb, as if in a silly stupor.

For the first time I am scared to death. It has little to do with Jay's marriage on the horizon. But it has everything to do with the realization that I am at a surprising distance from the real me. Somehow I have become surgically separated from familiar and reasonable emotions that should be a part of who I am. I am also frightened and a little disgusted that, once again, I am consumed with thoughts about myself.

It all happens so quickly. Jay and Rob celebrate their wedding on Friday afternoon after the last Maryland scene is shot. The sky is gray with heavy clouds, diffusing what fall colors remain. Nothing is diffused about the ceremony, however, as our pastor reads from the Book of Common Prayer. Amid lilting strains of classical music, they exchange vows before family and a few friends in the farmhouse living room. The warmth of the wedding matches the simplicity of their love for one another.

CHOICES

My life is full of ups and downs. The phrase rolls over and over. I am happy for Jay, of course. But what does such a change free *me* to be? To do? Just who *am* I, and where, in God's name, am I going?

Streamers of water flatten against the window beside me as our plane slices through the fog and rain on the flight back to Los Angeles. Once on the ground, we find the freeways slippery and slow; our rented house is damp and dark. It is the first time I have seen bad weather in L.A.

As Judy and Jay unpack and settle in, I glance over the script and call sheets for next week's filming. Names of actors are missing. They are no longer needed in the story line. There are several crew changes. We have more short pick-up shots than usual, and the schedule looks slower-paced. The production on *Joni* is definitely winding down.

Monday morning is still gray and chilly, but I am warmed by the friendly greetings from the crew and cast at the studio. The heavy lights on the make-up mirror drive the chill further away. Jim Collier pulls up a chair. "You look rested." Our eyes meet in the mirror and he waits for a smile. We both understand that I have been through a lot of changes lately. "I know many people have been praying for you. I've heard you got a pressure sore." He takes off his glasses and wipes them with a corner of his shirt.

I lower my head. "Yes, just a small one. I suppose I've gotten a little too thin."

"A little?" Jim replaces his glasses and rubs my shoulder. "Those hospital scenes were months ago."

"Well, I'll try and gain some." I tell a lie. "And Jim, I need the prayers." I tell a truth. Strength is what I need — physical stamina — to give my fullest energies to these last weeks of filming. But I know that emotionally, even spiritually, I am still backed against a wall.

"Listen, I know the rest of the crew has missed you. How about speaking to them as a group before we start in this morning?" Jim suggests as he leaves, tucking his clipboard under his arm.

I wheel downstairs to the sound stage where the producer has gathered everyone. "Good to see you, kid." The camera assistant gives me a hug. "She's back!" The prop man spreads his arms in welcome. The wardrobe and sound people greet me with hugs and kisses. James, the art director, waves his brush as he paints a backdrop. The gaffer, who is looping a cable on his elbow, waves and smiles from the other end of the set. My emotions are just below the surface as I mentally collect a few ideas to share. I do love these people. I have prayed for them, talked to Jesus about them, and talked to them about Him. But to avoid tears, I avoid the heavy, heartfelt speech on the tip of my tongue.

"I just want to tell you how much I've . . . I've enjoyed being with you these months. This film . . . uh, work of art, is . . . has meant so much to me. It has stretched us all creatively. It has put us all through many changes. And because of our teamwork," I say as I gesture toward the sound stage, "very many people will learn about the Lord . . . as I hope you have too."

The crew applauds. Their appreciation is warm, sincere. I want to say something more, something specific about the gospel, something more direct. To challenge these people about where they are with God. But some inkling of a double standard keeps me from going further. Tears spill over. I cry, not only because I love these people, but because I have let them down. I've let God down.

"Joni, we have a little surprise for you and the crew," interrupts Bill Brown, the executive producer, as hand-clapping subsides. "Billy Graham is at the other end of the building for a World Wide board meeting. He has asked if he can come over and talk with us for a few minutes." There are oohs and aahs and another smattering of applause.

Mr. Graham and several board members walk onto the sound stage. The tall, striking evangelist takes time to greet everyone personally, shakes hands, chats in a relaxed way as if he's known us all for years. Although I have met him several times before, I am nervous as he approaches. Stammering a bit, I keep my greeting brief. I want to direct his eyes off me and onto the crew.

"This film will speak to millions," he says as he turns to the group. "Millions who are paralyzed spiritually. People without Christ are crippled far more than Joni here." He motions toward my wheelchair. "But this movie you fine people are working on will tell of Joni's victory in Christ. What a great encouragement to so many who are suffering in so many different ways."

The group is quiet. Some lean on stage props; a few stand behind lighting tripods or sit in directors' chairs. Billy Graham is saying what I am too weak to utter.

"World Wide Pictures thanks you for the hard work you are doing," he continues as he turns to me. "And we thank you, Joni, for selflessly giving so much . . . reliving so many difficult memories for the spiritual benefit of thousands."

The image of thousands of nameless, faceless people crowds my mind. The powerful message of this true story — a young teenager's struggle to believe in God from a wheelchair — will, as he says, benefit thousands.

But what about the "me" behind the scenes? I'm afraid that people will think I'm a superhuman saint. Because of this movie, they may assume I am far more than I really am. I don't know what to say, how to respond. I manage a weak "thank you" and muster the courage to look Mr. Graham straight in the eye.

I have the sinking feeling he can look right through me.

One of the last scenes we shoot is an important one. We are re-creating a conversation I had with a man who attended my first art show. I have a lot of dialogue, and I've been memorizing it for more than a week now.

The wardrobe people have planned a nice outfit for me. I'm allowed to wear my current hairstyle and even my own make-up. Jim hasn't guided me much either. He knows I've said these lines scores of times before. It should come naturally.

On location at the small restaurant reminiscent of the little downtown café back in Baltimore, I sit across the table from an actor dressed in a marine uniform. He has an eyepatch and wears a metal hook on his right arm.

"Lights . . . camera . . . action" cues us to begin our off-the-cuff conversation.

> MARINE: "Hey, when did you get outta high school?"
>
> JONI: "Oh, sixty-seven."
>
> MARINE: "Yeah, me too. They never told us about this in Senior Problems." (*He gestures with his hook.*)
>
> JONI: "No, they sure didn't. I think in our school they called it Contemporary Issues in Social Sciences."
>
> MARINE: "Exactly."
>
> JONI: "There are a million questions, and only a couple decent answers in life."
>
> MARINE: "Half the guys in my class went to college, the other half went to Vietnam. Some lived, some died, some of us

got caught in the cracks." (*Long pause.*) "No one ever told us the world's an outhouse! Did they?"

JONI: "I am sure of only one thing. I know who put me back together."

MARINE: "How can you know?"

JONI: "I sleep nights and I laugh a lot. . . . Look, if there really is such a place as heaven and if . . . if Jesus really died on that cross because He wanted to bridge the gap between God and us, then getting to know Him and all that that means . . . well, it should be worth looking into, even for you. You see, I'd rather be in this chair, knowing Him, than on my feet without Him. And I never really knew that for sure until this moment."

I'd rather be in this chair, knowing Him, than on my feet without Him. That piece of script replays itself long after the director calls a wrap, long after I've gone back to our little house.

How can you know? I hear the actor say tauntingly.

"I sleep nights," I whisper into the darkness as I lay in bed, wide awake.

I am going home. This time for good. I lean back against the headrest of the TWA jet and think about what lies ahead. For me, right now, the movie seems to be the only thing heading forward in a charted direction, and even it is not in my life any more. Other people have the film now. Color processors. Editors. Musicians. And eventually promoters and distributors. People will pray. The movie's message, just as Mr. Graham predicted, will change lives.

The mask of that seventeen-year-old girl and her long-ago experiences must be torn off. Somehow I must pick up where I left off a year ago. The cast and crew have gone their separate ways. Judy Butler has returned to her work with the Billy Graham Association to set up a crusade in Nashville. I glance at Jay and Rob, asleep in their seats beside me. Perhaps now my life can get back to normal.

The plane drops within sight of the patchwork of snow-covered fields, farmhouses, and pastures. Our farm will be a picture postcard of drifts shouldering up to the stone house with its candlelit windows. Horses in their winter coats will be stamping their feet in the corrals, and pine trees dressed in heavy white will frame the scene. Leaving palm trees and freeways, I wonder how quickly I'll ease back into life at home.

Rob and Jay and I drive from the airport through the snow-plowed slush on the highway till we reach the country lane of the farm. Inside the house a few things have changed since Jay married — a new rug, a different chair, the living-room furniture rearranged.

I glance around the corner into my study. My desk and books are as I left them, along with a new stack of folders and letters that need attention. The Mason jars holding my brushes and paints await my return. My sketch pad lies opened on the art easel. The page is blank.

The setting is the same. I'm the one who has changed.

I don't fit any more.

And I'm not sure why, I think to myself in my own not-so-familiar bed that night. The blankets suddenly seem as heavy as the darkness, and I'm tempted to call Jay to pull down my covers. *It's probably just a little anxiety, the strain of adjustment to the months away from the farm. I'll try thinking about some Scripture verses . . . or praying.*

"They are darkened in their understanding . . . separated from the life of God . . . hardened in their hearts, having lost all sensitivity." The words, as clear as black ink on a white page, come back to haunt me. This time, the verse from Ephesians seems neither stuffy nor out of place.

God, are those words for me? The conviction, like darkness, presses in. *Darkened . . . hardened . . . could that be me? Not so much people in Hollywood, but me?* Where are the thoughts coming from? I am too dull to discern. God? The Devil? Is the Holy Spirit doing the talking, or am I shadow-boxing imaginary problems? I'm tired and I'm weak and I've been through a lot. Maybe I just need sleep.

Late December comes blustering across the fields, whistling through every crack in the farmhouse. Rob, between researching and scripting his new film project, dons a heavy coat and scarf to split more wood for the fireplaces. Jay sets up a little space heater in my study as I go back to work at my art easel.

It is winter 1978. I try desperately to keep my attention on the present, on my sketch pad. But every time I look away from the paper, my eyes focus on the movie. The people. The places. Photos of the gaffer and me framed in brass on my desk.

I look at Rob, still a new face in the farm setting. His smile and voice are linked so closely to those memories I battle. I stare at him and think of the dinner we all enjoyed in the little town of Solvang behind the mountains of Santa Barbara. Candlelight dinners around the farm table somehow seem empty by comparison.

I watch a program on television, oblivious to the story line and dialogue. Instead, I scrutinize the lighting. Are the shadows too harsh? Why aren't they using a fill card? My gaffer friend would have put in more backlighting.

A late-night movie comes on, with Burt Lancaster playing the Bird Man of Alcatraz. Don't they realize he has two shadows behind him in his cell? What sort of a professional did that? How would "our" crew have lighted it?

The bars on the cell window . . . the prison . . . the Birdman won't be released. He's in there until he dies. . . . Oh help me,

God — I'm in this wheelchair till I die. A cell. A prison . . . I can't breathe.

"I can't breathe," I call out. "I can't breathe!"

Jay rushes in, knotting her bathrobe. She quickly sits me up in bed. "What happened?" She presses her hand against my abdomen, helping me get my breath. My gasps quiet when I feel her arms around me.

I force myself to take long controlled breaths. "I don't know." On the television screen, the prison movie has broken for a commercial. I inhale slowly. "For a minute I felt like that man behind bars."

Jay lowers me back into bed. "Shh. It's only a movie." She smooths my hair back and waits by my bed in silence.

Only a movie, I think to myself as she flicks off the set. "Only a movie," I mumble in exhaustion.

The next day I am back at my easel. It has been months since I've drawn anything. I am rusty, out of practice, and everything I sketch looks wrong. Maybe I've lost my talent, my creativity. Perhaps I'm so dry I will never be able to draw again. Evil, ugly panic raises its head once more. With eyes wide, I glare at my feeble attempts on the art pad. I can't even draw a straight line.

Pushed to the brink, I spit the pencil from my mouth. Lodging my shoulder against the easel, I sweep my arm across the desk. The pad, the pencils, the books — everything goes flying, crashing against the wall and hitting the floor. The noise attracts Jay who is vacuuming in the next room. She comes running.

"I can't draw! I can't do anything!" I scream hysterically.

Jay stands dumfounded, looking at the mess on the floor, her hands open in question. Incredulous, she raises her eyes to me.

I shake my head and sob, "I don't know who I am . . . I don't know who I am." My voice cracks. Tears blur my vision. My nose runs and I lick my lips. Helplessly, I look at my sister.

I don't know who I am.

God is putting pressure on.

I debate with Him, having enough faith to doubt and still believe that He is there and listening.

"God, this movie was all Your idea. I didn't knock on anybody's door, anxious to bare my soul and share the struggle of those early years in my chair. I didn't want to be anybody's idea of a star. . . . I just wanted to do something for You, for Your Kingdom.

"What You have here is not sin, God. Give me a break. Look at all the sacrifices I've made. I'm drained. Tired. I've lost weight. I've been slapped with hospital memories. I've been tempted, sure, but You must know I'm in a wheelchair. . . . It's only understandable that my heart would get out in front of my head. And isn't it about time? Look, I've been content with my singleness for years. So what's the big deal in going out with somebody, even if they don't know You? What's wrong with an occasional date?

"And look at all those other changes. Living in 'Hollyweird' is bound to make anybody a little batso. Besides, there was so little time to read or fellowship with lots of Christians. . . . It was up at dawn, run to work, scarf down dinner, cram a script, and into bed early.

"And Jay's married now. Shouldn't that give me every reason in the world to wonder about my own future?

"And look what else those months away from home did. I sacrificed weeks away from my art easel. It's going to take me forever to feel comfortable with that pencil in my mouth again. Little wonder my creativity has shriveled up.

"This isn't sin! This is life. I'm expected to be exhausted. I am *not* darkened in my understanding or hardened or insensitive. I've made big sacrifices, and I deserve a little time off and a bit of understanding on Your part. On everybody's part."

But the pressure doesn't let up.

Another morning dawns after another fitful night. My first thought is that the sunlight pouring through the gauze curtains will, I hope, stick to my senses. Will somehow brighten me from the outside in. But I am antsy and bored, still tired, and anything but peaceful.

Doors click shut and faucets run. Somebody flicks on "Good Morning America" in the other room. I smell sausage frying and coffee brewing.

"Morning," Jay says as she enters my bedroom carrying two mugs. She wedges my coffee next to my pillow, placing one end of a flexible plastic tube into the mug and the other end in my mouth.

"You're in here early," I comment, sipping coffee.

"Well, there's somebody at the door to see you," she explains.

I give her a puzzled look.

"It's Bill Mock, Dad's old wrestling buddy." She sounds equally puzzled. Bill is not a regular visitor to the farm. He comes only for special get-togethers that my parents occasionally have with Daddy's wrestling crowd.

"Bill says he has a message for you," Jay explains. "Do you want him to come in or shall I tell him to wait until you get up?"

I know Bill has come some distance at such an early hour. How peculiar that he didn't call last night. "It's okay. Let him come in now."

Jay smooths my blanket, straightens my pillow, and leaves to get my unexpected guest.

It's odd to see Bill walk through my bedroom door. His face

and hands are still red from the cold. That makes him look even more out of place in my warm, cozy room. I can sense that he feels the strangeness too as he takes off his cap and approaches the foot of my bed.

"Joni, I know this is unusual," he begins. "When I woke up this morning, God gave me a clear message. And He told me to give it to you right away."

I am stunned by Bill's directness about something that obviously has nothing to do with my father or wrestling. I am numbed by his seriousness. But I nod with a smile and watch him turn to a marked place in his Bible.

"First Samuel 15:22," he announces, his voice steady. "'To obey is better than sacrifice.'" He closes his Bible, and for an awkward moment we are both quiet.

"I don't know what to add," he offers meekly. "Do you know what this is about, Joni?"

"Obedience . . . is better . . . than sacrifice," I repeat quietly. "Yes, I know . . . I mean, I think I understand the message."

As quickly and oddly as he came, Bill leaves.

Bill Mock's visit haunts me, though I do my best to rationalize it away. It couldn't have been a message from God. Come on now, really. It just appears that way because of the timing. It was just a coincidence. . . . Yes, that's it. Just a coincidence, a strange twist of timing. . . . Besides, I can't get all hung up in figuring out that kind of thing right now. Old Testament messages will have to wait. I've got more urgent concerns.

The Billy Graham Crusade in Tampa, Florida, is coming up soon, and World Wide needs one last bit of filming for the movie. The ending. I am to speak from the crusade platform to conclude the movie *Joni,* and I've got a script to memorize.

Jay spreads the three pages neatly on my desk. I read words that are — were — mine:

> When I think of Jesus paralyzed on the cross simply because He loved me, even when I couldn't have cared less about Him, I know I've discovered something priceless. And that healing is His gift of love to you and me. You know, trusting Christ is not necessarily having trustful feelings. It is an act of the will. We need to *believe* it; lay our sins and brokenness at His feet and receive spiritual healing that will start us on a great eternal journey.
>
> I became a Christian when I was a high-school sophomore. I believed my grades would go up, homework would be less boring. I'd be more popular. It didn't exactly work out that way, though. To follow Christ may cost something — you may be asked to fellowship in His suffering. But I can promise on my own experience that over and over again you will see, feel, and touch His sustaining power.

CHOICES

I look up after reading the first page. A wet glaze blurs my eyes. I am sincerely moved by my own words. Honest words. Ever since my accident I have clenched and clawed my way by God's grace to say those things from the heart.

My tears are nostalgic, telling me I have now, somehow, lost the heart for these words.

Judy Butler leaves her office in Nashville to fly with me to Tampa. It is the day before I am to speak.

Florida is a refreshing change from the last weeks of panic and pain. The sun, the fragrant breeze, the coconut palms with their silvery tips clicking in the wind. I sit beside the motel pool absorbing it all, rehearsing my lines silently.

> I'm glad this life is *not* forever. That's a dark subject, right? We all get so caught up in *now*. It's hard to think about heaven when it seems so far away. Besides, you have to *die* in order to get there.
>
> But if God were to take us to heaven today without changing us inside, the purity and holiness there would only repel us. And we'd become terribly bored after a while just as we do with even the most exciting things on earth.
>
> Can you imagine what it will be like to never again have the desire to sin? To never again feel guilty, alone, or depressed? Heaven will be heavenly because God will give us new bodies and new minds, and the Bible promises that we will *enjoy* Him forever.

I find myself in that crazy, unreal world again, listening to this *Joni* character tell me things I should already know. But I do wonder as I lean my head back and gaze up the skirts of a coconut palm . . . I wonder . . . at never having the desire to sin . . . at never feeling guilty or depressed.

An hour before the Saturday night crusade begins, I sit in front of a large mirror ringed with bright lights. The make-up man — nobody I know from the old crew — sponges thick pancake color on my face and neck. He works quietly while I nervously scan my lines one last time.

So many words. Important words Jim Collier has carefully selected to wrap up the message of the movie. And they've just told me that 30,000 people are seated out there in the stadium. I swallow, trying to clear my dry throat. I stare distractedly at the crinkled sheets of script on the counter.

> And I can't wait! I intend to stand before the Lord with legs that walk and arms and hands that work, and I will lift them high and shout out to the whole universe that Jesus Christ is who He claims to be as the very Son of God, the King of Kings and Lord of Lords, and *that's* only the beginning!
>
> If I hadn't decided to go swimming in Chesapeake Bay on that hot July day in 1967, I wouldn't be sitting here, speaking to you about the glory of God. But *I am!*

The make-up man has finished with me. I'm now sitting in a draped and carpeted corner of the stadium locker room. Couches and chairs disguise the ugly concrete. This is where the platform party, including Mr. Graham, Cliff Barrows, and Bev Shea, will meet and pray. I'm glad, privileged, to be included.

After we pray, Mr. Graham greets me. He is flanked by several men in dark suits holding walkie-talkies. He reminds me how happy he is about the progress on the movie. He's been told that the editors have nearly finished; all that's needed is the last minutes of footage to be shot tonight. Then he turns and walks out the stadium tunnel. The rest of us follow.

Our small group steps onto the field and moves past the television crew and press tables to the platform. The glaring stadium lights are blinding, and I have to squint to see the thousands filling the stands.

In the moments before I'm introduced, I fidget. My eyes dart to the script folded open on Judy's lap. A knot grips my jittery stomach. I am afraid. I try to smother the butterflies, to breathe calm to my pounding heart. It is not like me to be this unnerved.

"Joni, move. That's your cue!" Judy elbows me.

Startled, I realize that I somehow missed my introduction. I power my wheelchair up the makeshift ramp to the microphone. I smile and acknowledge Cliff Barrows who welcomes me with applause. After a quick, silent *God, help me,* I launch into the beginning of the script.

> "Someone once asked how I had managed it — getting my life together. At the time I couldn't say much more than that Jesus had done it. I only knew a handful of Bible verses then, but I did feel that God had taken the broken pieces of my life — physical, emotional, spiritual — and made something beautiful!"

Each word, each phrase that booms and echoes across the huge stadium flashes in black ink on the white page of my mind. This isn't so bad. I relax.

> "This was at least eight years ago. Today I know that the Lord is creating something in me that I could never create for myself. That is not to say that I now understand all the 'whys.' But I know *who* holds the answers, and I can wait!"

This is a breeze. And what powerful things are being said. I can't see expressions on the faces of people seated so far away in the stadium, so I say my lines to the cameramen. Oh . . . oh! It is . . . one of the cameramen from the movie. And the gaffer. He is another one of the crew people they've flown in from Hollywood. For a split second I lose my place, then quickly rivet my focus back on the script.

> "And anyway, the exciting thing is that you don't have to break your neck to find God!"

The audience laughs, as the script suggested they would. I nervously join them, welcoming the break to gather my thoughts. When the rumble of laughter subsides, I zero in on the next line of black-inked words imprinted on my memory.

"I wanted to put you at ease about that. Suffering can help the search along. Your priorities get rearranged. But I imagine most of you would catch on faster than I did.

"Still, handicaps come in all shapes and sizes . . . broken homes, broken hearts, anxiety feelings that threaten to take over. Burdens of doubt. A deep loneliness. The confines of your soul may seem as limiting as — a wheelchair. I *know* that feeling. But I also know that . . .

"I also know that . . ."

Oh, God! What is my next line? Seconds tick by. Nothing. It's not coming. Here I sit in front of 30,000 people . . . *God, what is my line?*

I drop my head. Tears well in my eyes. Several more seconds tick by. I don't dare look at Mr. Graham or Mr. Barrows or Judy, who has my script. I raise my head and start pulling something, *anything,* out of the air.

"I know that . . . that God's Word is real. And . . . and Romans 8:28 has meant . . . so much. And all things really do fit together for our good . . . and, and His glory."

I ramble, repeating bits and pieces of things I have said so many times before. All the while, through tears, I try desperately to pick up the script. I can't. Several minutes later, I finish.

The crowd stands and applauds. Mr. Graham does the same, leading the rest of the platform party in an ovation. It is only then that I realize my tears have moved these people. I'm so ashamed — my words didn't make sense — not to me anyway. I'm certain the film shot cannot be used to adequately conclude the movie. But, incredibly, God has made use of my ramblings.

"I blew it!" I whisper to Judy as she wipes my tear-streaked face. "In front of all these people . . . I blew it!" I begin to cry again.

I leave Florida, humiliated and defeated.

My soul seems as dull and dim as the gray sky outside my study window.
Snow is threatening. How I wish it would come. Late winter is
never pretty on the farm. A fresh coat of white would at least cover
the mud and manure around the barn and blanket the stark leafless
trees and barren fields.

My Bible reading is just as muddy and barren. Try as I will,
nothing gets through. God's Word is supposed to be sharper than a
sword to my soul. But I don't feel the cutting edge.

Yet I refuse to think of myself as hardened. Insensitive.
Darkened in my understanding. I understand plenty — I'm tired.
Just taking a little longer than usual to get my spiritual bearings.

The movie editors call. They want me to return to California
to do some voice-dubbing sessions for the film where the sound is a
bit garbled. They also want me to repair those lines I flubbed in
Tampa.

The idea of escape appeals to me. A getaway to palm trees and
sun and warmer weather. More than two months have passed since
I left California, and it will be odd to work with new people. All of
the original crew will be busy on other projects by now.

While in Los Angeles, I visit Grace Community Church for a
Sunday service, a church I had occasionally attended during the
many months of shooting. I sit in the back and watch people file in,

their faces clean and fresh. They all look alike. They have notebooks and Bibles in their well-manicured hands. Their pencils are sharpened, their skirt hems are at the proper length. Their hair is cut neatly over the ears. I wonder if they ever get their hands dirty with the world's problems.

I'm being a snob.

The choir enthusiastically sings a triumphant hymn. But only after the last note do I realize that my spirit was not lifted by the tune nor did my heart respond to the words. The service is for the other people sitting in the pews, not for me.

The pastor, John MacArthur, begins to preach his sermon. His topic, the obedience that marks the Christian. He quotes the Bible. His voice is urgent. He talks about narrow gates and straight paths. He punctuates his words with a pointed finger aimed at his congregation. Everyone around me listens attentively, nods in agreement, scribbles notes in notebooks and Bible margins. The deeper he gets into his sermon, the more distant I am. Above it all. On the outside looking in.

Listen to him. MacArthur has really changed . . . gotten legalistic lately. I don't remember him being so uptight and hardlined. He's become so narrow since I heard him last. I watch with amazement as people around me take it all in without a questioning look.

We've been freed from living out a bunch of rules and regulations, I argue with him. *A whole book in the New Testament was written about that. Life can't be that black and white when we're led by the Spirit. And what about God's grace? Doesn't it cover a multitude of mistakes? Life's too short to sweat the small stuff. We're not under law.*

The microphone picks up his words and booms them out over the sanctuary. " 'What then? Shall we sin because we are not under law but under grace? By no means!' "

I am stunned at the uncanny timing of that verse. Why, I was just thinking about the law and grace. I quickly try to explain away the painful truth of the text, while keeping up in the race with MacArthur.

He cites another verse from Romans. " 'Shall we go on sinning so that grace may increase? By no means! We died to sin; how can we live in it any longer?' "

Now the congregation has faded into the background and I am the only person in the entire church. MacArthur is speaking to me.

"'If they have escaped the corruption of the world by knowing our Lord and Savior Jesus Christ and are again entangled in it and overcome,'" he reads about apostates from 2 Peter 2:20, "'they are worse off at the end than they were at the beginning.'"

Apostasy? Ugh! What an awful word! That's not me, I am relieved to think. *But corruption?* I linger on that word while MacArthur passes me. *I know Christ, and He's pulled me from the corruption of the world — there's nothing even appealing about a walk down Sunset Boulevard. The sordid materialism and dog-eat-dog decadence.* To my dismay, I'm being arrogant again. It is the corruption of little things — snobbery, pride, toying with temptation or rebellion — that makes a fool of me.

It is not John MacArthur who has changed! This sudden realization is a shock. It is I! And it isn't his words that are needling me. It is God's words!

I pick up his roll of verses as he quickly flips back to Matthew 23. "'In the same way, on the outside you appear to people as righteous but on the inside you are full of hypocrisy and wickedness.'" I listen wide-eyed. The verse is about religious leaders who fool themselves into thinking they are right with God when actually they don't know Him at all. Again, I'm relieved to think I'm not a false prophet. But hypocrisy? My heart sinks. I've edged awfully close to seeing black as white. Bad as good.

MacArthur expounds a bit further and then goes to 2 Peter to close. "'Therefore, dear friends, since you already know this, be on your guard so that you may not be carried away . . . and fall from your secure position.'" Another sigh of relief — my position in Christ is secure. But my experience with Him? Oh, I grieve. I know I've let down my guard. Gotten carried away.

My heart is racing and I am short of breath. I've been grabbed and jerked up short, as though I were dizzily peering over the edge of a dark and murky pit, thankful that someone has caught me.

"'The word of God . . . judges the thoughts and attitudes of the heart. Nothing in all creation is hidden from God's sight.

Everything is uncovered and laid bare before the eyes of Him to whom we must give account.'" That verse from Hebrews seems fresh, brand new, as though I have never heard it before. It isn't so much that MacArthur is right or that my father's friend Bill is right. It is God's Word that's right — alive and active. It has sliced into me sharper than any double-edged sword. Dividing my soul and spirit.

I leave church deeply humiliated, my soul wounded and cowering. But in the deepest part of my spirit I know that truth has gotten through.

I'm back at my desk on the farm, feeling shaky and a little sick. And I gingerly take Scripture now as though it were a healing prescription, reading portions as if I were swallowing medicine.

I lean my head back and stare at the ceiling, remembering what it was like to be sick when I was a child and have my mother or father take care of me. They would hold a spoon of medicine to my lips. Touch my fevered brow. Walk quietly in and out of my room. I was always comforted by the sound of their voices downstairs. It was also a comfort to know that soon I would get better. I wouldn't always be sick.

Judy sends me a postcard with a get-well message. She simply pens Philippians 1:9: "And this is my prayer: that your love may abound more and more in knowledge and depth of insight, so that you may be able to discern what is best and may be pure and blameless until the day of Christ." She knows. She knew all along, just as Betsy, Diana, Steve, Jay, and the others did.

Could it be? . . . Yes, it could. The movie, the very piece of creativity I was most proud to be a part of, was God's way of pressing me up against myself. And I don't like what I see: hidden resentment, discontent in almost every situation, envy, the pull of temptation, a lazy attitude toward His Word, self-centered prayers.

The list looms and my stomach gets queasy again.

For months I have been wrestling with my problems, not even certain what is at the bottom of those struggles. *Could all that "struggling,"* it slowly dawns, *be nothing but a polite word for postponed obedience?*

Even though I still feel the burnt edges of exhaustion, the taint of humiliation, I very much want to be well. I know the answer, somehow, is in the Lord Jesus. The compassionate, sensitive way He dealt with sick people is always comforting. Sweet and gentle Jesus.

But now as I read the stories of His dealing with sin, I notice that He overthrows tables and flails a whip at people who pollute His Father's temple. He confronts those who try to mask their sinful attitudes. He exposes uncleanness in the lives of His disciples. He even sharply rebukes His closest friends.

I don't like reading these things, but they are there. He does not let selfishness or pride slip by His notice. He squares off against sin.

And He squares off against the sin in me. My sin — the word itself stings — has gone from a tiny trickle to a raging torrent that cannot be ignored. And now it's as if Jesus Himself is holding it up before my face and saying lovingly but firmly, "See! This is what you've become. What are you going to do about it, Joni?"

Do I hate sin in my life as much as He must? My heart breaks. The answer is no. I'm nowhere near as close to Christ as I had assumed.

I read from the book of James: "Wash your hands, you sinners, and purify your hearts, you double-minded. Grieve, mourn and wail. Change your laughter to mourning and your joy to gloom. Humble yourselves before the Lord, and he will lift you up."[8]

Tears stream down my cheeks and splatter on my desk. This verse, I'm ashamed — no, pleased — to say, was written for me.

I read a page from an old Puritan book. It becomes my prayer:

O God,
I know that I often do thy work without thy power,
 and sin by my dead, heartless, blind service,
  my lack of inward light, love, delight,
  my mind, heart, tongue moving without thy help.

Help me to rejoice in my infirmities and give thee praise,

to acknowledge my deficiencies before others
and not be discouraged by them,
that they may see thy glory more clearly.

Teach me that I must act by a power supernatural,
whereby I can attempt things above my strength,
and bear evils beyond my strength,
acting for Christ in all, and
having his superior power to help me.[9]

Oh, how I want to do His work in His power. Not mine. And I want very much to serve. But not heartlessly. I want to admit my weaknesses and not be discouraged by them. *And Lord, if I attempt things beyond my strength, may I always find help in You.*

The healing is happening.

I reread my book *A Step Further* with great interest, swallowing the advice Steve and I wrote for others to read. I notice in the introduction the words, "Oh, I'm still paralyzed. . . . But I'm no longer depressed." I smile at the confidence with which I penned that phrase. Little did I realize then that depression would one day hit me so hard. And I cannot presume that it will never return. I call my editor and ask her to delete that line in the next printing.

My mind, much clearer now, wanders back to that sermon on obedience I heard in church just weeks ago. What about my argument against law and for grace?

I realize that I can hardly abuse a religion where I am slavishly chained to obey a bunch of rules and regulations. But I have abused the freedom Christ has given me. The hazard in any system of choice is that I take the risk of misusing it.

I'm a prisoner of Christ. Me, this humbled and sorely disciplined child of His. But I am also free in Christ, and I pray with wrenching and heaving pleas that God will take a risk with me — that is, let me keep making my choices.

Yes, I admit to God, there will always be the danger of choosing the wrong thing, the sinful thing. But instinctively I know that if I am to change into a responsible, mature, and godly woman, I must still make choices even if, occasionally, they are wrong.

And Father, I want to yield to your Holy Spirit who can make those choices the ones that best honor You. And I believe You will sovereignly perfect me no matter what I choose.

The Ministry

Serve wholeheartedly, as if you were serving the Lord, not men.
—Ephesians 6:7

It is 1979 and a chilly, early spring day in Maryland. The yellow forsythia along the pasture fence promises that the barren farmland will soon be green with life. A gust of wind stings my cheeks, and I'm grateful when Jay takes off her sweater and wraps it around my shoulders. Standing behind my wheelchair, she leans forward and folds her arms around me. I can tell a question is coming.

"Are you sure you know what you're doing?" she asks as we watch my other sisters, Kathy and Linda, carry boxes, packages, and suitcases out to the waiting pickup truck. *Am I doing the right thing? Is this move to Southern California really in God's will?* My carefully packed books, clothes, medical supplies, and keepsakes seem to know where they're going. Do I?

Thinking back, I marvel over the circumstances that have brought me to this decision. A book and the recent movie have detailed the long journey toward accepting my paralysis. But I have learned, all too painfully, that you can't live in a world of books and movies. They can only reflect, in part, who you really are. Their glitter fades quicker than a spotlight.

Now I must get on with living.

I am thirty years old. And I sense a conviction, a certainty that things must change — just as surely as Jay and Rob, the farm and I are changing. The circumstances are right for it.

I cannot continue to be the girl whose faith wavers and weakens at every new juncture. I must grow. That faith must stretch further. And I cannot just be a "hearer" of God's Word. I must be a "doer" and practice these new lessons I've learned.

It simply is time. Time for me to launch out on my own.

Another cold gust of wind whistles through the pines in the pasture. "Brr . . . I'm freezing. Jay, pull this sweater tighter around me, would you?"

Jay knots the woolen sleeves, tugging their warmth snugly around my neck. Without prompting, she reaches up and pulls my stocking hat down around my ears. I feel instant relief and watch appreciatively as she holds my hands in her warm grip. She knows just what to do. In fact, she knows my routine needs better than I do.

Oh, I love her. I will miss her.

As I watch her adjust my feet on the wheelchair footpedals, I push a frightening thought out of my mind: life without Jay will mean the loss of a great deal of security. Our lives have been intricately entwined for years. We have lived together on the farm, traveled everywhere, done everything together. Jay is more than my sister. She is my confidante, my nurse, my roommate. Above all, she is my friend. Though she has her own life — her daughter Kay and now Rob — I know she will miss me too. That hurts.

The pickup truck is packed tightly now, engine idling and ready to go. The driver, a friend who is heading to the West Coast on other business, pulls off his gloves and climbs into the truck. Gunning the motor, he calls good-by and heads down our driveway. Within a week he and my things will arrive in sunny Southern California.

"Well, Joni, you're next!" My sister Linda smiles as she walks toward me, rubbing her hands together.

"You know, it's still not too late to change your mind." Jay reminds me that I have not answered her earlier question. She scoops Charlie, our farm cat, into her arms and rubs his chin.

"I know, Jay. I know all of you . . ." I swallow and glance at each one. "You want what's best for me. But I believe this is the right choice. . . . Besides, spring days in California have got to be warmer than this!" Our laughter breaks the poignancy of the moment, and we head into the house for some hot coffee around the log fire.

Sitting alone by that fire later in the afternoon, I think more about my decision to move so many miles away.

Decisions. Choices. I'm forever bumping up against those words. The decision to write a book about my life. Should I make the movie? Just what is God doing in my life, and where am I going? Who am I? Is a move away from the farm wise or not? And choices bring change.

My track record with God hasn't been the greatest this past year, but I've confessed inward rebellion, and I believe He is faithful in cleaning and clearing the slate. I sense the presence of His Spirit as I read the Bible. More than ever, I want to delight myself in Him. And if my life is truly lined up with God's will in these areas, then I know I can follow my heart's desire.

Mentally, I list those things making up my "heart's desire." I feel it is time to step out on my own. To step into a new dream. To be a "doer" of God's Word, I must help others — *disabled people with dreams of their own.*

I keep remembering my brief conversation with Debbie Stone that day at Rancho Los Amigos Hospital. Her words have haunted me as I have pondered my decision to begin such a ministry: "Joni, you wouldn't believe the problems most handicapped people face. Spiritual struggles, yes, but down-to-earth practical problems too."

I am a handicapped person who has experienced the overwhelming love and grace of God. I have the added advantage of loving family and friends who have cared for me faithfully, whether by lifting my spirits or lifting me into a wheelchair. Out there beyond the pasture and the walls of my cozy home are thousands of men and women, young people and children, who have none of that. They need not only comfort from God's Word, but practical caring from His people. I know I have been called to give it . . . somehow.

As incredible as it seems, the call includes Los Angeles. There, I can put together such a dream. I already know a few rehabilitation professionals from my own stay at Rancho years ago. I'll be returning to Grace Community Church. I have friendships with people connected with World Wide Pictures. And I do love the climate. I will have to face some painful memories — and the smog. But even after weighing these things, Los Angeles is still ideal.

As the afternoon fades into the early dusk of a spring evening, I sit alone in the shadowed living room; my only light, the glowing fire. Peace settles in my heart. No doubt. No panic. Just peace.

I don't know what lies ahead. But I do know who I am. I have a dream, and I know where I am going.

"Have you got the tickets?" I call to Kerbe as she unloads her bags at the airport curb.

"Uh . . . no, I don't think Jay gave them to me." She rummages through her purse, searching for the airline envelope. "Maybe Rob has them!"

Rob pats his jacket pockets. "Nope, not here," he says.

What a way to begin my new life out on my own! I can't even find the tickets to where I'm going! I scan the travel bags and carry-on luggage stacked around me on the sidewalk. Something tells me to look on my lap. "Here they are," I call out. Someone has wedged the ticket folder between my leg and the side of the wheelchair.

Kerbe grabs the tickets and shoves them into the hands of the impatient skycap who has already tagged most of our luggage and loaded it onto a cart. Making one final check, my eyes catch sight of the purple check-through tags. *Purple . . . that's not Los Angeles. Those tags will send our luggage to San Francisco!*

"Rob, stop that cart!"

Jay unlocks my wheels and hustles me through the automatic doors. "Don't forget to find a good doctor and a medical supply store," she reminds me as we rush through the security gate. "And don't forget to order new catheters and legbags. You're almost out."

Frantic moments later the tags are changed, the tickets stamped, good-by tears shed too quickly, and Kerbe and I are settling in our seats on the plane.

As the engines whine to full power, I strain to look out the window, hoping to catch a final glimpse of Jay and Rob, Mom and Dad, Kathy, and the others who came with us to say good-by. It was such a maddening rush at the gate. There wasn't time to say all that I wanted to say. Not that we won't see each other again. It just feels that way right now.

I picture Daddy standing at the curb, leaning on his crutches, wanting to help but unable to. He didn't know I was studying him. I could tell he was hiding concern for his youngest daughter about to leave the nest — in a wheelchair no less. He worries about where I'll live and who will help me, though I've told him at least ten times that John MacArthur, the pastor at Grace Community Church, has arranged for me to stay in a little house next to the church. And Kerbe, my cousin, will be living with me, along with Judy Butler, on loan for a year from the Billy Graham Association to help set up my new ministry. "Everything's okay, Daddy," I have told him loudly and repeatedly, pushing past his hearing impairment.

"Anything you say, hon." His blue eyes twinkle but his lip quivers.

Mother, on the other hand, was a pillar of strength this morning. Giving directions to everyone. Helping unload luggage from the station wagon. Like the calm in the eye of the storm. I hope I'll carry some of that family trait in the unknown months ahead.

Our jet takes off and banks left, heading west, and I let my head sink comfortably into the cushion. Fields and towns below us become obscured by clouds as we sweep higher into the sky. The edges of the morning's memories grow fuzzy, blurred by time and distance. Just as my eyes close on the edge of sleep, I feel the presence of someone standing by my seat.

"Aren't you the girl who just did that movie?" I look up into the smiling face of a woman in a high-fashion suit heavily accented with jewelry. "I'm sure I saw your photograph in a magazine recently."

"Well, I guess it could have been me. I just finished playing my own part in a movie about my life."

We chat about the movie. She explains that she and her husband prayed for me during the filming. They had difficulty imagining how anyone could relive such painful memories, and I assure her it was only possible because of the prayers of people like herself.

Kerbe puts down her magazine and listens in. After the woman returns to her seat, Kerbe turns toward me, tucking one leg underneath her. "What *was* it like, Joni? I mean, you know, doing a movie?"

I look into my cousin's clear blue eyes. She is a pretty girl — young, excited, and happy to be starting this new adventure with me. Just entering her twenties, she is anxious to follow the Lord's leading in her life. But her question reminds me that few people really know what I have been through emotionally and spiritually in the past year.

"You've got to understand that it wasn't very glamorous," I sigh.

Choosing my words carefully, I describe the pretty actress in the blue bathing suit — her grace and elegance, her striking figure — and the contrast of my embarrassment over my own appearance that day. The awkwardness. The ugliness. I rein in any temptation to enlarge the facts and become a spiritual exhibitionist.

As I wind out the story like the string from a ball of yarn, I wonder to myself what God saw that day. How He viewed me that afternoon on the beach. I was so concerned about the way I looked, but that was nothing compared with what God must have seen on the inside. If a mere bathing suit exposed useless, puffy legs, how could I ever have thought I could hide a resentful spirit from the Lord?

As I tell Kerbe about the rest of the movie months, the remaining hours of our flight pass quickly. The jet shifts altitude, and we begin our descent into Los Angeles.

We can see the gleaming white HOLLYWOOD sign propped like a billboard on the hillside overlooking the city. It reminds me that I must never again say I can't be touched by resentment. Never again take God's grace for granted. I am free in Christ. But I am a prisoner of Christ.

We land smoothly and taxi to the gate. Kerbe and I wait as the other passengers grab carry-on luggage from the overhead compartments and shuffle up the aisle to the front exit.

I feel a hand touch my shoulder and look up into the smile of the fashionably dressed lady. As she is pushed along by the flow of people, she turns and says, "We'll be looking for the movie . . . you're a really great person."

I want to say thanks but I can't. She has no idea of what went on in my heart behind the scenes of that film. But I know. And God knows.

"You're kind, but," I call after her, "don't we have a great God!"

"California, here I come, right back where I started from," I hum as we speed along the Hollywood freeway past borders of dusty oleanders that hide endless subdivisions.

Traffic thickens and we close our windows against the heat and fumes. Air conditioning brings cool and quiet. Images of the Maryland countryside flash before my eyes: spreading maples rustling in a fresh breeze, the spring house beside the pasture creek on our farm, and the sweeping valley down to the nearby river. What a different life I will have in Southern California. The only valley I've seen here is the San Fernando Valley, and it is overflowing with spreading housing tracts and sweeping freeways. Will I find a real home here?

We exit at the turnoff that takes us to Grace Community Church and arrive at the little stucco house that will be our temporary home. We see that someone from the church has hammered a sturdy ramp in place at the front door and widened the doorways. Others have provided a couch, a dinette set, lamps and cushions, pictures and plants, all arranged by someone with decorating skill. It is a welcoming, friendly place to begin.

Church people detour from their car-pool routes and grocery shopping to drop by and introduce themselves, casseroles in hand. Housewarming cards nest themselves in our mailbox. Freshly baked chocolate-chip cookies appear on our doorstep.

In all these ways and more, Grace Community goes out of its way to show kindness. Even John MacArthur takes time from study and appointments to visit. He comes as a brother, informal in slacks and a pale blue golfing sweater. I thank him for arranging all this, nodding toward the little house.

"We're just glad you're here," he says and taps the armrest of my wheelchair. I'm pleased he feels comfortable enough to touch. "How are plans for your ministry coming along?"

We discuss the budget Judy and I have laid out and the small office we plan to rent nearby. We are wasting no time in putting my dream into motion.

"You're welcome to look at what we've got going here." He gestures toward the church buildings. "But . . ." He hesitates. "You should spend more time with Dr. Sam Britten, one of our elders. He started our handicap outreach. He's also the director of quite a big center at the university."

I have already met Dr. Britten at our first board meeting. He was very personable, asking to be called Dr. Sam, putting his hand on my shoulder, and pulling up a chair to talk. I suppose that sort of warmth comes from his twenty years of working with disabled students.

The day after John MacArthur's visit, Kerbe makes an appointment for me to visit Dr. Sam at California State University.

The campus is not far from the church. Kerbe drives me there, and we search out the Center of Achievement for the Physically Disabled, which Dr. Sam directs. Kerbe parks her Camaro in the student lot and hails a passing student to help me out of the car.

I immediately feel comfortable on this campus. A row of parking places for the handicapped lines the front of the physical-education building, our destination. A girl in a power wheelchair, like the one I use at the house, is lowering herself from a van on a mechanical lift. A muscular young paraplegic in a tank top wheels by me in his sporty racing chair, books on his lap and bag draped over his wheelchair handle. I follow the dusty tracks of his wheels to the entrance. This, I figure, must be Dr. Britten's center.

Inside, the shiny linoleum of the long corridor reflects the sunlight streaming through the glass door at the far end, and we follow the echoes of laughter and voices to a door on the left, which opens into a large room. We stand in the doorway and watch.

Young men like the student we passed on the sidewalk are out of their wheelchairs, doing sit-ups on red gym mats. A girl who looks like a staff person braces the elbow of an elderly man as he takes shaky steps with stiff legs and the aid of a cane. Leg braces hang on the walls like pots on a kitchen rack, each in its orderly group. Canes, crutches, and walkers are neatly lined by the parallel bars at the far end of the room. Pulleys with weights fill one wall next to a floor-to-ceiling mirror. The place has all the trappings of Rancho Los Amigos but is somehow different.

Weights slam, straps buckle, people chatter and laugh.

Laughter. That is the difference.

I spot Dr. Britten. Tall, with a clean-cut athletic build, he stands by a young quadriplegic whose gloved hands are strapped to the pedals of an exercise cycle bolted to a table. He gives the boy encouragement while adjusting knobs on the machine. The boy leans forward in his chair, straining to throw his weight into each turn of the cycle. Dr. Britten smiles and squeezes the boy's arm. When he turns away, he spots us in the doorway.

"Come on in," he calls above the clamor. "I've been expecting you."

Kerbe wheels me into the room, and I feel as though I belong here. I can tell this is a place where things get done.

"Nice to see you again," I say as I balance myself forward and extend my arm in an awkward greeting. Dr. Sam takes my hand in his and smiles, clasping my elbow. His brown eyes are warm, sincere.

"Have you thought more about my suggestion that you can drive?" he asks as he glances at his clipboard. I am surprised, having entirely forgotten about our discussion at the board meeting a few nights ago. At that time he said he thought I could drive a van, but I politely dismissed it as impossible. "The best universities in the country have tested me. Everybody knows I don't have the muscles to turn a steering wheel," I told him.

"If you're open to it, I've got you scheduled for an evaluation," he says. "Now."

"Well, yes . . . but do you really think someone like me ought to be on the freeways. I mean, honestly?" We slowly make our way through the maze of people and machinery. Before he answers, he takes time to introduce us to various staff and students. We end up at an exercise table neatly piled with evaluation forms and medical consent slips.

"Did you see those vans parked out front?" He scoots a stool next to me and extends my arm, feeling my bicep muscles with his fingers. I nod absent-mindedly, absorbed by his work. He bends, twists, and stretches my arms, asking me to offer resistance now and then. As he jots notes on several of the forms, he motions with his pencil toward a handicapped girl wheeling by. "She drives one of those vans."

I stare at the back of the girl as she wheels away. She looks far more disabled than I. I return my attention to Dr. Sam, who begins to test my coordination and reflexes.

Later in the day, after I've talked with several disabled people who drive, Dr. Sam pushes me up to one of the exercise cycles — the same one I saw the quadriplegic boy cycling with his arms. He takes a pair of leather gloves off the wall and rips open the velcro straps.

"Your evaluation looked great." Dr. Sam smiles. "I see no reason why you can't begin some simple strengthening exercises right now."

"Driving, huh?" I challenge him with an unbelieving smile.

"You can do it." He looks directly into my eyes as he straps my hands to the cycling machine. "I know you can. We'll worry about the steering wheel later."

What in the world does he mean? I begin pedaling. Maybe answers come later. Then again, I did come here to ask questions. Sam Britten's obviously an expert, and I do need direction on starting a ministry to disabled people. I just didn't realize I'd be the first one on the receiving end.

Heaving my shoulders to push the cycling pedals, I begin to

feel a part of the pulse of the place. My heart rate quickens within minutes, and I breathe deeply, remembering athletic advice from days when I was on my feet. It feels good. For the time being I forget my questions. I think about how my father could benefit from a place like this.

Everyone is busy with routines except one young woman, who sits in the corner like a statue, her arms propped on the wheelchair armrests. Her lovely Latin looks and her mass of curly dark hair overshadow her wheelchair. An attendant speaks to her in Spanish, and I wonder whether it is her striking appearance or the distant way she observes the rest of us that sets her apart so distinctly. I wonder about her and her almost tangible isolation. Perhaps she is some movie star from South America.

Puffing and panting, I take a breather as Sam Britten approaches.

"That's enough for one day," he commends as he loosens the velcro straps on my gloves. "After I design an exercise program for you, you'll be on those freeways in no time."

We laugh — he with sincerity, I with skepticism. I do like this man, though. And I like the positive atmosphere of this place. I'm looking forward to coming back to his center on a regular basis.

"If I gather a group together," he says, "would you mind saying a few words to my students before you leave? They all know you . . . your book is required reading in my class."

I say yes, of course. Talking to these people about the struggles I've faced — dealing with pity and stares, learning how to live on my own and yet depend on others, and seeing God's part in it all — is what my dream of a ministry is all about.

Dr. Britten introduces me to the cluster of people in wheelchairs and walkers, and then joins the small group of staff members standing at the back. I can tell he is pleased to have me talk about my faith and my acceptance of my wheelchair. I sense that my having worked alongside these people today has helped. We're on common ground.

All except the beautiful lady with large green eyes that rarely blink. She sits in the back, as statuelike as before.

The full moon hangs pale and mysterious over the orange tree behind the little stucco house. It evokes memories of summer evenings on the back porch of the farmhouse when Jay and I would sit around the redwood table and sing old country songs. Tonight I sit in the backyard and sing a favorite hymn to the moon and hear Jay's harmony in my head. I wonder what my family is doing tonight.

It was good to talk to Jay on the phone earlier. I imagined her sitting on the kitchen steps, leaning her shoulder against the doorsill, twining the phone cord with her fingers. I had lots to tell her.

Our ministry, now christened "Joni and Friends," is a month old. Volunteers who type and take shorthand are helping me answer hundreds of letters that have come as a result of the movie and the two books. An office with job descriptions and procedures is unfamiliar territory to me, but Judy, having helped set up Billy Graham Crusades across the country, is right at home. Kerbe and I soon fit in with the typewriters and telephones.

I wish Jay were here.

I ward off creeping homesickness by keeping busy — working at the office and my art easel, looking through real-estate ads for a permanent home, and visiting Dr. Britten's center.

Sam is teaching me more than muscle-strengthening exercises. I watch how he deals with people who have no hope — people who have been shifted from one hospital to the next, people who feel they are a burden to families or friends. But not to Sam. Like

Jesus, he seems to be moved with compassion, not pity, when he sees the crowds. I marvel at how he keeps up with his overloaded schedule. He takes time, so much time, with the young girl, alone, without a ride home, or the boy with cerebral palsy who confesses his shame over uncontrolled drooling. I watch him kneel on the floor next to a student stretched out on his lab table. Sam seems to be talking to him, but he is probably praying.

I am making headway on the cycling machine. I pedal it faster, easier. I still am not convinced I will drive, but all this exercise isn't going to waste. I haven't felt this well, this strong, in a long time. I am gaining some weight and sleeping better.

"That's not bad," an attractive woman in blue warm-ups observes as she eyes the counter clicking off my number of cycles on the machine. I have often seen her here working with people and assume she is Sam's assistant. She introduces herself as Rana Leavell.

"How much longer on this thing?" I get dramatic with my huffing and puffing.

"I'm the wrong one to ask." She looks around for Sam.

"You don't work here?" I slow my pace. "I've seen you helping out."

"Well, I'm just here to earn a credential to teach phys. ed. to handicapped high-school kids. I'm near burnout with my junior high schoolers." She laughs. "In fact, see that girl in the wheelchair over there?" She points in the direction of the attractive Latin woman with abundant coffee-brown hair. "She just told me she had me for junior-high phys. ed. years ago. Talk about feeling old."

I stop pedaling. Rana knows the mystery lady. "Who is she?" I try to make it sound like a casual question.

"Her name's Vicky Olivas. She's only been paralyzed a few years. She's had a tough time." Rana speaks quietly. "She can't move much."

"Yes, I . . . guessed that." Sam is stretching Vicky's arms, both of them preoccupied, so I feel free to watch her as we talk. Suddenly I'm conscious of staring and in embarrassment say to Rana, "I've been praying for her."

"Praying?" Rana looks at me with a strange smile. "Yeah, well . . ." She slaps the cycle machine. "Let me get somebody to take you off this thing." She walks away.

So the mystery lady has a name. As Sam unstraps my hands and we talk about my progress, I watch from the corner of my eye as Vicky Olivas is pushed outside by her attendant. I wish I could catch her before she leaves, but I don't want to hurry Sam. Time and talk are an important part of his work. So by the time Kerbe pushes me outside, the lady in the wheelchair is gone.

"You need help?" Rana walks out the door behind us.

"Yes, if you would. You can help Kerbe get me into the car." I nod toward my cousin who is crossing the parking lot. Late afternoon shadows stretch across the campus toward a group of students kicking a soccer ball. The shade and the trees remind me of the cool earth smells of home. I wonder if I am making any progress. Not the sort Sam is after, but progress in making this area my home. A home with a ministry and a house and friends.

Friends.

Rana, standing next to me, rummages through her purse and pulls out a pack of Virginia Slims.

"Would you like to get together sometime?" I ask.

"Yes, I'd like that. Your cousin," she says, pausing to strike a match, "has already said something. I told her she could exercise my daughter's horse while she's visiting friends in Europe." She shakes the match and pulls deeply on her lighted cigarette.

"You have a family?"

"You could say that," she says as though she's given this information many times before. "I'm divorced." She sighs, then adds, "My daughter — she's twelve — and I are very close. I really miss her." She fumbles with the cigarette pack. The shadows shift and the sun reflects on her hair. It's much more blond than it appeared inside.

"Well, I couldn't help Kerbe with the horse," I laugh, "but the offer is sincere. It'd be fun to get together."

Kerbe steers her Camaro close to the curb, and Rana pushes me to the passenger side and takes off the armrest of my chair. My cousin reaches through my arms and grabs my waist while Rana positions herself in front and locks her hands under my knees. Together they lift me onto the car seat. While Kerbe heaves my folded wheelchair into the trunk, Rana buckles my seatbelt.

"Speaking of getting together," I comment as Rana adjusts the belt, "I'd like to get to know Vicky Olivas."

"So would everyone," Rana says without looking up. She slams the car door and leans down to look through the open window. "This setup is not the greatest in the world." She slaps the door. "A van would do better."

"That's what Sam keeps telling me," I say as Kerbe backs the car slowly from the curb. "But me? Drive fifty-five on the freeway?" I call as we pull away.

We go home to the little house by the church. Home. I call it that, but the three of us are still camping out of suitcases, our bedroom floor cluttered with open luggage, hair dryers, and boxes of books. So many things are borrowed. Even our pots and pans are on loan. But as we wheel up the wooden ramp to the back door and smell the dinner Judy is preparing, it feels like more than just a house.

That night I lay in bed by the open window and watch the waning moon cross the curtains. I think about the sounds of a summer night on the farm — crickets clicking, frogs croaking, and the distant bark of the dog over the next hill. Nothing like the noise of speeding cars on the boulevard that rattle the warm night air here. But the homey sounds of Judy in the kitchen and Kerbe murmuring to one of her new friends on the phone drift in to me.

Perhaps home is not that far away after all.

I wheel alongside the wrought-iron fence of the hilltop house which is for sale. The manicured lawn is bordered by a wall of pink bougain-villaea on one side and Indian paintbrush on the other. I stop beneath three silk oak trees. I decide they are the tallest of any as I scan the neighborhood from the edge of the backyard. It's not the farm — the house and the lot are small, and it's nowhere near as private. But it's beautiful. I take a deep breath and smile at the realtor.

I will have to draw up papers, get a loan, buy a washer and dryer, contact the telephone company and post office. And just a month ago I was biting my nails over opening a new checking account.

But my confidence comes and goes.

The same day Judy pushes my chair down the aisle of the supermarket. My lap is a catchall for a can of soup, a package of hamburger, mustard, and Comet cleanser. I block the aisle when she leaves me to backtrack for a forgotten item.

A woman with a loaded cart inches closer to me as she examines the shelves. I am sure she is wondering how she will maneuver her way around my chair. I decide not to speak until our eyes meet. She will have to follow my instructions and parallel park my wheelchair closer to the pancake mix in order to pass. I wonder if she's nervous, as I choose carefully what I will say. As I'm about to speak, Judy returns with the tea bags.

The woman smiles — with relief, I imagine — as Judy pushes

my chair past her loaded cart. I suppress the urge to apologize for almost being in her way. The rest of the trip down the aisle, past boxes of cake mix and sugar, I argue with the urge. I'm welcomed here just as much as any cart pusher in the place, wheelchair or no.

These mental gymnastics are silly, I decide after Judy enlists the help of a bag boy to load the groceries and me into her car. But how do others handle life out on their own? I picture the faces of the people I've met at Sam's center. How do they feel in situations like this? What does Vicky Olivas do? Or does she manage at all?

It is another day at the center. As my cousin and I approach the entrance, I spot Vicky sitting in the shade at the corner of the building with her attendant. She comes out here to smoke and, presumably, to escape the others. I gather courage. This is the day we will meet.

"We've both been so busy we haven't had a chance to talk," I begin as I'm pushed up to her, disguising the fact that we really haven't even met.

"Yes, I've noticed you too." She speaks perfect English with a heavy Spanish accent. Close up, she is lovelier than I imagined. Sophia Loren, I think to myself, as I grope for a comparison. She sits straight, almost too rigid, her hands propped on a flowered pillow, spread fingers displaying perfectly polished nails. Her jeans, ironed and starched to a sharp crease, come to a precise point over high-heeled sandals. Even her toes are painted. Her attendant holds her cigarette and coffee.

"What's your reason for coming to the center?" I ask the safest question I can come up with to try to begin to dispel the mysteries that surround her.

She looks at me incredulously with the expression of an aristocrat. "To get healed," she says. After an awkward pause, she adds, "Isn't that why you're here?"

I'm not prepared for this. I'll be late for my appointment if I get started. But this opportunity is answered prayer, and I do want to get to know her. "I'm just trying to strengthen whatever muscles I've got," I say truthfully. "If I get more in return, that would be great." I shrug my shoulders. "Whatever God wants."

"God?" She pauses. "My psychologist says it's all in my head."

"Your paralysis? In your head?"

Vicky Olivas looks down at her lovely lifeless hands. I realize I've said too much too soon. I start to say that perhaps, yes, such things happen . . . rarely, but . . .

"My psychologist says I may snap out of it if I keep coming here." She talks slowly, as though speaking is difficult. "I went to a hypnotist . . . that didn't work. The spiritist didn't work either." My heart twists at her last statement.

The mysteries surrounding this woman are not unfolding. If anything, she is more of an enigma than before. "Healing is really important to you," I conclude, filling the space while her attendant lifts the styrofoam cup of black coffee to Vicky's lips.

"Yes." Another pause. "I was in Russia not long ago. I read about research going on at this institute in Leningrad. My relatives in South America are involved in international politics, so the arrangements for my trip were easy."

"And?"

"And so you see," she says, pointing to her hands with her chin, "the Russian doctors couldn't do much. But," she adds hastily, "I had pneumonia and I got a bed sore. I was too sick to work that hard." She goes on to describe the battery of people who gave her deep muscle massage, braced her legs to help her stand, and told her to concentrate on moving her fingers.

"But I can do this." She leans ever so slightly forward in her wheelchair and shrugs her shoulders. She is proud of the small bit of movement, convinced the trip to Russia helped. "And I'll do more. I know I will." She tilts her head toward her attendant, a signal for another puff of cigarette and sip of coffee.

I wonder if she sees the strange contradiction she presents as she sits in the shade and talks about what she will do, while the real work of pushing and pulling toward such dreams goes on even now inside the walls behind her. Although Vicky Olivas is convinced she will begin moving at any time, she is doing nothing more than waiting. Waiting as she sits in a corner of Dr. Britten's lab, watching the rest. Waiting as she avoids the group and takes a cigarette break outside the center. Waiting while conferring with a psychologist, a hypnotist, even a spiritist.

It also occurs to me that Vicky Olivas probably does not go to supermarkets. Instead, others do her living for her while she waits to be healed.

"There you are!" Rana rounds the corner of the phys. ed. building. "Sam's been looking for you. You're late for your appointment, you know." She lifts her arm and points to her watch. "Hi, Vicky," she adds as she joins our circle. "Are you coming in, too?"

"No. I think I'll catch the early van home."

"Suit yourself," Rana replies in her matter-of-fact tone. I sense she's trying to make a not-so-subtle point.

Rana pushes my chair through the open glass door and down the long corridor to the lab. "What did you find out?"

I listen to the rhythmic squeak of my rubber wheels on the shiny linoleum, measuring my words. "She's got a lot to learn." I try not to sound condescending.

"Haven't we all." Rana sees people like Vicky all day long. Her comment adds a healthy perspective.

I do have a lot to learn. How can my dream of helping other people with disabilities become a reality unless I know how to put God's love into practice with someone like Vicky Olivas. Isn't that what sharing Christ in a real way with a real world is all about?

"By the way," Rana adds, "wasn't that some story of how she landed in that wheelchair?"

"I'm afraid I didn't get that far," I confess. I can't believe I didn't even ask Vicky the obvious question.

"You didn't?"

I shake my head.

"Well, I'd like to know where God was when all that awful stuff happened to her!"

A neighbor's swimming pool provides a good place for Rana to stretch and exercise my arms and legs. But now we take a break and float lazily as the currents from the wind and the pool filters send our rubber rafts in slow circles. Her hands drape in the water, her fingers splashing an occasional ripple.

It's a quiet Saturday afternoon and I'm not anxious to get back to my exercises. Instead, my mind drifts back to my conversation with Vicky Olivas. So many unanswered questions. I seize this moment as a chance to hear more about her.

"Rana, what can you tell me about Vicky?" I tilt my head and squint against the sun to see her.

I relax into the damp cool towel folded under my neck and listen to what she tells me. . . .

March 26, 1976, is a beautiful Friday morning in Los Angeles. But for Vicky Olivas it is a grim reminder of happier, brighter mornings. Her husband has turned his back on their young family, broken his marriage vows, and left Vicky alone to care for two-year-old Arturo. Saddened and shaken, facing an uncertain future, Vicky must get a job to support herself and her young son.

A woman at the employment agency has just called, and although it is Friday, with the weekend fast approaching, she insists that this one job interview could be an opportunity Vicky won't want to miss. "Probably by Monday the job will be taken by someone else," she has warned.

It means taking Arturo to her parents' house, a long drive back to Hollywood to change clothes — she will have to borrow gas money from a neighbor — and another trip back to the Valley. Vicky sighs and shrugs. Why not?

Driving her sporty car makes the distance a pleasure — something she hasn't felt since her husband packed his bags and left. A rush of air through the open window revives her hopes. Maybe with a job and a new apartment her life could begin again.

Vicky has difficulty finding the address she has been given. There seem to be only factories in the general neighborhood. She debates about forgetting it and just going home. But after showing the address on the slip of paper to a receptionist in one of the buildings she passes, she is directed up the block. She parks her car at the curb, then hesitates again when she walks to the corner and looks down a long dirty alley. The address, the receptionist said, is at the last door on the right.

I've got to start somewhere, Vicky thinks as she listens to the click of her high heels on the cement take her closer to the warehouse at the end of the alley.

The door is unlocked and she steps into a dim front office. There is dust on the typewriter, the floor is strewn with papers, and a damp closed-in smell fills the place. *I hope I don't get this job,* Vicky thinks. Peeking around a corner, she cautiously makes her way down a hallway. "Hello . . . is someone there? Hello?"

She walks through the warehouse and comes to another office where she finds two men, one sitting behind a scarred formica desk and the other slouched in a molded plastic chair with his arms folded.

"My name is Vicky Olivas. The employment agency sent me over."

The man behind the desk, obviously the boss, leans back and looks her up and down. Suddenly, Vicky is aware of her peach pantsuit. She feels the weight of her waist-long hair. She blinks her eyes, her lashes false and feathered and heavy. Everything seems weighted under his stare.

"Yes. I've been expecting you. Do you have a resume?" he demands.

Tell him you left it in the car and get out of here, something warns her.

"Well, do you?"

"No . . . no," she stammers, "I don't have one with me."

"Here." He slides an application across the desk. "Go into the front office and fill it out while I finish."

Vicky, shaking slightly but resigned to seeing the interview through, obediently begins to fill in her address and social-security number. She checks the box which indicates that at her former job she was an accountant's secretary. She glances up once and notices the two men loading television sets and stereos into a van parked at the open doors of the warehouse. By the time the other man pulls away in the van she has completed the form.

At that point the owner enters the room, closes the door behind him, and clicks the lock. Another chill of apprehension goes down her spine, but she dismisses it as nerves.

"Are you finished?"

"Yes. I just have to sign my name," she says and pens her signature at the bottom of the document.

"Let's go into my office." He motions her through a door. Vicky walks in front of him as he points the way. They are in another warehouse.

Then the nightmare begins.

Suddenly the man grabs her from behind, wraps his arms tightly around her chest, and throws her against the wall. She hits a tool chest and stumbles, her back against the bricks. The man stands several feet away from her, hands at his side, and says, "Do you realize this is all planned . . . all planned."

"Wh–what are you talking about?"

"I asked them to send somebody just like you," he says as his eyes hungrily scan her again. "I've sent everyone home," he hisses through clenched teeth and steps toward her.

He grabs her blouse, and Vicky twists and squirms violently to break free. Out of the corner of her eye she spots the glint of something metal. A gun! She wrestles even harder to free herself. Suddenly, a loud bang. The room and the man spiral round and round as Vicky slumps to the floor.

Her thoughts spin out of control as her body slides across the floor. She is being dragged. But to where? And what? She feels the cold tiles of a bathroom against her face and smells urine and dirt. Something wet and warm trickles down her neck. That is the only sensation. No pain. She strains to see where her legs are. She can't feel them. She struggles to brush her hair from her face but cannot lift her arms.

The man leaves the room, then returns after a few moments. He wipes his brow with his hand, nervously shakes his head, leaves again, and returns. He repeats this pattern several times. "I didn't mean to shoot you. . . . I didn't mean it."

The odor of the filthy bathroom and his sweaty body make her dizzy. She tries to think of something to save herself. "Would you be kind enough to call my brother," she says. As she makes this calm suggestion, she tries to keep her tone polite, cooperative, tries to control her panic and fear. "He'll come and get me. We won't say a thing. Everything will be all right." She gauges each sentence with a breath. She recites the phone number.

Amazingly, the man dials. He listens, then slams down the receiver — a busy signal. *Oh, Arturo, stop playing with the phone.* The man dials again. No answer.

He paces in and out of the bathroom rubbing sweating hands on his pant legs. "Please take my keys out of my pocketbook," she says. "If you would get my car . . . a Camaro, light blue . . . just up the street. You can't miss it." The man nervously struggles to decide what to do. Finally he leaves. In a few minutes he is back.

"Okay, I've got the car," he says as he reaches under Vicky's armpits to help her up. Her legs refuse to support her weight. They seem numb. Useless. He becomes angry and lets her go. She falls back to the tile, hitting her head and shoulder.

"Why aren't you helping me?" he yells. He storms out of the room, switching off the lights as he goes, and slams the door. In the dark stillness the odors of sweat, urine, and filth are suffocating. The silence is eerie. Has he left her to die in this awful place?

The room begins to spiral again. In her dizziness, Vicky thinks she hears a woman's voice, urgent and angry. She takes a deep breath. "Help! He-e-e-e-elp!"

A girl in her late teens rushes in. "What have you done?" *She must know the man,* Vicky reasons through her faintness. "What are we going to do?" Vicky can feel the girl's panic as she stuffs a dirty towel under her bleeding head. *Are they going to kill me?*

The glaring light and the girl's presence revive Vicky's senses. "How about if we say that the two of you were walking down the street and saw my car pulled off to the side with me slumped over the wheel." Hope is in her voice. She doesn't know whether she is making sense, whether they are even listening, but she has to try. "And you pushed me over to the passenger side and drove me to the hospital. You could say that you didn't know what happened to me or anything." Vicky's eyes dart to the man, to the girl, and back to the man. "I won't say a word. You won't be dragged into this. I promise!"

The two deliberate over the story, with Vicky coaxing to make it sound better and better. Finally, the perspiring man threatens, "We'll do it. But you'd better not say anything. We have your application. Your address. If you say anything . . . I know you have a son. I'll kill him."

"So then what happened?" I press Rana. Behind her sunglasses, her skin shining with Bain de Soleil, Rana, the no-nonsense lady with sharp wit and ready words, seems sincerely moved by the story she has related.

"Well, those jerks threw her into the front seat of her car. The girl drove and Vicky gave her directions." Rana lifts her sunglasses and looks at me. "Isn't that incredible?"

I shake my head and awkwardly splash my hand in the water to keep my raft facing her.

"So . . . they pull up in front of this hospital, and the girl runs into the emergency room and says, 'I found this woman. I don't know if she was shot or stabbed.' Amazingly, there were several police there on another matter, and Vicky was taken in on a stretcher. Feeling safe at last, she told the whole story to a policewoman while the doctors worked on her. Anyway," Rana says, taking another deep breath, "nobody believed her until they went back to the warehouse and found her purse and sunglasses, blood, and a gun in a trash pail. The guy was arrested."

This story sounds like a murder mystery or a television movie-of-the-week — unbelievable, improbable — but it is not fiction. And the ending has an even sadder twist.

"He was released after three years in jail. And Vicky spends the rest of her life completely paralyzed in a wheelchair."

"How does she live?"

"Although the employment agency wasn't connected, they

should have known the guy's record — three other convictions of attempted rape. Because of a small settlement, Vicky is able to live alone with her attendant and son. It's the only security she's got."

For the moment all is quiet except for the pool pump at the far edge of the backyard.

"It'll be a real miracle if that woman ever smiles again," Rana concludes, after sensing I have no comment. The fact is, I am thinking that Vicky's story must not end here. Not if my dream to help other people has anything to do with it. But where do I begin?

"I don't see how you handicapped people do it," Rana says in mild disgust. "And I don't know how you can believe in a God who would allow all that stuff."

I am still silent, but my thoughts have shifted from Vicky to Rana. I sense a pressing need much closer to home. I recall my conversation with Rob exactly a year ago on the movie set. Something about having the faith to doubt and yet believe. As then, but for a different reason, I am not quick to mouth a stock answer. Rana is asking about one of the great mysteries of my faith. It can't be handled in a trite or prepackaged way. That's something else I learned from the movie.

I also can't ignore her comment. Yet movie memories bring other concerns to the surface. *Who am I to tell anybody about the gospel?* Barely months have passed since my own time of rebellion against God. I'm still slightly shaken from the trauma of those months, even though I know God has forgiven me. My head knows He has wiped the slate clean. My heart is still having a hard time catching up. So who am I to tell anybody anything?

Besides, I hear whispers from an even more distant past, *Vicky's story would test the faith of the most steadfast of saints. Who could explain it?*

"Well?" Rana is waiting, lazily splashing her hand, making little eddies in the water.

Well, I asked for the chance to talk to real people in a real world. Here it is.

"What we need here is wisdom," I begin, leaning my head forward to shade my eyes so I can look directly at her. "And wisdom is not the ability to figure out why God has done what He's done and what He'll do next."

"Then what is it?" she says flatly.

I plop my head back on the raft. "It's trusting Him even when nothing seems fair." I add what is fresh on my mind. "You know, we can have faith to doubt and still believe."

Rana has come out from behind the dark lenses. She props her sunglasses on top of her head. I sense that in expressing her doubts she is truly asking for understanding. "So what's the big deal about God that He's worth that kind of trust?"

I grin, liking her honesty. "Look, Vicky's case is bad — no getting away from it. But far worse is *why* people pick up guns and shoot and rape and . . . whatever. In other words, sin. And not only the sin in crazy jerks like that man in the warehouse," I add quickly. "I'm talking about you and me. We're sinners too."

"Sin. There's something I know about," Rana says in mock pride. In the next breath she begins to tell her story. How she has come out of a divorce and gone looking for good times with reckless abandon. Why should it matter what she does as long as she doesn't harm anyone? As she exposes more seamy details about herself, I nod thoughtfully. The flow of words stops. She waits. For what, I'm not sure. Shock? Disgust? Astonishment?

My expression doesn't change. My ears are no longer tender, having been toughened by the movie experience. And my own sin is a glaring reminder of the sorts of things I am actually capable of doing, of being.

"Sin should never surprise us," I finally answer her unspoken question. "I am really . . . really . . . no different . . . no better than you." I squint through the glare of the sun. "The surprise is that God forgives any of us," I say, convinced that Rana knows her past of deeds and pleasures is wrong.

"And that," I say, turning my face back toward the sun, "is the big deal about God."

"I don't believe I understand," Rana concludes. She cools her skin with handfuls of pool water.

"Well, don't worry. I think it'll all come clear," I say, feeling my raft drift away from hers.

Several days later Rana and I find ourselves sitting at the edge of the same pool. I'm not surprised when she brings the subject up again.

As we talk she becomes even more real, opening the inside of her heart, describing her pain and disappointments. I describe for her the Savior who entered this real world and died on an agonizingly real cross for our terribly real sins. He was buried in a real tomb of cold hard stone. He rose in a real body.

"I'm sure God's Word would do a better job of explaining things to you than I can." I show her several verses in the New Testament and several in the Old, including Isaiah 53. She thinks the descriptions of Christ in the Old Testament are rather amazing. So detailed. So accurate.

She goes home that afternoon with a Bible in her hands. She promises, without prompting on my part, to read more. The next afternoon she comes for another visit. An unexpected one. "I have something to tell you," she says.

My new friend has prayed to acknowledge Christ as her Lord.

The thrill in Rana's voice, the new light in her smile, are like a fresh wind that blows new strength and excitement into my own soul.

Clunk! My head hits the edge of the car door frame. "Drat it!" I exclaim, squeezing my eyes against the pain. Kerbe's car is easy enough to be lifted out of, but grabbing a novice off the street to help has its disadvantages.

"I'm so sorry," Kerbe apologizes as she lightly rubs my throbbing head. "Uh-oh. A bump."

"Oh, it's nobody's fault," I groan. "Rana's right. Getting lifted in and out of a car all the time is a real pain — no pun intended."

Kerbe begins to smile. Rather cheeky, I think, still wincing from the mishap. My head smarts, and I want to ask her what's so funny.

As we wheel to the center, I spot Dr. Britten beside a new cream-colored van. He is wiping the shiny fender with a cloth. Kerbe stops my chair beside him as Sam straightens and spreads his arms.

"Well, how do you like it?" he says.

"Nice." I wonder why he wants my opinion on a van.

"Our church wanted to help your ministry. The elders put it before the people, we took an offering, and it's yours to drive." Sam beams as he opens the sliding door to show me the interior.

I don't look at the van. My gaze is fixed on Sam as he chatters on. "Of course, it has to be adapted. The mechanical lift will go here." He motions with his arm. "We'll take out the driver's seat so your wheelchair will fit there."

"How can this . . . be?"

Sam stops his tour of the interior and leans against the passenger door. "Still don't think you can do it, huh?"

"No, it's not that. This van — ," I say, sweeping my head in a scanning motion. "How . . . I mean, it's a gift . . . to me?"

"Joni, you've been asking me all kinds of questions about churches helping disabled people. Just think of this as an example of what a church can do." Sam gestures toward the van. "And you can get the word out better than I or anyone else in our congregation."

Sam's idea intrigues me, but I'm still not certain I can drive. I push myself even harder, lifting wrist weights, cycling at the machine, developing my balance in the chair.

Weeks fly by as my power chair and I are measured for width, height, and weight to fit the van. The mechanisms are fine-tuned to the strength in my arm. The new van is fully equipped. The moment of truth is here.

Sam and Rana climb into the van while I jab at the outside controls to open the automatic door and lower the mechanical lift. Once I am lifted into the back of the van, I power my wheelchair into the driver's alcove. My chair couples and locks into place. Sam fits my hand into a cuff on top of a metal joystick that rises from the floor where the "four on the floor" would ordinarily be. He explains that I should push forward to accelerate, pull back to brake, swing my arm to the right for right turns and vice versa for left.

"Very simple," he concludes.

I lean my head to reach for a mouthstick. With it, I jab at the ignition button on the control box bolted to the door. The engine turns over easily and roars when I lean my shoulder forward slightly, applying pressure with the joystick. I examine other buttons on the box — a red one for the emergency brake, white for air conditioning, blue for windshield wipers, and yellow for headlights. I press another button with my mouthstick and shift into drive.

"I can't believe I'm doing this!" The van inches out of the parking lot onto the street. "What if a policeman stops me?" I ask Rana, looking at her in the rear-view mirror.

"Got your learner's permit?"

I nod nervously.

"Well," she laughs, "you'll just have to pretend we're not here. He'll have to get it out of your wallet himself. Simple!"

I drive through back streets, a little disoriented to be sitting on the driver's side. Teeth clenched, I brace myself for an approaching stop sign. Trying to remember all that Sam has taught me, I cautiously flex my bicep, pulling back on the joystick. The van jerks to a halt several yards before the sign. "Stay calm. Every move is carefully planned," I say in my best Inspector Clouseau accent. As my muscles relax, the drive becomes smoother.

I breathe deeply and glance at the houses that flow by. I am driving. I am moving. Just like everybody else.

After a few more days on the road, I am convinced I can drive — even the freeways. The only people Sam and I need to convince now are those at the Department of Motor Vehicles.

Rana, who has learned to manage the sensitive controls on my van, drives me to the D.M.V. building the following week. She grills me on questions from the student-driver's handbook.

Although we are early, the lines are already long. We wait. Time and the people in front of us inch forward. *This is crazy.* I look around at the scores of people waiting at other windows. I grin, imagining their thoughts. *I can't even lift a glass of water to my mouth and here I am about to tell these people that they ought to let me on the road!*

Finally, it is our turn at the window. The official-looking woman sitting behind the desk stamps a few papers and gives a "next please" look to Rana.

I clear my throat. "Good morning. I'm here to take the written exam for drivers. I . . . uh . . . can't use my hands, but my friend here — "

"May I have your learner's permit please," she replies in a monotone, reaching for an application.

"As I was saying," I continue, "I can't write with my hands, but my friend here," I nod toward Rana, "can help me take the exam."

The government lady thumbs through more papers and without looking up says, "I'm sorry. You'll have to come back next Friday morning a little earlier. Handicapped people may only take the oral examination with one of our employees in the conference room." She glances at her watch. "The room is closed now."

Rana and I look at each other in disbelief. It took a mountain of effort for her and Judy to get me up and out of bed even *this* early. I whisper to Rana through the side of my mouth, "We're not leaving here until I take this exam."

I reassume a smile and clear my throat again. "Well, I think we can come up with a creative alternative here." I adopt a tone of official authority to match the woman behind the window, who continues to look at me without expression. "You see, I'm a mouth artist, and I hold brushes and pencils between my teeth." The woman's eyes widen. "And if my friend will be allowed to hold the test on a clipboard, I can take it that way."

She sits rigidly now, ignoring her paperwork. She rises and walks from the window, advising us to wait while she finds her supervisor. In a few minutes she returns and motions Rana to the window. Leaning forward, she whispers, "I do think she'll be too much of a distraction to the other people taking the examination. Do you know what I mean?"

"Do you know what she means?" Rana turns to me.

Those old feelings of inadequacy begin to encroach. I will not be intimidated by this woman and her silly red tape. "Well," I say, my smile in plaster by now, a tinge of anger in my voice, "how about this. Let's tape a pen to my wrist. And if you don't mind my straying out of the little true and false boxes a bit, I can take the exam that way."

"I don't believe this," I say to Rana through clenched teeth as the woman leaves to confer with her supervisor again.

"Hmm. I felt like telling her that tall guys with big noses and glasses distract me." We smother our chuckles.

The license lady returns with a roll of masking tape and leads us to the examination area. We are pleased with ourselves — until I look up and see the desks. They are designed for people to stand and take the exam — too high for me to reach from my chair! But I am not about to back out now. We devise a scheme to place a waste basket on my lap and prop the exam paper on top within easy reach. "Although frankly," I say to the woman, "I believe I am far more of a distraction doing it this way."

Later I do prove to be a distraction, however — to the examiner riding with me as I take my road test. He is so fascinated that he keeps forgetting to tell me where to turn and when to park.

But I pass the exam, and move one step closer to independence.

Oh, if my Maryland friends could see me now. I can drive to meet someone for dinner. I can drive myself to work at Joni and Friends. I can drive to watch a sunset. I can drive alone. For the first time in fifteen years, I can actually go somewhere . . . anywhere . . . by myself. It's almost like getting healed!

My driving is an occasion that calls for my parents to make a special trip out to Los Angeles. They've heard I can drive, but they must see it for themselves. As they clutch their seats, I drive them to meet Sam. They are amazed at my accomplishment and immensely impressed with his work at the center. Meeting some of his disabled students gives them a better perspective on what I'd like to do through Joni and Friends.

Mother and Dad bite their nails as I sign the papers for my new hilltop home. They stay an extra week to help move things from the little stucco house to my new address. I am proud of my home and anxious to copy decorating details from the house on the farm — Indian rugs as wall hangings, a George Washington spread on my bed, and a stained-glass lamp over the kitchen table. Daddy has brought a handmade driftwood lamp, a wooden chest, and several oil paintings of cowboys and horses. I even buy a miniature schnauzer puppy who reminds me of one of our old dogs on the farm. My California home has an air of the Maryland farm, but it is distinct, unique, and mine.

I take more steps toward independence.

Mom and Dad help me pick out a washer and dryer, a dining room set, and a rug for the kitchen. They buy dog toys for Scruffy, my new pup. Pushing aside shrubbery with his cane, Dad examines the backyard fence to make sure Scruffy can't escape.

Mom enjoys a game of tennis with Rana. Vicky Olivas and I watch from the sidelines and keep score. My parents take great interest in my friends. They think Judy and Kerbe are absolutely wonderful for taking such excellent care of me. (Parents never change.)

Every time I see my mother smile or my father nod, I am further convinced that I did the right thing in moving to Southern California. They approve of and enjoy my independence.

"Joni, this decision you made to move was a good one," they say.

"Just imagine," my mother says, shaking her head in the back seat of the van, "Joni driving us down the Ventura freeway. I can't wait to get home and tell everyone about it."

I laugh as I savor the proud smile on her face. And I recall Sam Britten's comment: "Just get out there and tell other churches what they can do."

"Okay, how are we going to pay the bill?"

I think for a minute. "I don't know. Maybe it could be my treat. But then again ..." I hesitate. "I don't want to offend her."

"Maybe if I treat, it would look a little less patronizing," Rana replies. "Vicky has a lot of pride."

"Okay. So she's disabled and doesn't want a handout. Then she pays for her own dinner."

"Maybe she can't afford it. It's an expensive restaurant."

"We're making this into a big deal." I sound exasperated. "You treat. Judy and Kerbe and I will even up with you afterward."

"Then it's set. I'll pick her up, and we'll meet you all at Benihana's on Friday."

We smile good-naturedly. Perhaps we're both overly concerned for Vicky Olivas. But Rana has seen the emptiness in Vicky's life. And she has felt her own emptiness vanish with her new peace in God. I'm proud that she wants to make a difference in Vicky's life. I want to also.

Finally, it seems to be happening. Vicky has agreed to go out to dinner with us. If I can really spend time with her, perhaps I can get behind the enigma.

We will be friends, I plan. We will learn from each other, as friends should.

The evening of our dinner engagement arrives, and we gather at the well-known oriental restaurant. We sip fruit drinks while we wait to be seated. In the corner, a man plays background music on a piano. After a few tunes we are ushered to a large U-shaped table, the middle of which is a metal cooking surface. Vicky and I have to have the footpedals on our wheelchairs dismantled so we can fit under the table.

Vicky sits across from me, and I glance at her over my menu. She sits straight and rigid, her hands on the flowered pillow, towering over the girls beside her. She wears a silky blouse, low cut and belted. I wonder if she does something special to her hair to make it so thick and full. Someone has pulled part of it back with a pearly comb and a flower.

A Japanese waitress in a kimono greets us politely with a slight bow as she places our plates and chopsticks before us. I look at the chopsticks, then at Vicky, shrug my shoulders, and laugh. A busboy carrying a tray of water glasses bumps into her wheelchair and mumbles a quick apology. It's an awkward beginning.

"We almost didn't get here," Rana says with a hint of exasperation as she shakes the folded napkin and places it on her lap. "I got a phone call today from Arturo wanting to know where his mother was." She smiles at Vicky as she places her napkin on her lap.

"A call . . . from Arturo? He's only five years old," Judy responds.

"I know. Don't ask me how he tracked down my phone number." Rana shakes her head and takes a sip of tea. "But he knew I was somebody from Sam's center. The thing was . . ." She pauses. "He was desperate. Not out of fear for himself, but for his mother. He told me that somebody should have had her home from the center hours ago."

Vicky looks at Rana, waiting for her to continue her story. I take that as permission to probe. "What'd you do?" I ask.

"Well, I told him not to worry. That I'd find his mom. But honestly . . ." She opens her menu as she speaks. "I didn't know where to begin looking. I figured she missed the van, so I tried the campus. There she was," Rana says, gesturing toward Vicky, "quietly, patiently, waiting."

"Wow, Vicky . . . that's some kid you have."

"Yes, he's that all right," Vicky replies. Rana lifts the small porcelain teacup to her mouth. After a sip, Vicky continues. "He takes good care of his Mamita." She blushes a bit, and I wonder if it is from pride in her son or embarrassment over the incident. Does she wish she could take better care of him?

There is a lull in the conversation as we examine the menus and order.

"'Mamita.' Is that his special name for you?" Judy asks.

"Yes." It seems she doesn't intend to say more. No one offers to change the subject, however, and Vicky finally continues, "Arturo and I depend on each other. We live alone." Her tone is matter of fact. "That is, except my attendants who never seem to stay very long. I'm always training someone new to help me out."

When I hear this, I squirm a bit in my chair. I never seem to lack for someone to help. I live in a brand-new house with new furniture. I can paint. I travel. My van — an expensive gift — sits out in the restaurant lot. And I think of Vicky and five-year-old Arturo clinging to each other.

"Just the other night, I was feeling so . . . so sad." Vicky glances at us as we sit listening intently. "I was in bed, thinking how nothing is really going very right. Dr. Britten's exercises aren't helping . . . that is, I'm not getting any better. I couldn't help crying." She laughs, trying to make light of it. "And there was Arturo, sleeping next to me in his bed on the floor. He does that when he gets sick," she explains. "Anyway, he had a cold . . . his breathing was stuffy. And that made me feel worse. I couldn't get up to check his temperature or give him an aspirin, wipe his nose, or cuddle and cover him." She shakes her head, emphasizing each phrase.

"My crying woke him up. Then, without saying anything, he got up and found a Kleenex, wiped my nose and my tears. He went and got this big blanket — he's only a little boy, you know — and climbed up onto my bed so he could pull up the covers." She smiles broadly. "Isn't that something? He's such a good boy," Vicky says as she leans toward Rana, a signal for more tea.

At this point the Japanese chef approaches the stove with a tray of raw shrimp, chicken, and steak. He smiles and, with a quick bow of his head in the tall white chef's hat, scrapes the meat and raw vegetables onto the sizzling stove with a sharp knife. Steam hisses and billows and rises to the copper ceiling vent. Rana, Judy, and Kerbe lightly applaud as he begins his fanfare of cutting and slicing.

I watch the flying steel, but my thoughts are absorbed by the beautiful woman sitting across from me. I can hardly believe she's revealed as much as she has. Yet I know it has not been to gain sympathy. Rather, she has told the story to boast about her young son who is so responsible for his age.

"So you don't live with your parents?" Judy asks, reaching for a fork rather than chopsticks.

"No. You see . . ." She hesitates. "Although they don't live far away, I really want . . . need to be my son's Mamita, to raise him by myself."

No one presses her further. She is obviously a private person. Perhaps she feels she has shared too much already. For the remainder of the evening we talk about the food, Judy spins some yarns about her days as a midwife in England, Kerbe chatters about the career group at church, and Rana describes her daughter's recent trip overseas. Like life, our conversation just rambles on.

Rana feeds Vicky. She holds a morsel of chicken poised in question over the dishes of hot mustard and soy sauce. With a nod, Vicky selects the mustard. Rana cups her hand underneath the chopsticks and lifts the chicken to Vicky's mouth. Vicky leans forward and daintily takes a bite. I'm suddenly aware of my own way of eating as I lift my shoulder and angle the bent spoon attached to my arm splint. In a practiced motion, not quite smooth, I bring the spoonful of food to my mouth. I chew and swallow, feeling a bit guilty because I can feed myself. I wonder if Vicky will be able to feed herself one day.

That strange feeling urges me to say, "Your level of injury is about the same as mine, Vicky. I'll bet you'll be using your arms like me one of these days." I remember her poor attitude about God and exercise, and add for encouragement, "I know, I'm convinced God has some wonderful plans for you. With prayer and hard work, I've seen it happen."

After our dessert of green tea ice cream, the waitress presents the bill on a porcelain dish. I shoot a glance at Rana; I've forgotten what we decided to do. After a second of hesitation I announce that dinner is my treat and ask Judy to reach for my wallet.

Before anyone can quibble about the bill, I grab for Vicky's attention again. "I can't say that I know what you've been through. But I do know that God is a big part of the answer. Maybe," I continue, with a questioning look, "we can talk about it sometime." I look for a response. "I'd love to meet Arturo," I add, hoping that will be an incentive.

Vicky doesn't reply. Instead, as Rana backs her wheelchair from the table, she tosses her thick hair in that aristocratic manner and turns her head in the direction she wants to go — the door. Rana repositions her hands on the pillow and pushes her toward the exit. I back my power wheelchair into the aisle and follow them. Whatever closeness we had gained has somehow been lost.

Judy and Rana lift Vicky into the car while I watch and wait to say good-by. A valet slams the door. Vicky sits slumped, the comb in her hair beginning to fall. I don't want her to feel self-conscious, and I wish I could reach in and fix it for her. She turns her head slightly and offers a stiff smile, mouthing the words, "Thank you," through the closed window.

I move to the back of the car where Rana is loading Vicky's folded chair into the trunk.

"Well?" I say.

Rana shoves the spare tire further into the luggage compartment before she speaks. "Well, everything went fine up till the end there." She straightens and dusts off her hands. "Look, I'm a novice at being a Christian, but . . . I don't know how to put this . . . but, you . . . we just can't waltz into her life with ready-made answers, no matter how much we want to help. For anybody to pattern their life after you is a big order. Things just don't happen for others the way they happened for you." She slams the trunk.

I am hurt. God has used this baby Christian to point an admonishing finger at me. I am humiliated. I want so to do the right thing, say the right thing, say the right words to help Vicky and her young son, but I am embarrassed as I realize that she has become less of a person and more of a project. My own thoughts, my plans, condemn me: *We will be friends.*

I think about formulas, plans, designs, programs, and organized efforts. Perhaps I am relying more on these than on demonstrating God's love to a real person.

I wonder, what would Jesus have done?

I've observed Sam Britten for months now. His hands communicate love as he gently lifts a boy from his wheelchair or stretches the sore and spastic muscles of an elderly woman stiff from years of inactivity. Even his voice is tender and gentle. I am learning a lot from Sam's love and compassion.

"How do you . . . where do you . . . begin?" I ask as he unstraps my hand from the cycle machine. "So many people need so much."

Several cerebral palsied boys bide their time by the classroom door, waiting to begin their treatment. There are not enough classroom aides. Not enough equipment. Not enough room. And there is always a long waiting list.

"Just one at a time, Joni," Sam replies, motioning for an aide to greet the boys at the door. He returns his attention to me and the velcro strap on my other hand. "All you can do is try your best to help one person at a time."

He neatly refastens the straps to the gloves, smoothing the leather over and over again. Exasperated with his own limitations, it's obvious he wants to say more, and I stretch my aching arms, waiting for him to continue.

"I visited Tante Corrie ten Boom this weekend," he says, plopping tiredly into an empty wheelchair.

I've talked with Sam about Corrie before. In her late eighties now, this old saint of God, who survived Nazi concentration camps and went on to a worldwide ministry, has recently suffered another stroke. Severely disabled, she can no longer travel and speak. Now she lives a quiet life in a sunny little house south of Los Angeles. Disability is the great leveler, and Tante Corrie, like millions of others, now must struggle through the confusing world of wheelchairs and pressure sores, tubes and catheters.

An edge of excitement creeps into Sam's tired voice. "Joni, it was . . . was indescribable. Walking into that woman's room was like entering a sanctuary. We talked, although she could only answer with lots of smiles and nods." He shrugs his shoulders and his eyes focus on something far away. "When I rubbed her feet, I kept thinking about the hundreds of thousands of miles that woman has traveled. I kept thinking about her bare feet on the hard, cruel dirt of that death camp."

I don't speak at all — just listen and learn.

He straightens his back, hands on his knees. "I devised a pulley system so she can do some exercises and get more strength in those frail arms of hers. And I instructed her companions on how to properly lift her in and out of bed, positioning her in her wheelchair, things of that sort.

"It's amazing to think that at almost ninety years of age that devout woman should have to start all over again . . . a whole new and different ministry."

I look at him questioningly.

"A ministry of waiting . . . of silence. Of being still before the Lord. Of, uh . . . prayer." Sam looks back at me with his own questioning expression. "She was such an active woman — "

I nod. "Now she is the one who needs help."

"But you know what's strange?" Sam smiles. "Doing those few things for her, meeting those few needs — I was the one who came away blessed. She ended up giving more to me than I could ever possibly give to her."

We are interrupted by a sudden call from one of the aides who needs Sam's help to lift a young girl back into her wheelchair. He gives my shoulder a friendly squeeze and hurries to the other end of the room.

I watch him switch gears as he gives the young girl on the mat his entire attention, his complete devotion. I bite my lip at the poignancy of the moment, recalling his words about helping people one at a time. He gives as much to this girl as he would to Tante Corrie. To anyone.

Each person is special.

I learn another lesson.

The weekend brings a new month with a promise of cooler days. Welcome days. But how I wish the weather would act like it's supposed to in November. Instead, the California sun lingers lazily high in the sky, smiling warmth on palm trees and swimming pools. I long for the rustling of crisp leaves in the wind. The fragrance of burning cherry wood from a neighboring chimney. I miss the steam of frost on my breath and weather cold enough to wear a wool scarf. Fall of 1979 has been so busy that I have forgotten such things.

I call home on Saturday. I tell Mom and Dad about our progress with the ministry. I ask how Jay and Rob are doing. How's Charlie Cat? How's Kathy's new Appaloosa colt doing? Does everyone miss me?

"And how is your friend Vicky doing?" The three thousand miles of telephone lines cannot filter out the warmth in her words.

"Oh . . . we went to dinner last week. It was nice. I feel so bad for her though. Mom, you wouldn't believe what she's been through."

"Give her our love." I can hear the smile in my mother's voice.

"I'll do that," I say sincerely. I do want to give Vicky love.

After I hang up, I think about my closing words. Like Sam Britten, I want to love and help people as individuals. See each person as special and unique.

But somehow I got bogged down at Joni and Friends this week. Every day there were scores of letters to answer. Tuesday I met with Sam and Greg Barshaw, another elder at Grace Church who works with disabled people. On Wednesday I contacted Debbie Stone at Rancho Hospital and found that she's going to move into the little stucco house and work full-time at the church. We talked about new programs for the church. Thursday and Friday I studied independent-living manuals, attendant-care manuals, source books for the disabled, architectural codes, and anything else about "handicaps" I could get my hands on.

It's so hard to think of people as special and unique while absorbing overwhelming statistics and impersonal manuals.

On Sunday morning I drive to church alone. There are dozens of handicap parking places in the church lot, and almost all are taken. I poke along, mindful that many people are unloading from vans and cars, wheeling their way across the lot to church. Several wave.

First service is just letting out. I glide down the ramp and greet the people walking up the ramp who must squeeze against the wall to avoid my wheels. Church is crowded, and I'm glad I'm early enough to get a good seat. Or, I should say, an aisle.

People in wheelchairs line up like a row of parked cars alongside the end of each pew. I stop and greet a few who aren't preoccupied with friends or the church bulletin. Then I wheel into place beside Kerbe, who is already seated at the end of the sixth row.

The choir sings. We are led in prayer. The congregation stands and sits, appropriately, as Scripture is read or hymns are sung — all except those who sit at the ends of the pews next to the wheelchairs. They hold our hymnals and turn pages for those of us who cannot.

It is time for the morning message. People pull out their Bibles and look for pens and paper. John MacArthur walks up to the pulpit. I smile, remembering a time not too many months ago when I couldn't wait to pull his sermon apart. My attitude sure is different now.

Somewhere near the beginning, MacArthur flips to a verse in the Gospel of John.

His voice carries across the congregation of three thousand. "And the Lord cried out from the cross, 'I thirst.'"[1] He makes his point and moves on.

My attention, however, is still on that verse from the Gospel of John. I close my eyes and picture the cross. The scattered crowd. The dark clouds and the soldiers. I picture Jesus crying out in thirst.

I wonder what I would have done. I ponder as the minister's voice fills the background. I imagine myself huddled in that crowd. If I had heard Jesus say He was thirsty, what . . . just what would I have done?

Well, I wouldn't have stood there like a nincompoop, as my mother would say. I think — I hope I would have run, not walked, to the nearest well. Forget the sponge and vinegar. I would have brought Him the real thing — a cool cup of water.

Then it hits me. I inch my chair closer to the edge of the pew where Kerbe sits. She is listening intently to the sermon, but I interrupt her briefly as I whisper, "Flip to Matthew 25 for just a second."

She thumbs back a few chapters and lays the Bible open on my knee. My eyes scan the page for a particular phrase. I glance at the second column where Jesus is having a conversation with His disciples. There it is.

"I was thirsty and you gave me something to drink. . . . I tell you the truth, whatever you did for one of the least of these brothers of mine, you did for me."[2]

I raise my head and straighten my shoulders, staring into the distance. I am struck with the obvious. This is what Jesus wants me to do. To do for others with the same sense of urgency and concern what I would do for Him. Not just talk. Not just give advice. Jesus wants me to *do* something. For others. For Him.

I imagine something else. I picture Jesus being moved with compassion when He encountered the blind or the hungry or the widow who had lost her son. He was not overwhelmed by needy crowds. It was just part of His nature to roll up His sleeves and help one person at a time. That's what Sam Britten is doing every day at his center. Seeing needs. Making a difference with love and compassion.

I try to place myself in that picture, and squirm, knowing that so often what I feel edges close to pity. *"I feel so bad for her."* My response to my mother's question yesterday about Vicky haunts me. Pity, I decide, sees a need at arm's length. Compassion reaches out to touch. Pity never becomes more than a feeling. Compassion compels us to act.

I look around at the people in their parked wheelchairs. A man with cerebral palsy wails his way through a hymn. A woman taps her cane in time with the organ music. Each one in this crowd, myself included, has needs.

Vicky Olivas has a need. I place her here in my imagination — sitting across the aisle, singing, smiling, surrounded by friends. She, like these people, is neither a statistic nor a sociological grouping in a manual.

And I can . . . I really can make a difference in her life. But not with pity.

Jesus wants me to do something about it in a loving and compassionate way.

"And this Scarlett O'Hara contraption is my corset," I say as Judy pulls up on my blouse and down on the waistband of my jeans to reveal the stiff, white garment of stays and buckles around my middle. "It helps me breathe and sit up straight. Honestly," I add, as Judy tucks my blouse back into my jeans, "it's the only reason I can sing or even talk loudly."

"Hmm . . . interesting." Vicky inspects my posture.

"I've got an extra one here." I motion toward my dresser drawer. "Would you be willing to give it a try?" I don't want to sound pushy, so I add, "It's no big deal. You can take it home and try it on there if you want to."

"No, I'll try it on here. I'd like to see what a corset does for me." Judy and Rana lift Vicky onto my bed and shift and roll her body to position the corset under her middle. She grunts and puffs as they tug at the straps and fasten the buckles.

"I betcha feel like John Wayne's packhorse, don't you? I always do," I say laughingly.

Back in her wheelchair, Vicky fights to gain her equilibrium from her new center of balance. "This isn't easy," she comments. And then, "Oh, my! Oh, my goodness! What a difference this makes in my voice," she says, surprised at the depth and projection she can already hear. Rana tucks in her blouse while Judy reshapes her corduroy cuffs to a point. They stand back and we all take inventory.

I am so pleased that she has responded to our help, but I want to make sure she understands that the decision is hers. "Look, I'm not pushing corsets. And a lot of people don't wear them and do quite fine. But for some, it's a real plus."

Vicky looks at me directly with a broad grin for the first time since I've known her.

"Watch out for pressure sores, though. I'm still battling a leftover one from the movie days."

We spend the rest of the afternoon talking, crowding in practical ideas and suggestions. I show her more of the tried-and-true hints I've accumulated in my many years in a wheelchair: support hose for better circulation, attractive leather armsplints to stabilize wrists and hands, and a portable easel to begin learning how to write with a pen between her teeth. She asks about the kind of catheter I use. We talk about exercises and the importance of drinking lots of water. Transferring properly to and from bed. Vitamins. Nutrition.

And bed baths.

"Yes, I know about those," she says with a blush. "There are just some things I'll never get used to. Like showing a stranger how to give me a bath."

She hits a sensitive chord. "Yeah, I have those feelings too." I try to throw some light and laughter on the subject. "But, listen. Even the disciples protested when the Lord Himself washed their dirty feet. Maybe they too had a thing about being bathed by somebody else, even if it was God wielding the washcloth." After I say it, I realize I've just mentioned a story from the Bible in a totally real and natural way.

Again, Vicky smiles. "Legbags. Corsets. My, there's so much to learn." She glances over Rana's shoulder at all the notes and scribbles she has made on her yellow legal pad.

"I'd like you to have that corset . . . but," I caution, hoping I'm not saying too much, "you should see your doctor and get measured for your own. And the easel is yours too if you'd like it. I have an extra."

Vicky is an aristocrat. Proud. Untrusting. Skeptical. Mostly unsmiling. But she says yes to my gifts.

"We could get together with your attendant and explain how to put the corset on and — "

"I'd *like* to get together with my attendant," she sighs. "The last one just left. Thankfully."

"What do you mean?"

She hesitates, as though deciding whether to trust us with her personal problems. "We got into this argument. I don't even remember what it was about. She got so angry. She took a pillow and . . . and she put it on top of . . ." She looks up, her eyes iced with tears. "On top of my face. She was so mad she wanted to . . . to kill me," she says, as though she still can't believe it.

The room is silent. At the far end of the backyard, Scruffy barks. The spray from the lawn sprinklers patters on the concrete ramp outside the sliding glass door. This woman, like many others I am beginning to discover, lives in a world that is foreign to anything I have ever known.

"Luckily, my brother was upstairs. The woman didn't know that. We both thought the house was empty. He ran down the steps when he heard me scream. He grabbed her by her hair and threw her out the front door. Then he raced upstairs, dug her things out of her room, and threw them off the balcony to her, yelling, 'Don't ever come back!'"

I lean on my arm propped on the wheelchair armrest. Judy sits slumped on the edge of the bed holding a corset. Rana dog-ears the corner of her tablet over and over. Just like that night in the restaurant, it is clear that Vicky has not shared this story to tug at our emotions. She has simply told us the facts.

I finally break the silence. "Well, we'll just have to . . . to *do* something." I look toward Judy and Rana, shaking my head. "I don't know what." I look back at Vicky. "But something."

Vicky tosses back her thick hair and sniffs. "I need someone . . . anyone. Arturo and I can't go on alone this way."

"Let's start by praying," Rana says softly. Her suggestion is sudden and jarring. A trace of a smile crosses my lips as I look at her sitting calmly with hands folded on top of the tablet on her lap. A soft breeze gently rattles the blinds of the glass door, and we wait for someone to second the motion.

"Jesus can't help me." Startled, we look at Vicky who continues, almost questioningly. "It isn't Jesus who can put me to bed or get me up in the morning. He can't get me a drink of water. It's nice that you all believe in God, but I need somebody more . . . more real than God. I need people."

"I need them too," I say out of nowhere. "The difference is that I know Judy and Kerbe and others are like . . . like the hands of God for me. I guess you could say it *is* God who gets me up in the morning." I pause and then add, paraphrasing a Bible verse, "Things happen that we might not rely on ourselves, but on Him."[3]

"And has one of your people ever tried to murder you?"

I don't answer.

Vicky hangs her head, embarrassed at the sarcasm behind her words. Swallowing hard, I divert the conversation back to something positive. "As I said, we all want to help. Corsets and the easel are a beginning. I don't know what is next, but we're in this together."

I think of Jesus and a glass of water.

We have begun.

I am painting today in the quiet room adjacent to the office at Joni and Friends. The brick floor is cool. The brilliant color chart is a treat for my eyes. My art books and cloth samples are stacked on top of a metal art file in the corner. Mason jars filled with brushes and tubes of acrylics are lined, soldierlike, on wooden shelves. Even the clutter of papers and color swatches tacked to the cork board are a relief from the office efficiency of telephones and typewriters on the other side of the closed door.

When I paint, I am supposed to think of nothing else. Just the brushes and colors and canvas.

But that's impossible today.

I keep thinking of Vicky and her new easel, wondering how she is progressing with a pen between her teeth. I recall my first easel and my feeble first-time efforts. I glance around —

"Phone for you, Joni." Judy sticks her head in the door. "Want to take it or are you still painting?"

I wheel to my desk phone and tilt my head to the receiver clamped to a gooseneck. "Hello?"

"Yes . . . uh, my name is Bee. We met the other night at a concert. Remember? I was the guy in the striped shirt with my friend Jack Fischer?" He is speaking fast. "I'm calling with really bad news. Jack just broke his neck in a parallel bar accident — "

Details come into focus. One night last week I went to a concert. There, I met two young men, both national gymnasts. Yes, one was named Jack, a handsome and happy fellow. He just wanted to meet me since he had finished reading my book *Joni* a few days earlier. He said something about using gymnastics in some way to talk about his faith in God. And now . . .

"An accident. But . . . but . . . I just met him — ," I interrupt.

"Yes, well, he wanted you to know that you and your book . . . you know, what you said to him that night . . . everything is really helping."

I get Jack's address and tell Bee that I will write to him. "And please," I urge, "please tell Jack we will be praying for him."

I hang up, wishing my parting words hadn't sounded so hollow. "We will be praying for him" doesn't ring true in a situation like this. It sounds like a convenient way to end a distressing conversation. I need no further prompting. I bow my head and pray for Jack Fischer.

Later, at dinner with Judy and Rana, I tell them about Jack. We talk about Vicky. These are not statistics in an attendant-care manual. They are people with very real needs.

"What program could be set up to help them?"

But our discussion lacks energy. Our ideas seem stale. We play idly with our cheesecake.

As we lean back and wait for the busboy to clear our table, I think about needs. *Suppose a brother or sister is without clothes and daily food. If one of you says to him, "Go, I wish you well. Keep warm and fed," but does nothing about his physical needs, what good is it?*[4]

"What was it that helped *you* most, Joni?"

Judy's question seems naïve. "My situation was so different," I say as I brush her off. "My family's unusually close, and I've got great friends."

She stares at me. "Well?"

"Well, what? Do I stick you two in a Xerox machine and pass out the copies?"

"Sort of. Why don't you train others to help like we do?"

"Who?" I ask.

Rana rolls her eyes. "Look at all those people in churches on Sundays. Some of them must have some free time."

"Hmm. You're thinking of a class or something? Teach folks how to push wheelchairs or whatever?"

"Yeah," Rana says. "And maybe they'll even learn how to empty a legbag. Why wait around for social-service groups to teach those things? I've always heard Christians should set the standards for caring. Right?"

Judy fumbles in her purse. "Rana, have you got a pen? . . . Thanks. Hand me that napkin. Let's see . . . how to greet someone whose hands are paralyzed . . . how to talk to somebody who is mentally retarded or who can't speak . . . how to lift people out of a car into a wheelchair."

Judy pulls out her calendar as the ideas gather momentum. She scribbles on another napkin.

"Maybe we can use Dr. Britten's center."

"Or a room at Grace Church."

"We need compassionate people — both to teach and to learn."

Judy interrupts, jabbing her pen at us to emphasize her words. "Gene Newman over at church writes great curriculum. And Greg Barshaw can lecture," she adds as she jots down more names.

"The office girls can help with registrations. We'll invite church people from all over the Valley."

The ideas go from paper napkins to planning sheets, from lesson plans to notebooks, from brochures to a professional workshop. But as registrations from scores of churches begin pouring in for our first "People Plus" in the spring of 1980, a conviction deepens in my heart: a program — even one well-planned and well-prayed for — is not the entire answer.

The night before the launch of our weekend workshop I read a story about Jesus in the Gospel of Mark. "Some men came, bringing to him a paralytic, carried by four of them. Since they could not get him to Jesus because of the crowd, they made an opening in the roof above Jesus and, after digging through it, lowered the mat the paralyzed man was lying on. When Jesus saw their faith, he said to the paralytic, 'Son, your sins are forgiven.'"[5]

It's people who must make the difference. Not a program. People who will go to the same kind of lengths as those four friends, I think to myself.

Somehow we need Christians who will push through crowds, scale walls, and rip up roofs with that same urgent yearning to meet an ordinary human need.

Our first People Plus workshop. Crutches and cycling machines have been pushed aside to make room in Sam's lab for the more than one hundred people present: college students, some nurses, teachers, mothers, several businessmen. I listen from the sidelines along with a smattering of others in wheelchairs. A tall man with curly blond hair rests his chin on the mouth control that operates his power wheelchair. The wheezing rhythm of someone's respirator drifts across the classroom, and I spot the woman who, I surmise, has had polio. Her attendant occasionally leans over to adjust knobs on the machine.

The speaker is Greg Barshaw, the elder at Grace Church who helps disabled people. He shuffles his pages into order, adjusts the level of the microphone, and grabs our attention with a story. In his Sunday school class for mentally handicapped teens, it seems there was a young girl who was catching on rapidly . . .

"The girl's mother called me on the phone the other day," Greg explains. "She said she couldn't understand how her retarded daughter was learning so much, grasping concepts far beyond her natural ability. Her daughter wasn't doing anywhere near that well in public school. This lady couldn't understand what was going on. 'What are you doing different?' she asked me."

At this point Greg puts his hands in his pockets and strolls out from behind the podium. "This mother was shocked. But she shouldn't be. We don't discern biblical things with the brawn of our brain, so neither do the mentally disabled." He reaches for his

Bible on the lectern. "It says in 1 Corinthians 2:12 and 13, that 'we have . . . received . . . the Spirit who is from God, that we may understand what God has freely given us. This is what we speak, not in words taught us by human wisdom but in words taught by the Spirit, expressing spiritual truths in spiritual words.'" He looks up and smiles. "Time and time again I've seen the Holy Spirit by-pass the mind and teach mentally handicapped people truths that are far beyond their comprehension."

I turn to Vicky Olivas and Rana beside me. We give each other the look that says, "Hey, I never knew that." Obviously, the students in this workshop aren't the only ones learning.

"Look at Peter's famous confession of Jesus as the Christ," Greg goes on. "Immediately the Lord pointed the finger and said, 'Flesh and blood has not revealed this to you, but my Father who is in heaven.' He wanted to remind Peter that no one needs a super IQ to interpret God's Word. Just the Spirit within us."[6]

He looks directly at the audience and asks, "So who's mentally handicapped?"

A young college student raises his hand and says quietly, "I guess we all are."

"That's right. Any one of us is mentally disabled when we try to think our way to God. He doesn't need the muscle of your mind to get His truths across. In fact, pride of intellect sometimes gets in the way."

We laugh.

"All we need is faith. And the mentally handicapped have plenty of that. Remember, 'God chose the foolish things of the world to shame the wise.'[7] . . . Bet you came into this workshop thinking folks like that couldn't teach you a thing." Greg grins and shakes his finger at the class.

Again I glance at Vicky and Rana. The notebook they share is marked in the margins, with points underlined. More than a few Bible verses are circled or marked with asterisks. Greg holds their attention.

When coffee break is announced, people close their notebooks and several walk to the front to ask Greg questions. I am curious to know what Vicky and Rana think.

"So . . . do you think we're getting through to these folks?" I ask as Arturo stands on tiptoe to give his mother a sip of coffee.

"Oh, yes. You can tell they're learning a lot." I watch Arturo stretch his little arms around his Mamita to pull her to him and give her a hug. Then, as if it were a perfectly natural way to end a hug, he pushes Vicky back to an upright position.

Vicky is relaxed, at ease, a far cry from the aloof woman I met a few months ago, the woman who viewed other disabled people from a distance.

Rana pats the cover of her notebook. "You know, I understand what Greg means about learning from handicapped people. I remember giving this guy — he was cerebral palsied — exercises when I was at Dr. Britten's lab. And all the while I kept stretching and bending his legs, he kept telling me how I ought to know God. I thought the guy was sweet," she says, using a syrupy tone. "I mean, I thought, 'Isn't that nice . . . he's religious and he wants me to be too.'" She scoots forward in her chair. "And you know what? In my own mind I was set — absolutely determined — that there was no way anybody was going to talk me into thinking about God. I could not have cared less. But here I was listening to this guy talk my ear off about his faith." She laughs. "I only put up with his preaching because he was handicapped." A softness enters her voice now. I hear the difference and wonder if she does. Rana too is far different from the tough, calloused woman I first met.

"It must have been the Spirit of God that got through to me. Honestly," she says with surprise, "I was more handicapped than that guy with cerebral palsy."

Vicky listens intently as Arturo leans on her shoulder. "Actually, I'm learning a lot too," she admits to us. "I used to have a million questions and no answers." She draws a deep breath. "I still don't have any answers. But I'm learning that the questions aren't . . . aren't — "

" — aren't as pressing as they once were?" I finish her thought for her.

She tilts her head, thinking. "I guess you could say that."

"I know what you mean," I say, feeling myself drawn to some

other time of my own. "It's just like Greg was saying. Sometimes the intellect gets in the way when we try to think our way to God." I ponder a moment and then add, "That doesn't mean there are no answers. It just means they don't come all at once."

I wonder if Vicky has found an attendant yet, I think as I watch Kerbe. She and Judy take turns giving me a bath and exercises each morning, fluffing my pillows, straightening my sheets, and making breakfast.

They work compassionately, yet efficiently. They have to. My speaking and traveling, the driving, workshops, and painting have cost me. I've been sitting up too many hours each day, and now I am in bed with my old nemesis, a pressure sore. The old one from movie days is now a full-fledged wound, open and oozing.

A week has passed — it seems like two. My doctor says I've got two more months to go. Two months in bed. Somehow God provided the grace to handle years in a rehabilitation institution. But that was long ago. Now time ticks by with slow monotony.

I read the Bible. This is not easy, though. The book must be pillow-propped on its end as I lay on my side. Words are hard to read sideways. Gravity works against me. And it is impossible to turn pages.

I read about the "day of evil" in the book of Ephesians.[8] *This must be it,* I brood. In the few places I can feel, I ache from inactivity. My hair is greasy and matted in back where my head has pressed on the pillow. Which reminds me, I must get a flatter, harder pillow. This puffy feather thing poofs around each side of my face in a suffocating, claustrophobic way. Little things — fitted sheets snapping their elastic corners, crumbs under my neck, a stuffy nose — irritate me.

"Therefore put on the full armor of God, so that when the day of evil comes, you may be able to stand your ground . . . take up the shield of faith, with which you can extinguish all the flaming arrows of the evil one."[9] . . . I reflect on verses like this. But in the hours idling by, my imagination does silly things.

I picture darts with red-hot tips coming at me while I weakly hold up a shield. Ha! Missed! I act out the struggle against "rulers, authorities, and the powers of this dark world."[10]

The truth is, my prayers seem to ricochet off the ceiling. I picture myself heaving heavy petitions on my shoulders, pushing them past the roof to heaven, clawing at the prison wall of my backyard. My life doesn't go past the border of yew bushes outside. I conjure up weird designs and scary faces out of the shadowy textures in the ceiling. I turn my head on the pillow and pull the same meaningless patterns out of the wallpaper.

Why do I tempt myself with such nonsense?

Depression does this. I remember that from my early days in the hospital. So I ask Judy to come up from the office in the afternoon. She sits beside me on the bed and goes through the mail. She gets me "outside," takes my mind off myself in this room and out to other people's concerns. Yet it's strange to be writing advice to others when I'm having a difficult time swallowing my own prescriptions.

She relates all the latest happenings at the office. I feel left out. I wonder if anyone has missed me.

"Of course you're missed." Judy smooths my dirty hair from my forehead and smiles warmly. I have discovered over these years that Judy, so very British and easily perceived as uncaring or unthoughtful, is truly compassionate. She folds back the blanket and examines the pressure sore, dabbing it with a swab and ointment.

"We need to keep the circulation moving around this area," she comments absently, her attention focused on massaging the skin around the sore.

But even with all the care and kindness, depression continues to eat away at me in my weaker moments.

I watch a videotape of *Gone With the Wind*. Hey! There's the name of the prop man from my movie. *That's right,* I recall wistfully. *He said he worked on that film in his younger days.* Memories of the *Joni* movie — the crew, Solvang, the challenge of film making — make me more restless during these doleful days.

I play backgammon lying on my side with the board balanced on the uprighted end of a suitcase pressed next to my bed. Frustrated, I search for exact words to describe where on the board I want my chips moved. I listen to the radio. I watch television. *Why do game shows depress me?* At least I have enough sense to avoid dumb reruns of "The Twilight Zone."

I look forward to meals. I eat a lot. The rest of the time I just lie here.

From my bed I hear Vicky's wheelchair coming up the short hallway. She and Rana have come for a visit. I want to see them. Then again, I don't.

Judy has smoothed down the greasy cowlick on the back of my head and tucked in my sheet with nurses' corners. I wish I could be propped up in bed with pillows, but it would be dangerous for my sore.

Vicky enters and Rana positions her chair beside my bed. Vicky's olive skin has tanned nicely in the summer sun. Her hair has been cut for the hot weather. It's short but stylish. Her make-up is perfect. She sits so straight — the corset is helping. Wearing armsplints now, she appears to have more movement in her arms. As always, her corduroy slacks are perfectly creased. She has a new pair of summer sandals.

"So, how's the sore?" Vicky asks as Rana leaves to fetch some Cokes.

"Oh, it's coming along," I say, gesturing with my head toward the side of my hip. "How have you been?"

"Fine. I got a new attendant."

"Really?" I say with hope in my voice.

"It's working out great." It's wonderful to see her smile. Not stiffly as before, but with a new confidence. I'm curious to know whether her smile reflects something as wonderful happening on the inside.

She talks about her new helper, about her discussions over the

Bible with Rana, about Arturo and the new van she's getting. I talk about the boredom of bed, about how behind I am on paintings and correspondence, and about how many speaking engagements I've had to cancel.

I stop short.

I'm whining. That makes me even more irritated with myself. Paranoia creeps in.

"Look, I guess you can tell I'm not in the best frame of mind at the moment," I apologize. "I'm not very . . . together." I laugh half-heartedly.

"That's okay. I guess the tables have turned."

I look at her in puzzlement.

"There was a time when I said the same to you." There's no spite in the tone of her voice.

"Go on," I urge her.

She seeks a kind of approval from Rana who is drinking a Coke. "Uh-huh," she says with her mouth full. It's up to you, she seems to say.

"Well, sometimes Rana would give me exercises, and I would snap at her with sarcasm, 'You want me to do these the way Joni does them, don't you!'" She searches for another example. "Or I'd look at you and sneer to myself, 'Joni can't be that happy, that together.'"

Vicky glances at my dresser, my walls. "And this house. And your van. So you wrote a book. And so what if you're a quad, I would taunt myself. Your problems are nothing compared with mine — or a lot of other people, for that matter. I used to think your life wasn't that big a deal."

She stops and shakes her head in a "tsk-tsk" manner. "I was so down on myself. I thought I could handle my problems better if I could cut you down to my size. I felt ashamed, though, when you wanted to be my friend. I couldn't even understand why you'd want me as a friend." She nods toward Rana. "Or why Rana was being my friend."

Openness. Honesty. The room — and me — are refreshed by the cross breeze of Vicky's candor.

"I guess it was just envy," Vicky says.

"I know what you're talking about," I break in. "I sometimes look at paraplegics even now and think they've got it made because they can use their hands and don't have to depend so much on others."

"Do you really do that?"

I nod sheepishly.

"I do too." Vicky laughs, delighted to discover a vice we have in common. I chuckle too.

"But it does help," she adds, her voice softened, "to see you . . . real. Struggling like the rest of us."

She whispers to Rana who leaves and comes back carrying a small potted prickly cactus tied with a bright bow. "Rana was showing me a verse out of her Bible that said something about looking out for another's interest as you would your own." She pauses as Rana places the cactus on my bedside table. "You've helped me. And although it's small, this cactus is my way of helping you along. You're tough . . . we can make it through these hard times. Together."

Her words glaze my eyes with tears. I recall something Sam once said of his visit with Tante Corrie: "*I* was the one who came away blessed. She ended up giving more to me than I could ever possibly give to her."

Vicky, in her unpretentious way of putting things, has given me much more than a surprise cactus. She has freely given me her friendship so that finally we can be real with one another. And that helps me see clearly through my depression.

Later that night as I fight off more demons in mad midnight moments, I grapple to hold on to the light of my friends' visit. *Being real hurts.* But this time it's easier to fight the battle. In the darkness the shadowy outline of a flower vase on my dresser could become a frightening form. Instead, I purposefully attach a brighter meaning to it. And in the dark and quiet, while crickets make peaceful, steady calming sounds outside, I am given something else. A new song inside.

C H O I C E S

I have a piece of china,
  a pretty porcelain vase.
It holds such lovely flowers,
  captures everybody's gaze.
But fragile things do slip and fall
  as everybody knows,
and when that vase came crashing down,
  those tears began to flow.

My life was just like china,
  a lovely thing to me.
Full of porcelain promises
  of all that I might be.
But fragile things do slip and fall
  as everybody knows,
and when my life came crashing down,
  those tears began to flow.

But don't we all cry when pretty things get broken?
  Don't we all sigh at such an awful loss?
  But Jesus will dry your tears as He has spoken,
  'cause He was the one broken on the cross.

Now Jesus is no porcelain prince,
  His promises won't break.
His holy Word holds fast and sure,
  His love no one can shake.
So if your life is shattered
  by sorrow, pain, or sin,
His healing love will reach right down
  and make you whole again.[11]

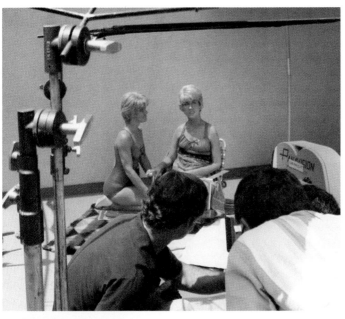

Doing a color test to make certain my double and I exactly match on film.

Face-to-face with "the girl in the blue bathing suit."

Make-up artist Bill Tuttle goes to work.

Bill and hair stylist Kaye Pow-
nall glue on the scalp line of
my wig.

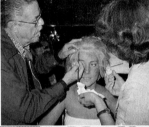

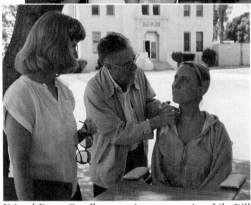

Friend Betsy Sandbower tries on my wig while Bill
pins my own hair tightly under a net.

Rob Tregenza, Assistant to
the Director, helps block
shots on the crane.

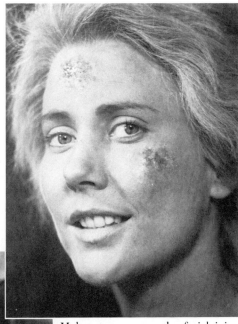

Make-up re-creates the facial injuries from my diving accident.

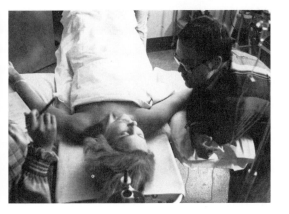

Jim Collier, Writer and Director, gives me direction for my scenes on the Stryker frame.

Dr. Sam Britten and Chris Ige.

Working at the cycling machine exercises my shoulders, biceps, and cardiovascular system.

Here Margie is helping develop my balance.

Margie Corbett, Dr. Britten's assistant, stretches my shoulder muscles to increase flexibility and reduce spasticity.

Dr. Sam Britten presents me with the van, a gift from Grace Community Church. These snapshots capture my range of emotions at the time!

On the left is my cousin Kerbe.

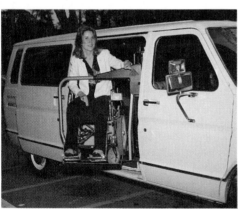

A mechanical lift enables me to enter and leave the van by myself.

Behind "the wheel." My right arm is locked into the handcuff that controls the steering, accelerating, and braking.

Visiting a rehabilitation center.

In my office, dialing a number with a mouthstick.

Our radio ministry is a vital part of Joni and Friends.

Joni and Friends staff and volunteers gather for a picnic.

The first Joni and Friends workshop in Southern California.

Steve Estes "talks" with a workshop participant who uses a wordboard.

A typical day's mail.

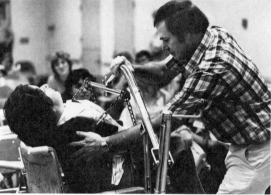

Some of the Joni and Friends staff and volunteers.

At a workshop Dr. Sam Britten and Debbie Stone demonstrate how some disabled people are transferred from bed to wheelchair.

Preparing a mailing.

Rana and I teach a People Plus class.

My armsplint and special spoon allow me to feed myself.

Having fun with my niece Earecka Tregenza and Ryan and Adrienne Estes (Steve and Verna's children).

Earecka feeds Aunt Joni an ice-cream cone.

I often borrow the hands of others. Here, Earecka, Ryan, and Adrienne help me shop, cook, and clean my wheelchair.

There are many important people in my life. Here are some who hold a special place in my life and in this book.

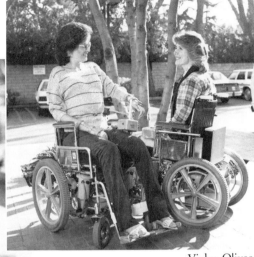

Vicky Olivas

Scruffy's not a person, but he is special!

My sister Jay

Vicky and her son Arturo

Judy Butler, thinking and planning as usual.

Rob and Jay

Rana Leavell

One of my favorite pictures of Ken, taken just as he was ready to leave for a game of racquetball.

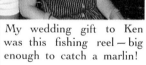

My wedding gift to Ken was this fishing reel — big enough to catch a marlin!

Mother and I wait for the ceremony to begin.

Left to right: Ken's parents, Takeo and Kay Tada; Ken and I; Grandmother and Grandfather Minoru Hori, Ken's grandparents; and his sister Carol.

Left to right: my mother, Rob and Jay Tregenza, Ken and I, my sister Kathy Eareckson, my father, and my nieces Kay Trombero and Earecka Tregenza.

Our wedding party. Back row, left to right: Ed Hill, Larry Bonney, Ken, Dr. Sam Britten, Pete Lubisich, and Jan Janura. Front row: Betsy Sandbower, Carol Tada, Kay Trombero, Earecka Tregenza, Jay Tregenza, and Kathy Eareckson.

Daddy and I prepare to walk down the aisle.

My relaxed groom.

Mr. and Mrs. Ken Tada

A few disabled friends gather to catch my bouquet.

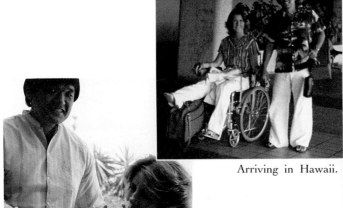

Arriving in Hawaii.

Some of our favorite moments are spent in the garden.

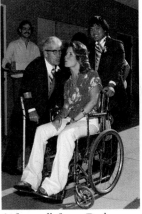

A farewell from Dad as we leave for our honeymoon in Hawaii.

Ken rigs a special easel for me to use during the long weeks in bed required for healing pressure sores.

Ken carves our first Thanksgiving turkey.

We visit a rehabilitation center in Poland.

Ken and I participate in a Wheel-a-Thon for the Center of Achievement for the Physically Disabled.

I follow the snaking line of Interstate 15 on the map spread open on my lap.
We pass the honor guard of eucalyptus trees that line the freeway,
breaking the harsh hot winds for the new breed of stucco homes
bordering the desert's edge.

It's exciting to leave Los Angeles behind. With pressure sores
healed, I can finally take this long-awaited vacation. And I get to
navigate while Rana is at the controls of the van. Judy and Vicky
are with us too. Free from the confines of my bed, I am again an
adventurer on the road of life.

We climb to the High Desert of sand and sagebrush, and
speed past the offramps toward Barstow. Great red arrows and
blinking neon lights warn us to stop at McDonalds or Burger King
before crossing the hot plains to Nevada. We have our cooler filled
with fruit and orange juice. We'll do fine, thank you.

On the dry and desolate outskirts of Las Vegas we find a
Motel 6. Vicky and I wheel to the pool deck while Rana and Judy
register. The desert sunset silhouettes date palms and hills in the
distance. Winds whip ragged flags around the pool, and the
halyards pinging against the metal poles sound like the sailboats on
Chesapeake Bay. My mother would think this was an adventure
too.

The next morning, dressed for the desert heat in a tube top,
pigtails, sunglasses, and plenty of lip gloss, it's my turn at the
wheel!

I drive slowly through truckstop burgs with names like

Mesquite and Salina and Beaver, dusty little towns roadblocked with detours and busy corner cafés. Over a hundred or more miles of passing lanes I make friends with two trucks — a Peterbilt hauling timber and a Kenworth carrying steel beams.

We stop often at roadside rest areas or scenic points of interest. Vicky and I sit side by side under a shade tree while Rana spritzes our faces and arms with cold water from a spray bottle. Neither of us perspire — something else we share in common from our spinal-cord injuries — and our temperatures will equal the desert's if we aren't careful.

We pass wind-sculptured mesas and a few wind-beaten armadillos. Finally, hours past sunset, we pull into Green River, Utah. Weary and dirty, we sit in the darkened van while Judy checks in at the front desk. It's a large motel, but several tractor trailers are parked in the lot with their engines idling, keeping air conditioners going.

"Tomorrow we'll make Colorado by lunch and then have a late dinner in Estes Park, don't you think?" I speculate.

"I've never been to a Bible camp before," Vicky says.

Through the windshield we see Judy coming, stepping her way around huge muddy potholes in the gravel parking lot. We're ready to collapse into bed. But just as we click open the locks on our doors and heave our suitcases into our rooms, the phone rings. We look at each other questioningly. Who knows we're here?

"It's for you," Rana says, holding the receiver toward Vicky. "It's your mother." Judy drops a hanging garment bag on the bed and slumps down beside it. A bewildered Vicky leans her head to the receiver in Rana's hand.

"Halo . . . Mamie, que paso?"

Seconds pass. No change in her expression. Suddenly, her eyes widen. "Que? Estas segura?"

I don't need my high-school Spanish to tell me that something is desperately wrong.

"Quando paso?" She presses her head harder against the receiver. "Todo?" Another stretch of silence. "No puedo es impossible. Mamie, yo te llamo mañana."

Rana replaces the receiver in the cradle, and we sit in silence, waiting. Whatever it is, Vicky can't take any more letdowns. Not now. Not when she finally seems to be getting a grip on her life.

"My mother says the peso in Mexico has fallen. All my savings are in those banks . . . everything is worthless." She finally is able to lift her head and look at us. "The peso is almost worthless."

"Everything you have . . . in Mexico?" Judy says, stunned.

Vicky closes her eyes tightly. "The interest rates were so good . . . I needed the income just to make ends meet."

Rana flicks on the television to catch the late news. The commentator gives the headlines of the fast-breaking international story, accompanied by film coverage of banks in Mexico City where anxious people wait in long lines. Vicky's income from her insurance settlement — everything she has to live on — will be cut to the core.

Rana lowers the volume after the report. "We can go back to L.A., you know."

Vicky sighs deeply. "No . . . no, we'll go on. There's nothing we can do. Let's just hope the value of the peso doesn't drop further," she laughs, "or I'll be flat broke. No house. Nothing." I can't believe she can laugh about it.

The news makes our time around the Bible that evening — a vacation ritual we promised each other — all the more meaningful. Amid open suitcases, heaped bedspreads, and scattered sweat shirts, we pray. Vicky listens. Before she and Rana go to their room, I ask Judy to flip to Psalm 50.

"This is . . . uh, . . ." I pause until Judy holds the Bible open in front of Vicky and points to the verse. "This is Psalm 50. The fifteenth verse says — "

"'Call upon me in the day of trouble,'" Vicky reads slowly in her heavily accented English, "'and I will deliver you.'"

"There's more," I prod.

"'I will deliver you, and you will honor me.'" She thinks for a moment. "Well, this is a day of trouble, no doubt about it," she says wearily.

I am convinced that in the night, alone in her bed, Vicky will call upon God.

The next day we travel fast, make fewer stops, and arrive at our destination at dusk. As we bounce up the rutted mountain road, our headlights freeze a doe and her fawn in our path. The large chalet that is Ravenscrest Lodge overlooks the twinkling lights of Estes Park, Colorado, a mountain resort bordering the edge of Rocky Mountain National Park.

We don extra sweat shirts against the crisp alpine air and haul our luggage up the small dirt path through the ponderosa pines to our cabin. Despite Vicky's misfortune, we still sense adventure.

In the morning, I finally see the world we've entered as I sit outside our cabin and wait for the others to get ready for breakfast. It is very quiet on the side of this mountain, yet the air seems to roar. Does it breathe and sigh through the pines? Or could it be a rushing stream? Pine needles sparkle in the sun, and occasionally I hear the scratching of a rake on a dirt path.

The wooden screen door creaks open, and Rana wheels Vicky out beside me.

"Did you sleep okay?" I greet her.

"Considering," she replies with a smile, "yes." She throws her head back and basks in the high-altitude sun. "That verse you gave me the other night about calling on God helped," she says. "I guess I have nowhere else to turn."

"I understand. Even though things haven't hit me as hard as they have you," I say, reflecting on her confession that day in my bedroom, "the fact is, I *have* had it easier." Her eyes are open now, as she leans forward to listen.

I look deeply into her eyes. "But you've taught me to be so grateful for the things I can do. Like something as simple as scratching my nose," I say as I lift my arm to my face. "We both know what it means, though, not to be able to scratch our backs. So in some ways I . . . I think I can understand."

We are two paralyzed people, with injuries so similar and lives so different. Yet together we draw comfort from the sun and the things we share in common.

That afternoon, after lunch and a class on the book of Colossians, I power my wheelchair across the crunchy gravel toward our cabin. Judy is going to set up my easel so I can sketch the bark on the pine tree outside our cabin window. I am intrigued with the platelet-like shingles, the color and the texture. I pass Vicky and Mrs. Thomas, a kind gray-haired woman in a fresh cotton blouse and full skirt, the matriarch of sorts around here. She has wisdom, and she sits on a rock wall and talks over an open Bible to Vicky.

Later, Vicky tells me about it.

"Saying His name . . . the name of Christ . . . is so different." God's name, spoken in a gentle and accepting way, is foreign to her. "But that lady, Mrs. Thomas," she says, bobbing her head in the direction of the chalet, "says His name so warmly. Just like the rest of you. She talked about a personal relationship with the Lord Jesus . . . that's what she called Him. And that if I receive Him — " She spots Rana coming up the dirt path. "Rana, show Joni this verse. Right where my Bible's marked," she calls.

Rana places her half-eaten apple between her knees and reaches for the new study Bible on Vicky's lap. She opens it at the bookmark and smooths the stubborn page against the breeze.

"'Just as you received Christ Jesus as Lord,'" Vicky reads, "'continue to live in him, rooted and built up in him, strengthened in the faith as you were taught, and overflowing with thankfulness.'"[12]

Rana replaces the Bible on Vicky's lap, folds her arms, and continues to munch on her apple. Vicky gets to her point. "I'm already weak — in every sense of that word. I have nowhere else to go but up. And it makes sense that I'll only get stronger if I put my faith in Christ," she says with profound simplicity. "Don't you think?"

I glance at Rana who, more than any of us, has practically and consistently poured God's love into Vicky's life. She tosses the apple core and leans down to give Vicky a hug. "You know, you really *don't* have much else to be thankful for. Just purely and simply Jesus — and that's where He wants all of us to be."

We hear that night that the peso has weakened further. But our faith has been strengthened.

The Bible study we began during our vacation spills over into the following months. I watch in astonishment as the lovely, statuesque Latin woman in the wheelchair exchanges the mysteries behind her for the mysteries of God's Word. Less stiff, more trusting, Vicky accepts love without pride or question. Even more, she wants — needs — to give love in return.

One night, months later, we sit around the table after our Bible study, relaxing and nibbling on chocolates. No one is in a rush to leave. I talk about the farm and my family — a recent letter from my mother, the missions film Rob and Jay are doing in the Philippines, the few horses they've sold. A year ago it would have pained me to recount such homey details. I ponder aloud about this, reflecting on how in my wildest dreams I never imagined I would write a book or have a part in a movie or leave the farm to start a ministry of workshops and radio programs, traveling, and speaking.

Judy leans on her elbow and says, "I never thought I would end up in California . . . full-time with Joni and Friends. It feels funny living in one place after moving from city to city with the Billy Graham Crusades."

"Yes," Vicky says, picking up the thread of our rambling conversation, "and a year ago I would never have seen myself in a situation like this." She scans the Bibles, scattered commentaries, pencils, and notes cluttering the table. Her eyes take on a faraway gaze.

"I think it all started with me when my husband left," she begins. "And then God really grabbed my attention when I was attacked. And, yes, the gunshot . . . and paralysis . . . the divorce — Jesus really pulled me through that one. Let's see . . ." She mentally gropes for the list. "All those attendants who never worked out and that one who tried to murder me . . ." She laughs, shaking her head. "Oh, and I never told you about the one who refused to feed me, did I?"

We all look at each other, dumfounded. She's really serious, recounting these matters in the same way we'd tabulate a day's minor irritations. "Uh . . . no . . . you never mentioned that one," I say.

Vicky checks off more of her list. "Raising Arturo on my own. The money crunch." She stops and asks Rana for a chocolate, takes a small bite, and continues. "But God has done it. And I never would have dreamed I could trust Him . . . after all those things. But I do." She smiles convincingly, even a little cockily.

Vicky has laid out the events like cards on the table, pleased to have been dealt such a good hand. "I don't need all the answers," she continues. "I just need the One who is holding those in trust for me."

What wisdom for one still so young in the faith. Yet it is wisdom I've heard before. *I said nearly the same thing in the movie, didn't I,* I muse with a smile, and an idea glimmers.

"You know, I got this letter the other day," I mention, "and I'm having a tough time answering it. Would you mind taking a look at it? Maybe even answering it?"

"Me? You're kidding! What do I have to say?"

"Listen. I'll send the letter to you. You tell me what you think."

Perhaps another part of my dream is beginning to take form: to see disabled people themselves reaching out to others in need. Before I send the Linda's letter to Vicky, I read it one more time.

I feel like I'm the only quadriplegic around. I so much dislike living in this nursing home. The only plus is its location — my mom lives only a block away and so I get to see my eight-year-old daughter. My divorce and custody battles are still not settled. It's so difficult at times to cope with first losing my husband, my daughter, my body, and my home because of some drunk driver. Many times I wonder if I'll make it.

I wonder if I'll make it. I've said those words too. Vicky has said those words. And somehow we must encourage this woman who has had her life jerked upside down and inside out by "some drunk driver" — let her know that she can make it. With the grace of God, she can and must.

After Vicky has had time to receive and read the letter, I press her, "What do you think?"

"I'm not sure I can help, but I'll give it a try," she replies.

Dear Linda,

My friend Joni shared your letter with me. Since our situations are so similar, she asked me to write to you.

Eight years ago I was shot in the neck. I needed the aid of a respirator but was lucky enough to be weaned off it in two months. During those months I had pneumonia most of the time, suffered from pressure sores, and was never really expected to live.

My son was eighteen months old at the time, plus I was in the process of a divorce. At that point my parents took custody of my son because they felt that even if I lived, I wouldn't be able to take care of him.

During that first year I felt I was in the middle of a bad dream, thinking any second I would wake up and everything would be okay. I went through all the motions of rehabilitation, but never allowed myself to learn. When I was released, reality hit me in the face. What to do?

Pity on me, poor Vicky! The pity lasted for two years — I refused to get out of bed or do anything for myself. I made everyone around me miserable.

Finally, it was like the Lord said, "Enough." Do I take the easy way and stay in bed in my parents' home while they make all my decisions, raising my son? Or do I move out on my own and start taking responsibility for my son and for my own life. How scary!

I got a house, and my attendant, my son, and myself moved in. I had to enroll my son in school — a giant step for me. Next, I had to go out shopping to furnish my home. I was faced with mortgage payments, utility bills, food expenses, finding medical supplies, no transportation, and a need to be a meaningful part of my son's life. I didn't feel I could handle it. But it can be done.

Linda, I pray that you will have faith in the Lord that He will help you too. He was with me through all those rough times and the triumphant ones too. You will worry and wonder, but with God's grace, you'll make it.

I'm enclosing a book and a Bible with parts underlined. And Joni and Friends will send you a list of agencies and resources in your area. We will help you find a good church.

This is only the beginning, and I hope to talk to you soon on the phone. Please write. I'd love to know how things progress for you.

Yours in His care,
Vicky Olivas

My secretary folds the letter and sticks it in a Joni and Friends envelope. I look at the name of our ministry in the lefthand corner. The "and Friends" now includes Vicky.

The dream is coming true. Not here on my desk, but in the lives of people like Rana and Vicky and perhaps even Linda. People who, with God's help, are finding out who they are and where they are going.

I read in a magazine this week that Corrie ten Boom has suffered another setback. It is simply a small paragraph at the bottom of a page, a few sentences highlighting her past ministry and a mention of this new stroke. *How old is she now? Eighty-eight? Eighty-nine?* I shake my head in amazement.

It's been far too long since I've seen her. And now, more than ever, we have much in common. My own battle with pressure sores is still fresh in my memory, and I recall the need to have visitors at my bedside, the comfort that people cared and prayed. I call Corrie's home and plan a visit.

Rana makes the long drive with me down to Orange County, to the single-story suburban house on the quiet tree-lined street that is now Corrie's sanctuary. We are greeted by Pam, Corrie's companion, a tall and strikingly graceful English woman. As we step into Corrie's home, it is like stepping into a different world. The air is fragrant with the rich aroma of good European coffee and Dutch chocolate. Old World clocks tick and a kettle steams.

Pam ushers us into the sitting room and asks us to wait while Tante Corrie is readied for our visit. Old photographs of the Ten Boom family crowd bookshelves and a buffet table. Photos in sepia of friends from Europe and from her travels. Each one is an individual treasure in a richly carved frame, proudly displayed on a lace doily. A reclining chair sits prominently in the room, and I wonder if it is a favorite of Corrie's, perhaps brought from the Netherlands.

A bunch of heavy, dewy pink roses crowd a vase on a small round table by the sliding glass door that opens into Corrie's backyard garden. A tree rustles and tulips sway. The breeze lightly wafts in the fragrance of orange blossoms. What a restful place.

Pam pushes Tante Corrie into the room in a wheelchair. She sits, slightly slumped, with her head resting in a forward position, but she greets us with a smile and a nod, waving her hand in a sing-song fashion with a finger raised. She mumbles a few garbled sounds.

It suddenly strikes me that this dear old saint who has ministered to thousands, even millions, with her speaking can now barely utter an intelligible word. I fight back tears of compassion and tell her how pleased we are to visit her. Her smile broadens. Her eyes sparkle.

Tante Corrie's silver-white hair, thin and wispy, is arranged in a soft roll. She wears a long white gown and a pink cotton robe. With her good hand she fiddles with the lace on the robe. Little round glasses perch on the end of her nose, and she peers over the rims at us.

I demonstrate my power wheelchair and recite some of the lessons we have both learned from long confinement. I do this not to exhibit my own spirituality, but to encourage her with what is really a litany from both of us to our loving God. "God's grace is enough for each day," I confirm, and she smiles and nods, pleased to agree.

I recall that Jim Collier, the director of *Joni*, had also endeared himself to Corrie in the making of *The Hiding Place*. She brightens when I mention his name, delighted to hear about his latest projects.

The mention of the movie triggers something else, and she gestures toward the shelf of video cassettes. Tante Corrie wants us to view one of her church films.

Pam puts on the video and leaves to prepare tea and cucumber sandwiches. I watch Corrie as she views her movie. She mumbles more sounds, accentuating her image on the film with a wave of her finger again. It seems she is not so much delighted with her appearance on the screen as she is with its message of hope from God's Word.

Corrie and I talk about heaven. It is a favorite topic for both of us. A new body. A new mind. A new heart. A new language. A new home. Even new ways to serve. Corrie underscores each of my words with a hearty Dutch "ja."

It seems appropriate to sing a song for her, one that has become particularly special to me because it captures all my thoughts and feelings about God and heaven and my disability. And as I begin, I realize how very fitting the words are for this dear friend of mine.

> Though I spend my mortal lifetime in this chair,
> I refuse to waste it living in despair.
> And though others may receive
> Gifts of healing, I believe
> That He has given me a gift beyond compare.
> For heaven is nearer to me,
> And at times it is all I can see.
> Sweet music I hear
> Coming down to my ear,
> And I know that it's playing for me.
> For I am Christ the Savior's own bride,
> And redeemed I shall stand by His side.
> He will say, "Shall we dance?"
> And our endless romance
> Will be worth all the tears I have cried.

I raise my paralyzed hand and clumsily place it on the arm of Tante Corrie's wheelchair. She balances her good hand on top of mine and taps in rhythm while I sing the last verse.

> I rejoice with him whose pain my Savior heals,
> And I weep with him who still his anguish feels.
> But earthly joys and earthly tears
> Are confined to earthly years
> And a greater good the Word of God reveals.
> In this life we have a cross that we must bear,
> A tiny part of Jesus' death that we can share.
> And one day we'll lay it down

And He has promised us a crown
To which our suffering can never be compared.

For heaven is nearer to me,
    And at times it is all I can see.
Sweet music I hear
    Coming down to my ear,
And I know that it's playing for me.
For I am Christ the Savior's own bride,
And redeemed I shall stand by His side.
He will say, "Shall we dance?"
And our endless romance
Will be worth all the tears I have cried.[13]

Another breeze stirs the stillness, and it occurs to me that Pam, holding a tray of tea and sandwiches, has been standing for some time at the edge of the sitting room. None of us wants to disturb what has become, unintentionally, a holy moment.

Tante Corrie carries on the moment by grasping her paralyzed hand with the good one and then with great effort entwines her fingers. Pam, understanding this gesture, immediately puts down the tray, kneels by Corrie's wheelchair, and looks up into that determined face. "Tante Corrie, may we pray with you too?"

Pam rises and seats herself on the sofa beside Rana, and we bow our heads. After a moment, Corrie begins. Her words are indistinct, but her voice rises and falls as she prays earnestly in the Spirit. The Spirit is, in fact, the only one who understands her.

That night in bed, I relive each moment of my visit with Corrie ten Boom. I recall how our eyes met as we were fed our cucumber sandwiches. Helpless and for the most part dependent, I felt our mutual weakness. Yet I am certain neither of us had ever felt stronger. It makes me think of the Cross of Christ — a symbol of weakness and humiliation, yet at the same time, a symbol of victory and strength.

A stream of faces now flows through my mind — Vicky and

Rana, Daddy and Jay, Debbie and Dr. Sam, Jack and Judy, Kerbe, Pam, and many more. Dependent or independent, being served or serving others, we are all trading our weaknesses each day for a far greater glory.

My thoughts focus on one of those faces — Vicky Olivas. I recall that day I first saw her at Sam's lab. The anger in her eyes and voice was iced over by her cool, calloused defense. She didn't seem then to hold the promise of one day being a child of God.

But through Vicky I have learned that, ironically, those who are icy cold — intensely belligerent — may be as close to the Kingdom as those who seem hotly interested in things of God. It is those who are lukewarm toward God who are in deepest trouble, Christ says. Suffering, in a mysterious way, pushes people to either extreme. And Vicky has now left the ice of anger and entered the warmth of heaven. I pray that our ministry may keep pushing thousands more of those who suffer out of their lukewarm complacency and into the vulnerability of either being hot or cold.

For a wheelchair may confine a body that is wasting away. But no wheelchair can confine the soul . . . the soul that is inwardly renewed day by day.

For paralyzed people can walk with the Lord.

Speechless people can talk with the Almighty.

Sightless people can see Jesus.

Deaf people can hear the Word of God.

And those like Tante Corrie, their minds shadowy and obscure, can have the very mind of Christ.

The buzz of Kerbe's hairdryer in the bathroom reminds me that it is Friday night. She must have a date. *We don't spend much time together,* I think as I look up from my book. I wheel out from under the kitchen table and down the hall to the bathroom. It'll be good to visit with her.

"Got a date?" I yell above the whine of the dryer. She turns, one arm held high above her head to stretch the strands of long brown hair twisted around a roller brush. She fans her hair with the heavy dryer and beams. The guy must be special.

"Yes." She raises her voice above the whine. "A potluck at church tonight."

We chat for a few minutes about her work at Joni and Friends, about the Bible study she's working on, a new milk-shake diet we're both trying, and the new colors Revlon is putting in their lipsticks.

I lean my head against the doorpost of the bathroom and watch her artfully handle her comb, teasing or pulling a curl here and there until her hair bounces like a thick mane.

"You look like a lioness," I laugh.

She turns to attack, threatening to paint a mustache on me with her blue eye pencil.

As I wheel back to my book, she heads for the door, shoulderbag and sweater draped on her arm. She's a gorgeous girl — so very popular at her church. Always a date. Always a party or a social or a Bible study to run off to. Yes, Kerbe fits right in to fast-paced California.

"Want some perfume?" She pauses by the open door and reaches into her purse for the spray atomizer.

"I'm not going anywhere," I say doubtfully.

"That's not the point." She sprays her neck and wrists as she walks toward me. "You don't have to be with anybody else to enjoy a little luxury." I tilt my head as she squirts the scent on my neck.

I like that attitude in Kerbe. On mornings when it's her turn to get me up and ready for work, I always arrive at the office looking like I've wheeled out of the pages of a fashion magazine. A contemporary hairstyle. A new blend of eyeshadow.

After she waves good-by and clicks the door behind her, I sit alone amid the lingering fragrance. My book doesn't hold quite the appeal it had earlier. My thoughts stray back to long-ago days when I was on my feet on a Friday night. Like my cousin, I'd spend an hour in front of the closet deciding what to wear and another hour at the magnifying mirror with a cover stick and make-up. I would leave the house polished and shined to a high gloss.

That was years ago. My only ventures into the dating scene now are when I catch a glimpse into Kerbe's world. I'm in my thirties — a bona fide single. I can't remember my last date. I sigh and shrug my shoulders.

That's not entirely true, I think abruptly. There was a dinner date with the movie gaffer. I shrink a bit, remembering those movie days when I abandoned my 20/20 vision and lived on blind feelings.

I push my attention back to the paragraph I have read and reread — several times. I glance around the kitchen. Judy and I may fix a snack later. We'll play a game of Scrabble. Maybe there's something good on television. I smile as I turn the page. *I could go out on dates like Kerbe. . . . But then again, no guy is exactly beating down my door,* I chuckle to myself.

Singleness. I have the gift whether I like it or not, whether I want it or not.

The evening slips by into a routine weekend. Grocery shopping, clothing sales at the mall, a few hours of painting, a phone call home to my family, an early night on Saturday. On Sunday, Judy and Kerbe get me ready for church.

John MacArthur is away, speaking at some conference, so we have a guest minister this morning. One of the elders leads the opening prayer and hymn. I peer over Judy's shoulder and scan the bulletin for the name of the guest speaker. Nobody I know. During the announcements people rustle in their seats, rummage in purses and coat jackets for pens, checkbooks, and wallets. A few reach for visitor registration cards in the little pew boxes. I read the fine print in the bulletin, yawn, and look around. Sam Britten and his wife are sitting in a pew across the aisle. Our eyes meet, and we smile our greetings to each other.

After the offering, special music, and another hymn, the guest speaker climbs the steps to the pulpit. I settle down to listen. He introduces his sermon with a story. It gets a little long, and my mind begins to wander. I slap my thoughts back in line. *Attention! Front and center! This is a worship service, Eareckson.*

My eyes settle on a dark head down front, four or five pews ahead. Thick black hair. My heart skips a beat. It's him. I can't see his face, but I know it's the gaffer. How is it that he's in church — this church? I strain to see, but . . . no, of course it isn't. It's just someone who looks like him from the back. The tension and adrenaline drain away.

The power of those dormant feelings takes me by surprise, knocks me off balance. From nowhere, I can taste the faint disappointment of old pipe dreams and false hopes.

The man tilts his head slightly, revealing a strong jaw and the smooth tanned curve of his neck. He leans to the left and in profile reaches for a Bible in the back of his pew. Other feelings force their way in — longings, wishful thinking, regret. Tiny darts of depression pinprick my resistance.

No. No. This must not happen. I will not sit here and squander this worship service on selfish notions! If I can't concentrate on the sermon, I will rivet these irksome thoughts into line — nail them down once and for all. *We take captive every thought to make it obedient to Christ.*[14] I remember the line from Scripture.

I find, though, that it takes a mountain of effort to pull my eyes away from the back of the man's head. In this instance, I cannot flee. That black hair—my heart knots. *Okay. Okay,* I challenge my feelings. *If that's the way you want to play, I can stand firm; if that's where the battle is, that's where I'll fight it.*

While the speaker drones in the background, I throw on my armor. I focus my eyes on the back of this stranger's head. *Oh, Father . . . You desire mercy rather than judgment. Now be merciful to me, a sinner. And bless You for not judging me according to these awful thoughts. Stupid, silly thoughts that distract me from worshiping You. Be merciful and help me win this battle—for Your honor and for the benefit of this man, whoever he is.*

I take a deep breath and gain more ground. *Father, if this man knows You, get him deeper into Your Word. Help him to obey. If he's dating somebody, convict him if he's messing around. If he's married, hold him to his vows. Don't let him get away with cheating, even if only in his thoughts. Strengthen him against the Devil and the world with all its temptations. Make prayer a big part of his life, and give him extra joy when he makes a stand for You.*

And if there are problems where he works, make his life shine as a real witness to his co-workers. If there is a lingering argument with his mother or father, resolve it, would You? Make his testimony at home consistent with what he believes here in this church. I stare at the man's head, his hair black and shining, and a wave of peace washes over me as I sense victory within grasp. *We're winning,* I smile to the Holy Spirit.

Save him if he's not in Your family. Strengthen him. Refine his faith . . . keep him from lies . . . clear up his bad habits . . . assist him in prayer . . . sustain his health . . . guard his mind . . . deepen his friendships . . . make him into the man You want him to be.

My heart is filled with honest-to-goodness joy. I know, through my prayer, that God is being exalted on this Lord's Day, even if in a most unorthodox manner. The speaker is winding up his message. It's too late for me to pick up his drift, so . . .

Almighty God, Father of all mercies—I begin a silent piece of liturgy I've known since I was a child—*we, Thine unworthy servants, do give Thee most humble and hearty thanks for all Thy goodness and loving kindness to us and to all men. We bless Thee for our creation, preservation, and all the blessings of this life. But above all, for Thine inestimable love in the redemption of the world by our Lord Jesus Christ, for the means of grace and for the hope of glory.*

As the speaker closes his sermon and asks the congregation to rise for the closing prayer, I continue my own petition. *And, we beseech Thee, give us that due sense of all Thy mercies that our hearts may be unfeignedly thankful, and that we may show forth Thy praise not only with our lips but in our lives — by giving up ourselves to Thy service and by walking before Thee in holiness and righteousness all our days through Jesus Christ our Lord. To whom with Thee and the Holy Ghost be all honor and glory, world without end. Amen.*

"Amen," the speaker says from the pulpit, and several in the congregation echo, "Amen." It is noon, and digital watches around me beep the hour in unison. The organist pulls out all the stops as the postlude permits everyone to gather sweaters, books, and purses. People begin shuffling out of the pews.

"I'm starved. Let's hurry home for lunch," Judy says as she steps out of the pew and over my footpedals.

"Let's!" I respond, but I am watching the man down front as he steps into the aisle and begins chatting with several people. I consider — only for a moment — approaching and introducing myself, perhaps mentioning my prayer for him. I instantly dismiss the notion. No. He'd think I was nuts! Or making advances or something. Besides, I don't want the morning's victory to be tarnished. I'll keep it between God and me.

A month or so passes. The memory of that morning battle with temptation has faded. I am at another worship service at Grace Church. Afterward, an acquaintance introduces me to a nice-looking oriental man. He looks familiar, and I study him with a puzzled air. Brightening, I ask him to turn around. He looks just as puzzled. "I want to see the back of your head," I explain. So he complies.

Sure enough, he is the man with the thick, black hair. We laugh when I tell him I prayed for the back of his head just a couple of months ago. I simplify my story, saying something about a boring sermon. We chat for a few moments.

As I start to power my wheelchair toward the exit, I realize I've already forgotten his name, and circle my chair around.

"Ken Tada." He smiles and waves good-by.

Our Marriage

As water reflects a face, so a man's heart reflects the man.
— Proverbs 27:19

It is May 1980, and Jay and Rob's new baby, Earecka, is barely a month old. A strong sense of nostalgia overwhelms me every time I see snapshots of their family or imagine Earecka's crib in the corner of the farmhouse bedroom where my things once were.

I recall my visit East last year for Jay's baby shower. Still in faded jeans — with a sewn-in blue elastic band — she didn't let her swelling tummy dissuade her from farm chores around the vegetable garden and horse barn. Sitting in her rocker in the corner of the dining room, she looked resplendent, if not a little self-conscious, among pink and blue crepe-paper streamers and piles of presents. It seemed she would rather get her baby born so that the two of them might tackle farm chores together.

I examine a photo of Jay holding Earecka in her arms and imagine what it would be like — if I could feel, if I had the strength — to hold her. It makes me want to be home. I send a gift and several cards, and telephone the farm often.

I become philosophic. The choices and changes in Jay's life and mine are remarkable. She, in a ministry as a wife and a mother and a farmer — a rich blend of earthy, pragmatic sensibilities like breast-feeding and nurturing and gardening and giving. Me, in a ministry with handicapped people — seminars and churches and curriculum. So different. Do I have regrets? I wonder.

No. I see a parallel between our lives in the rich blend of art and music and speaking and creating, all of which fill my time along with the work of Joni and Friends. I have no doubts. The decisions I have made are choices with which I can rest. Like my older sister, I feel privileged to enjoy depth and soul and meaning in what I do.

I still know who I am — a happy single woman. And I know where I am going — forward with a singular dream.

Somebody's up to something. Why has Ken Tada been invited to my birthday party? I'm certain I see the fine hand of Carol and Twila, two friends from church who are giving the party at their townhouse. Plus, I keep running into this guy. At church. At a recent Young Life function where I spoke. But this birthday party seems a little too suspicious. After all, I don't really know him. Yes, I bet Carol and Twila are trying some matchmaking.

There's no doubt about it. This Ken Tada is an attractive man. He seems comfortable with himself and with other people as he sits on the sofa, gesturing with a can of soda as he speaks. He looks directly at people when he talks to them. He smiles a lot.

When I think no one is looking, I study his face. His thick black hair frames his high, wide cheekbones and dark brown almond eyes. He has a blockish build, square and stocky. As tall as he is and with those broad shoulders, I bet he's Hawaiian. And I bet he's an athlete, judging from his strong neck and arms. He seems reserved, neither brazen nor boisterous, even at this party among many friends. In fact, he seems somewhat shy.

For most of the evening I sit in a corner between the foyer and a living-room chair — the Emily Post thing for me to do in a small room crowded with this many people. I wonder if, at some point, he'll talk to me. But the evening passes, the party dwindles, and the guests begin to drift away. Some help pick up empty punch glasses and dirty paper plates. Most of them stop to say good-by as they funnel toward the door. Ken does too but lingers longer than the others. He leans comfortably against the wall beside my chair and chats. I learn that he lives in the condominium next door and teaches social studies and government at a nearby high school. He also teaches a class called Minority Studies, and I learn that he is not Hawaiian, but Japanese. He coaches football. *I was right about the athletics.* I bring up the subject of mainstreaming handicapped kids in the public school system. He doesn't seem to have very strong opinions about it. Perhaps he's being polite.

Finally, I say I should go; I need to get up early. Ken leaves, apparently to get his coat, and I wave good-by to Carol in the kitchen, thanking her for the party. Twila empties my bulging legbag. I have a long drive home by myself.

As the bag slowly drains into a bottle, Ken returns with his coat over his arm. As he swings it on, he says, "How about if we continue this conversation over dinner next Friday night?"

"I suppose so," I reply. "Sure. I'd like to go."

"Can I pick you up about six?"

"That would be fine."

On the way home, it suddenly occurs to me that I have actually accepted a date from a man — an attractive man. It was so casual, so natural. And while my legbag was draining — of all things! I think back over the scene in my friends' living room and chuckle to myself.

Oh, who cares. I learned the painful way long ago that there's no pretense possible with a handicap. You might as well be real.

"*A bouquet of roses? For me? Who are they from?*" I *ask*.

Kerbe slips the tiny card out of its envelope and reads it to me. "Looking forward to Friday . . . Ken Tada."

I rub my nose against a soft yellow petal and sniff the delicate fragrance. "Um . . . nice gesture. They're really pretty."

"Is that all you can say?" Kerbe cries.

"Well, don't you think it's a bit much." I nod at the roses. "I mean, I hardly know him."

She places the vase on my bedroom dresser, fluffing and primping the buds and greenery. A garish satin bow tries to outdo the hothouse arrangement.

I feel slightly uneasy at the sight of the bouquet. Ken seems like a pleasant guy, but I don't want to make a big deal about this dinner date. I've had my share of distorting reality. And I had hoped he would approach it a bit more . . . more dispassionately.

Friday evening Ken arrives promptly, dressed up in a well-tailored blue suit. And with more flowers. I'm glad I dressed for the occasion in my white wool jacket and silk blouse. I just hope he doesn't pop a button on his dress shirt when he lifts me.

Judy and Kerbe give him a crash course in the essentials, explaining how to lift me single-handedly and straighten me in my wheelchair, how to tuck my jacket in the back so it won't wrinkle, and how to pull down the inseams of my slacks. He listens attentively and shows concern for details.

He wheels me outside to his car. I tell him, as graciously as possible, to be mindful of the steep ramp, cracks in the sidewalk, and turning sharp corners. He remarks that he never knew so much was involved in simply pushing a wheelchair. I hope I don't sound like a nag. "You should come to one of our workshops," I tease.

My housemates watch, arms folded, and somewhat amused, as Ken takes off his jacket, rolls up his sleeves, hikes up his pants, and squats by my chair to lift me. He slings my arm around his neck. I can tell from the way he gathers breath and strength that he has lifted weights before. With a mighty karate "hi-yah," he heaves me to his chest. I feel very heavy.

As Judy shows him how to fold my wheelchair and load it in the trunk, Kerbe leans into the car to straighten my jacket. "Have fun," she says with a coquettish smile and slams the door with a wave.

"You really aren't heavy at all," Ken says as he backs out of the driveway. "Light as a feather, in fact."

"Oh, really?" I say mockingly. "Judging from that weight-lifting exercise back there, I would never have known."

Ken steers with one hand while he slides a cassette into the tape deck. "Well, I *have* been working out . . . lifting weights and stuff." He's obviously missed my tongue-in-cheek joke.

"How much weight did you train with?"

"Oh, about 175 pounds."

"A hundred and what?!"

"I wanted to make sure I didn't drop you," he says with a smile. Perhaps the joke is on me.

"Just so you understand that I don't weigh 175 pounds."

"Oh, don't worry," he says with a mischievous grin. "I can tell how much you really weigh."

I return his smile. *So he knows how much I weigh. So he's held me in his arms. So I hardly know him. So what?* I don't have the luxury of modesty most women would on a first date. Besides, none of that really matters. What matters is that there are no pretenses. It's a lovely twilight, and our drive on the freeway moves swiftly, as easily and as unencumbered as my conversation with this unassuming and delightfully ordinary guy.

We drive into Marina Del Rey, the flashy neon-lit city on the edge of the ocean. Rows of condominiums rise like giant cylinders of concrete, glass, and metal overlooking the bay and boats and crowded tennis courts. Disco music and siren-red Ferraris, California blondes with their bronzed boyfriends create a kaleidoscope of shiny street color and action everywhere I look. Ken takes several side streets to point out a certain dock on the marina. He looks for the tall mast of a boat belonging to someone he knows. We don't find the boat, but behind the glitter I notice silhouettes of solitary benches, framed by oleanders and palms, that invite couples to sit and gaze at the quiet canals and watch the shadows of dark and silent cabin cruisers putter by.

It's a wild place but not unfriendly.

Ken parks his Oldsmobile in front of a restaurant called The Warehouse. The name fits, I think, as I scan the weathered siding and tin shingles. Barrels with rusty rims, and massive ropes with block and tackle decorate the steps and boardwalk leading to the front door. Ken lifts me out of the car and situates me comfortably in my wheelchair. We look for a ramp but find none.

"You could ask the maître d' about a kitchen entrance," I offer.

"No, we don't have to worry about that." He dusts off his hands as though ready to do more lifting. "I can easily handle those steps." He wheels my chair backward, lodges the large wheels against the first wooden step, tilts me back, and pulls me one step at a time to the boardwalk level. "Easy." He commends himself.

I like his cool-headed approach to those steps. And to me. He's not trying to impress me with a lot of macho muscle-flexing. He just wants me to know he can handle my chair in an unflustered and unconcerned way. He wants to put me at ease. We amble down the boardwalk, stopping to look at the carp that swim in the brightly lit lagoon below.

Inside, the maître d' seats us at a window table. He presents a large, leather-bound menu to Ken. I ask him to place mine on the table. With a smile he flips open my linen napkin and places it on my lap. As the busboy fills our glasses with ice water and the waiter removes our wine glasses, I look out the window at the hundreds of different sailboats moored at the docks. The skyline of masts against the evening sky makes a beautiful seaside picture. *I should paint something like this.*

"You look nice tonight. I like that jacket," Ken says when the waiter leaves.

"Thank you." I inspect my cuffs. "I usually wear it when I'm speaking."

"Like at the Young Life dessert?"

"That's right . . . you were there."

"And I like what you said that night," he says as he leans on his elbow. "You talked about how we can relate to people whose circumstances are different than ours. Like your wheelchair. People don't have to be afraid of it." He picks up his menu and reaches over to open mine. "Or of you."

"What do you mean?" I say as I glance at the menu.

"Well, your wheelchair is one thing . . . people not knowing what to say or do. And the fact that you are well known is another. Some people think you have it all together. That you never struggle." He pauses a moment to study his menu, then closes it and continues. "But I don't need to be afraid just because you're different."

I admire so much confidence.

Ken orders steak and I order shrimp. He leans across the table to give me a forkful of his appetizer. I ask for a drink, and he stretches his arm across the table again and lifts the glass to my mouth. We chat about Joni and Friends, his school, Judy and Kerbe, Young Life, and our mutual friends from church. Our dinners arrive. Before I can ask the waiter to cut up my shrimp, Ken has my knife and fork poised over the plate. "May I?" he asks.

I cannot get over how comfortable, how happy I feel with this man. And I can't help comparing it with that dinner date with the gaffer when I was so nervous, so apprehensive about my handicap — were my inseams straight, was my catheter going to leak, would my make-up smear? I could hardly eat that night, my stomach was in such knots. With Ken, there is no stage fright.

To the Reader:

If your life has been touched by this book, Joni would like to know about it. You may correspond with her in care of **JONI AND FRIENDS,** P.O. Box 3333, Agoura Hills, California 91301.

JONI AND FRIENDS is a Christian ministry reaching out to people with both visible and invisible disabilities around the world. **JONI AND FRIENDS,** and its CHRISTIAN FUND FOR THE DISABLED, helps churches minister to handicapped people through evangelism, encouragement, and practical services.

Dear Joni,

_____ Please keep me informed about the ministry of **JONI AND FRIENDS.**
_____ Send me information on your cards, art prints, records, and books.
_____ Send me information on **JONI AND FRIENDS** films, videos, and cassettes.
_____ Tell me more about being a friend to a disabled person.
_____ I am disabled myself. _____ A member of my family is disabled.

PLEASE print!

Name _____

Address _____

City _____ State and Zip _____

H6CC

To the Reader:

If your life has been touched by this book, Joni would like to know about it. You may correspond with her in care of **JONI AND FRIENDS,** P.O. Box 3333, Agoura Hills, California 91301.

JONI AND FRIENDS is a Christian ministry reaching out to people with both visible and invisible disabilities around the world. **JONI AND FRIENDS,** and its CHRISTIAN FUND FOR THE DISABLED, helps churches minister to handicapped people through evangelism, encouragement, and practical services.

Dear Joni,

_____ Please keep me informed about the ministry of **JONI AND FRIENDS.**
_____ Send me information on your cards, art prints, records, and books.
_____ Send me information on **JONI AND FRIENDS** films, videos, and cassettes.
_____ Tell me more about being a friend to a disabled person.
_____ I am disabled myself. _____ A member of my family is disabled.

PLEASE print!

Name _____

Address _____

City _____ State and Zip _____

H6CC

JONI AND FRIENDS
P.O. Box 3333
Agoura Hills, CA 91301

JONI AND FRIENDS
P.O. Box 3333
Agoura Hills, CA 91301

"It seems you've been around disabled people before," I comment, scooping another bite of shrimp.

"Well, yes and no." Ken leans back from the table and dabs the napkin to the corners of his mouth. "Sometime back I was switching channels on television and came across this program about Special Olympics. There were these great shots of mentally handicapped kids barreling down the track. Some stumbling. Some skipping. Others going flat out." He shakes his head with a grin as he folds his napkin and smooths it by his plate. "And there were these people at the finish line, cheering each one of those kids on. Everyone hugging each other. And then the announcer came on and said something about . . ." He searches for the exact words. "How in this world that seeks perfection, where is there room for those who aren't? Then they said, 'What really matters is not winning, but finishing.'" He is silent for a moment, stroking the folded napkin.

I admire so much physical strength mixed with such sensitivity.

He reaches for his water glass. "So, that's when I signed up at my school to get involved in Special Olympics. I've only worked with them, officiating and whatever, for a couple of years." He puts his glass down and leans on his elbow. "But dating someone in a wheelchair . . . no." He leans back shaking his head. "I've never done that before."

"Well, there's something else you're going to have to do that you've never done before," I say with a sly grin.

"What's that?" He reaches for his wallet to pay the bill.

"My legbag needs emptying."

"Okay," he says as he slips his credit card out of his wallet. "Just tell me what to do." Ken negotiates my wheelchair through the tables toward the door. We pause in front of the alcove that leads to the ladies' room on the left and men's room on the right. "Uh . . . we have a problem here."

"Yes. Well, I hadn't thought about this one," I tease.

"Come on, Joni. No jokes," Ken whispers as several people walk around us, going in and out of the restrooms. "What do I do?"

I try to be serious but I can't resist saying, "Is this the part where you're not afraid even though I'm different?" I look at Ken with a Cheshire-cat grin. "Okay. Okay. Let's head outside and find a tree."

"A tree?!"

"Well, it *is* more classy than a fire hydrant, don't you think?"

Ken, dressed in a T-shirt and warm-ups, holds his sport bag in one hand and opens the door with the other. "Can you make it through?" He flattens the glass door further.

I power my wheelchair into the lobby of the athletic club, slowing to let Ken catch up and lead the way. We head for the registration desk. A blonde in a club shirt with terry-cloth bands on her head and wrists greets Ken warmly and passes a clipboard across the counter for him to sign. He steps aside and introduces me. The girl, bubbly and effervescent, waves hello.

"Do I have to sign a guest registration?"

"Oh, no, don't worry about it," she says as she files the clipboard. "Any of Ken's friends are welcome here." She turns and slaps a key on the counter.

I follow Ken to another lobby, just off the main foyer, where tables and chairs in light wood and modern gray fabric are clustered in front of floor-to-ceiling Plexiglas panels through which we can view three racquetball courts. Track lighting illuminates two framed posters at the end of the lobby. A ceiling-mounted television is tuned to a football game, while the soft drumming of low-volume rock music pumps through overhead speakers. Men in sweaty shirts slouch in their chairs and sip juice drinks.

"How about sitting here?" Ken hikes his heavy sport bag onto a table.

I nod, and Ken shuffles a few chairs aside so I can maneuver my wheelchair close to the table. My legs don't fit underneath, and

I stick out into the aisle a bit, but checking over my shoulder, I see that people are able to make their way by.

"This will be a nice place to sit," I tell Ken.

"Then you won't mind watching these things for me while I change?" Ken empties his pockets of keys and a wallet, rolls them in a sweat shirt, and slides the bundle across the table to me. "I'll only be a minute." He twirls his locker key on his finger.

As he crosses the room, he stops to slap the backs of a few racquetball buddies. Then he disappears behind a swinging door, and I turn my attention to a man and woman battling on one of the courts on the other side of the glass panel.

"You're a friend of Ken's?" someone says from behind me.

I turn my head as far to the side as possible, straining to see the speaker. "Yes, I am . . . but, uh — "

"Oh . . . I'm sorry . . . let me move around here," he says as he rearranges a chair or two to get by. "Good to see you." The man extends a hand of greeting.

I'm a little slow in lifting my arm to his, but before the moment turns awkward he reaches forward and clasps his hand around my wrist.

"Yes, I'm a friend of Ken's, and I'm sure glad he brought me here. This is so fascinating." I nod my head in the direction of the two players on the court.

The man knots his hands around the ends of the towel draped over his neck and glances at the competitors. "Yeah, they're pretty good," he says. "That guy on the court is just warming up though." He leans toward the glass panel and slaps it hard to get the player's attention. He points to his watch and then thumbs in the direction of the locker room.

"He and Ken have a challenge game scheduled," he says as he flops into a chair and crosses his feet on the armrest of another.

Ken returns with his sport bag and shoes, greets the man beside me, and waves to the people on the court. His overstuffed bag is packed with towels and fresh folded T-shirts. A row of fifteen or more racquetball gloves dangles from the bag handle.

"Why so many?" I ask.

Ken unsnaps one and stretches it on his hand, securing it at his wrist. "When this one gets sweaty, I've always got more." He gestures at the row of gloves strung like scalps on the handle.

This guy means business, I think.

"Are you okay for a while?" Ken asks over his shoulder as he heads for the court, slapping his racquet against his shorts.

"Fine, just fine. Go for it," I call as he opens the court door.

Ken bounces the ball a few times, twists his body, backswings, and follows through, easily propelling the ball against the front-court wall. The ball bounces and returns to his racquet. He swings and hits, repeating the rhythm — hitting and striking and bouncing — over and over again.

His partner leans against the sidewall and wipes sweat from his forehead with his T-shirt. He grabs his racquet and stretches both arms over his head, waiting while Ken warms up.

Ken motions that he's ready and the game begins. His partner serves an easy ball and Ken, just as easily, hits it back. The pace quickens. The ball smacks against the wall with a loud hollow sound. Their shoes squeak, screeching as they stop and turn, each one jockeying for center-court position after he makes his hit. The partner finds his balance and slams the ball deep into the corner. Ken lunges forward but the ball is dead.

He positions himself for another serve. He's all concentration.

The game continues; the score flip-flops. I watch with wonder at the different styles of the two players. Ken's opponent bounces and jumps like a fly off the wall, smacking and swinging. Ken moves with grace; every swing of his arm is elegant. He shines on the court with style and symmetry.

A few passers-by idle near our table, watching the match. I eavesdrop on their comments, all racquetball jargon about style and form. I'm pleased they make so many good observations about Ken. I'm proud of him and feel special that he's sharing this part of his world with me.

The game ends and Ken reaches to shake the hand of his opponent. The man beside me slings his towel over his shoulder and rises to leave. "Not bad," he says. "Your friend's not bad."

I smile in return. I assume Ken has won.

The court door opens, and Ken comes out from behind the silence of the Plexiglas. Sweat pours from his face, and he reaches for a towel in his sport bag. "Are you okay?" he asks, pressing the towel to his neck and forehead.

"Am *I* okay?" I ask in amazement.

He unsnaps his glove. "Yeah . . . well, don't worry. I sweat pounds off like this all the time," he answers. He begins to grab the edges of his soaking T-shirt and then hesitates. "Mind if I change shirts?"

I smile, shrugging my shoulders. He tears off his shirt and throws it over one of the chairs. His dark skin glistens with sweat, highlighting each muscle. He leans near me as he reaches for a dry T-shirt from his bag. Suddenly, the moment seems very personal. Slightly embarrassed, I turn my eyes toward the television.

He rolls his wet shirt into a towel and stuffs it into the bag.

"Let's get something to drink," he suggests and leads the way to the juice bar. Gesturing with the Pepsi in his hand, he points out the locker rooms and clothes boutique, and explains where the sauna and Jacuzzis are.

"If we had time and if you were in your lighter chair," he says, glancing at my heavy power wheelchair, "I could show you the girls' aerobics room." He makes a motion above our heads. The ceiling shakes slightly, and we hear the muffled sounds of rock music and screaming, clapping girls.

"No elevator?"

He shakes his head no and shrugs his shoulders as if to say he's sorry.

"That's okay," I comment as I watch a group of girls leave their locker room and head up the stairs. They wear slinky leotards cut high around the thighs. Their tights, in high-fashion colors of hot pink, turquoise, and yellow, are made of some shiny slick fabric. Little belts and headbands, gold chains and fuzzy leg warmers complete what is obviously a certain "look." They giggle in a cluster and bounce up the steps. "Maybe we can go up there some other time. . . . I don't think I'd fit," I say with a knowing smile.

Ken and I head for my van. As I jab at a toggle switch to open the door, unfold the lift, and lower it to the ground, I applaud Ken on his game. "I don't want to sound gushy, but your coordination and athletic ability are tops."

My chair lurches onto the lift, and I jab at more buttons, which raise me to the floor level. The belts on my chair squeal and grind as I maneuver into the driver's position. My chair slams into the locked position. I am only slightly conscious of my own uncoordinated, jerky movements.

Ken climbs in and I head for home.

The house is empty and dark. Judy and Kerbe are out for the evening, but everything is arranged. Judy has set things up as I asked. The cutting board and knives are on the kitchen counter. The table is set for two, with linen napkins, placemats, and candles. The coffee maker is ready on automatic. The meat, onions, mushrooms, and celery are in the refrigerator. Ken is going to show me how to fix stir-fry steak.

While he uses our shower, I wheel around the house and flick on lights. After jabbing at the stereo buttons, I wheel into the kitchen and wait.

When he returns to the kitchen, clean and relaxed in a fresh T-shirt and warm-ups, I explain where everything is. He gets the cooking oil and neatly piles the meat and vegetables next to the cutting board. Examining the edge of the knife, he reaches for the celery and angle cuts a stalk with precision, as though he were one of those Japanese chefs in a sushi bar.

"I learned all this from my mom." He beams proudly and reaches for another piece of celery.

I power closer to the kitchen counter to see how he does it.

"It's the angle that makes for better cooking," he explains. "Here, let me show you how you can do it . . . put your hand here . . . hold the celery like this." His voice falters. "Then . . . then you tilt the knife like so." He glances down at me. He has forgotten, just for the moment, that I cannot use my hands.

Neither of us mention his slip, and he continues to cut up the mushrooms and onions. After fifteen or twenty minutes of cutting, the novelty wears off.

Finally, he lays the knife beside the slabs of steak and leans, straight-armed and silent, against the kitchen counter. I look down at the useless hands folded on my lap, then at his hands, strong and muscled, now white-knuckled as he clenches the edge of the counter.

"I wish you could help me," he whispers, staring out the window above the sink.

"I wish I could too."

After several seconds our eyes meet. He smiles, leans back, and takes a deep breath. Then, picking up the knife, he reaches for a piece of steak and continues cutting and explaining.

Judy, Kerbe, and I are flying East for Christmas 1980. I leave behind a cold locked house, a half-decorated tree that will dry out, a wreath that never made it to the front door, and greeting cards piled in disarray on the kitchen table. Ashes in the fireplace will make the closed-up house smell stale, I think, regretting that we didn't get it cleaned out before leaving.

Christmas is being divided between California and Maryland. But Christmas will be more like . . . like Christmas home on the farm. A year and a half in California hasn't allowed enough time to initiate new holiday habits and replace old ones, no matter how much I enjoy my life there.

Unlike any other holidays, Christmas draws me to the glow of homey images. Friends and family holding hands in prayer around a table of hot fragrant food. Creamy-skinned aunts who smell of lavender, fur, and silk. Distant cousins you haven't seen for years but greet like long-lost friends. Neighbors dropping by for a piece of pie and a few spirited carols around a cheery wood fire.

Nothing short of a Currier and Ives print can match the sight of the stone farmhouse with its candlelit windows and drifts of powdery snow shouldering the walls. Kathy, who has picked us up at the airport, drives by the barn where woolly horses stamp their feet and impatiently snort blasts of frosty breath as they wait for their bales of hay. We pull into the driveway, and old Charlie Cat, thick with winter fur, jumps up and makes his bed on the toasty hood of the car, tucking his head under his tail against the frigid night air. The thin sheet of ice covering the snow crackles and crunches underneath the weight of my chair as I wheel to the door. I breathe deep and my lungs sting.

"You're home!" Jay shouts with arms spread in welcome. "Just in time for hot chocolate." Cozy smells of vanilla candles and pine garlands invite us in. My arms are weighted and bulky under the heavy down jacket I've borrowed, but I lift them to show Jay I want a hug. She leans down and squeezes me, and the air hisses out of my jacket. "Where's Earecka?" I ask, eager to see my eight-month-old niece.

Jay points to where she sits in her pink pajamas underneath the gaily lit tree, eyeing the wrapped presents. She only half notices my entrance and the stuffed toy I picked up for her at the airport. The lights and tinsel fascinate her more.

"Earecka, come say hi to Aunt Joni," Jay insists.

She spreads her little hands on the floor, hikes her backside into the air, and crawls her way over to my wheelchair. She squats by the right wheel, plucks the wire spokes like strings on a harp, and at the twangy sound, beams me a toothy smile.

"No ordinary kid," I comment to Jay and Rob. "Most would just grab my tire and chew away."

That night I lay in bed and listen to gentle strains of Vivaldi waft through the farmhouse. All of this — the quiet, the music, the comfort of this old house — is mine for the moment. My mind wanders to other Christmases and pleasant memories often rehearsed. I recall one of the most familiar — the last Christmas I spent on my feet, just months before my accident. . . .

It has snowed heavily, and the afternoon has faded into a windy twilight. A high-school friend, Dick, and I decide to brave the unplowed roads in his tough little Volkswagen with chains. By the time we reach downtown Baltimore, the shoppers have left the streets. Dick and I exchange greetings with the smartly styled window mannequins as though they are in our private party. At the corner of Howard Street we pause, enchanted by the cathedral bells up on Mulberry Street ringing down the alley. The bells draw us to the church.

After climbing the slippery steps and stamping the slush from our boots, Dick and I quietly walk up the center aisle, rubbing our hands for warmth. The church is empty except for an old lady kneeling at the altar. We slide into one of the pews, and I lean back to look up into the vaulted silence of the cathedral ceiling, breathing in the scent of prayer candles and lemon-polished wood.

A roaring blast of wind startles me, and the logs of the cabin window creak. My memories fade like an old sepia photograph. As the wind dies, I wander further back to another Christmas. . . .

I am caroling on horseback with my family, clip-clopping down a wet street, stopping under a corner lamppost to sing in the falling snow.

My mind takes a sharp turn; this time toward a Christmas after my accident. . . .

My uncle and cousin have machined a pair of short, sturdy metal skis for my wheelchair. They push me to the top of the snow-packed street near my parents' house, clamp the wheels in place, and belt me in. We edge to the crest of the hill, and with a Geronimo yell, my cousin Eddie heaves my wheelchair forward and jumps on the back of the skis, steering with his weight. We reach the bottom, whooping and hollering, and in one piece.

Outside the frosted bedroom window of the present, bits of snow and ice spray against the glass. I wonder, burying my head underneath Jay's Norwegian comforter, if Charlie Cat has found refuge under the hay in the barn tonight.

The week slips by between parties, dinners, and midnight communion on Christmas Eve. Celebrating the birth of Christ has a wonderful sameness to it — sitting in the little candlelit Episcopal church, hearing the familiar story from the book of Luke, and singing old carols. I am glad this has not changed.

Yet I can't help thinking how very different home is. Our family is larger. Jay is a new mother. New friends from Rob's film business drop by. Daddy's hearing and arthritis are getting worse. Kathy is teaching a different grade level. Linda has a new car.

Even my old friends have changed. Betsy is with Young Life in Dallas. Diana is a car-pooling mother, carting her two boys to school and soccer. Steve and Verna are expecting another baby. Dick is married with children of his own. Others have also married. Some have moved.

The pine trees by the farmhouse are taller than I remember. A housing development is taking over a neighboring field. Charlie Cat is no longer the family favorite; a dog named Grizz now rules the roost. It is home, but it is not quite home. Life in Maryland has changed as much as I have.

The night before I leave for California, I sit in the kitchen and talk with my mother and sisters as they do the supper dishes. Mother turns from her place at the sink, her arms immersed in suds, and our eyes meet. I can tell that she is already missing me.

The kitchen phone rings. Mother reaches for a dish towel, wipes her hands, and answers it.

"Yes, this is Mrs. Eareckson. Yes . . . oh, really?" She shoots a glance at me. "Uh-huh . . . it would be nice to meet you too. Just a moment, I'll let you speak to her."

Mother untangles the cord and stretches the receiver toward me. "It's a friend of yours from Los Angeles . . . a man," she adds, widening her eyes. Kathy takes the phone and presses it to my ear.

"Yes? . . . Ken?" I can barely contain the excitement in my voice. I glance at my family. The three of them are silent now, gingerly stacking plates in the cupboard.

"It's my new friend, Ken," I say in a hoarse whisper away from the receiver. "He's the one I told you about . . . remember?" Jay and Mother look at each other questioningly.

"Yes . . . yes, the weather's nice here . . . It is?" I lift my mouth away from the receiver again. "He says it's eighty degrees . . . sunny . . . he's been fishing," I whisper. Jay throws the dish towel over her shoulder, folds her arms, and leans against the sink. She smiles and cups her ear, pretending to be hard-of-hearing.

I close my eyes and lean into the phone. Ken tells me about a party he went to by himself, a racquetball match with a buddy, church on Sunday, and John MacArthur's sermon. He mentions that he met Rana and Vicky for the first time and that he stopped by Joni and Friends.

"How is Judy? . . . Is Kerbe with her parents?" he asks. "You're missing some beautiful, bright days. . . . When are you coming home?"

"Tomorrow. . . . Yes, I . . . I miss you too, Ken."

I watch as Kathy places the receiver back on the wall phone. Ken's voice, warm and close, instantly seems thousands of miles away. I do miss him. Yet as I look around, in a strange way I miss my family too, even though we congregate here in the kitchen to sip hot tea and nibble leftover pie. I don't want things to change, but they have.

Yet I am the one who made the first move, uprooting myself and, in a sense, everyone else. I am the one who chose to leave. And I am the one who probably has changed the most.

In the morning my mother helps Judy pack my suitcase, folding sweaters and filling the corners of the luggage with Christmas gifts. Inside, I sense a nervous knot tightening. I don't know if it's excitement over our return to California or fear of leaving Maryland.

Mother straightens from packing and rubs her forehead. "I don't believe all this stuff will fit." She runs her fingers over a small stack of presents on the bed next to the suitcase, then picks up a package in each hand. "Why don't you leave these gift soaps here for the next time you come East? You don't have to take them home with you now."

"Did you hear what you just said?" I laugh.

"Yes, I did," she says, sitting on my suitcase lid to snap it shut. "I know exactly what I said." She grabs the luggage handle with both hands and slides the heavy suitcase off the bed and onto the floor. "I saw that look in your eyes when you were talking on the phone last night." She mockingly chides me with a shake of her finger.

"But Mom, I hardly — "

"Never you mind," she says as she smooths the bedspread. "Home, Joni, is where your heart is."

Ken carries me to the couch while Scruffy scrambles out of the way. It is good to be home in front of a crackling fire after spending a chilly afternoon down at the wharf in San Pedro with the wind whipping off the ocean.

"So you like going places?" I ask as Ken walks into the kitchen, picking up on the conversation we began as we warmed ourselves over Belgian waffles and tea in the corner window of a little café and watched the freighters from Europe and the Orient steam by.

"I do. But I haven't had the chance to travel that much," he calls from the kitchen. I hear a cupboard door open. "What makes you ask?"

"Nothing. I was just thinking of what you said about foreign places this afternoon." I am thinking about other things too. About how much I love being in my own living room with a cozy fire. With Scruffy curled at the end of the couch. With Ken.

"Maybe I'll get to go with you sometime," he says, returning with a jar of cashews.

"Maybe." The idea of Ken traveling with me is appealing. Of course, visiting hospitals and rehabilitation centers and churches, whether in the States or abroad, doesn't have quite the romantic appeal of those colorful, exotic travel brochures. And anyway, how would it work? We're just friends.

"What do you talk about when you go to those places?" he asks as he plops next to me and munches on a handful of nuts.

I sling my arm up on the side of the couch to gain my balance. "Oh, you know — how God is in control of our lives . . . our disabilities. Lots of disabled people get lost in their questions. So Joni and Friends helps churches reach out to them. But many congregations are at a loss as to what to do. We try to make a dent through workshops, financial aid, counseling letters, materials, and stuff." I tilt my head as he cups his hand and slides some cashews into my mouth. I chew for a moment and then add, "Are you really interested?"

"Yes, I am. What you do is so much different than what I do at school or in Young Life." He pauses and tilts the jar of nuts toward me. "Want any more?"

"Uh-uh, no more for me," I say absently. "What exactly is your work like?"

"Well," Ken says emphatically as he rises to get another log for the fire, "I teach kids all day long at school, one class after the next. I talk to them in the hallways, see them after the last period. Coaching football every afternoon . . . Friday night games." He moves the fireplace screen aside. "And then at Young Life Club every Wednesday night." He throws a log into the back of the fire and nudges the andirons together with his palms.

With his back to me, he stands and brushes the soot off his hands. I admire the way he looks in his blue cotton tie pants, navy sweat shirt, and thongs, with his hair slightly mussed. He remains in front of the fire, warming his hands. The sun drops further from the afternoon sky, and the living room suddenly darkens. His features dim in the fading light, and with his legs slightly spread, he becomes a silhouette against the flames.

"I know how it is to feel lost in your questions, like you're going nowhere. I felt like that in high school." He looks down at his feet. "And I felt like that when I was in college.

"And then somebody asked me to go along on a Young Life weekend to help out . . . you know, more coaching and games with the kids. I wasn't a Christian then." He turns to face me and rubs his forehead. "But when I heard about Christ and all that He did for me . . . even when I could have cared less about Him, well, I knew I couldn't go away the same man."

Although I cannot see his face, I know he is looking at me and that his eyes reflect the wistfulness I hear in his voice. He is silent for a moment, and I wonder at his strength and tenderness. I have seen this gentleness in him before. It is part of the reason I am drawn to him. Like a moth to the flame before him, I am drawn.

"Listen . . . I don't know why God brought us together," he says abruptly, leaving the fire and returning to his place next to me on the couch, "but I do know that I like . . . really like being with you." His almond eyes glisten with the fire's reflection.

"I like you too, Ken."

"No . . . I mean . . ." He shakes his head and twists on the couch to face me better. "I mean that I've never . . . well, never felt so sure about — "

"Yes?" I think I know what he wants to say, and I am getting awfully nervous inside.

"Joni, I tell you things about myself that I don't tell just anybody. And I feel strong . . . not just emotionally, but spiritually too, when I'm with you." He reaches for the cashew jar on the coffee table and twists the lid back and forth. "But . . . but, I am afraid."

He looks up. "It's like this," he says, placing the jar back on the table. "When kids in Young Life come to me, all mixed up because they're dating somebody steadily and yet . . . yet going nowhere, they ask the most unbelievable questions. Like, 'How do I know if she is God's will for my life, Mr. Tada?'" He gestures with his hand in exasperation. "Or, there are kids who break up with their boyfriends and then cry on my desk because 'he won't talk to me anymore, Mr. Tada.'" He waves the other hand.

"And you know what I tell them?" He looks at me directly, the fire highlighting the side of his face. "I tell them that when they decide to date somebody seriously, it's going to end up one of two ways. Either they will marry that person . . . or they'll break up and never be really close again."

There is a gentle rap at the front door. Scruffy bounds off the couch. The handle turns and Kerbe peers around the corner. "Hi, guys," she says a little timidly. "Sorry to interrupt."

Ken takes a deep breath, greets her warmly, and goes to help her with her packages. I sigh deeply too, uncertain whether I am pleased or sorry we have been interrupted. "No bother at all, Kerbe. It's time I got off this couch anyway." I yawn, stretching out my stiff arms and giving them a spasm. "When you get through, could you help me up?"

They walk into the kitchen, flick on the light, and pile her sweater, packages, and purse on the table. Ken returns to the living room, shoves the coffee table aside, and angles the wheelchair for a transfer. They heave me into my chair and straighten my sweat shirt.

"I'll, uh, I'll be in my room," Kerbe says a bit awkwardly. "I've got a few things . . . um, drawers to straighten, you know." She backs out of the living room with a grin and a little wave. Down the hallway, her bedroom door clicks behind her.

Ken stands in front of me, holding Scruffy in his arms, gently rubbing her neck. I wait a moment for him to speak and then pick up the thread of conversation myself. "So you're afraid that if we keep spending time together . . . as friends or whatever — "

"That's just it, Joni. It's awfully hard for two people . . . a man and woman in their thirties, single . . . it's hard to be just friends. I want it that way, really. But then again, I don't," Ken says. "I'm afraid I'm going to have to swallow the same advice I give those high school kids. . . ." His voice drifts off.

He sets Scruffy on the floor and places his hands on the armrests of my wheelchair. "I cannot imagine not being close to you." He wraps his hand around the back of my neck and leans to kiss me.

The fire crackles.

"I'm afraid," I whisper.

"I know. So am I."

"Okay, what's next?" Ken strides alongside my wheelchair, juggling two boxes of popcorn, an ice cream bar, and Pepsis in his hands. His Mickey Mouse ears begin to slip off his head, and he wiggles a hand free just in time to grab them. This is the other side of the serious-minded teacher — the grown-up kid at Disneyland.

"Let's try that wild roller-coaster ride on the other side of the park," I decide. "I've never been on it before . . . but you look strong enough. I think we can handle it."

"Great, let's go!" Ken moves into high gear, plops his Mickey Mouse hat on my head, and begins unloading his armful on my lap. "If we want to make it, we've got to really move. The lines to that thing are blocks long." He wedges a box of popcorn between my knees.

I smile smugly and sashay my wheelchair down the walkway at slow speed.

"What's with you?" Ken runs behind the back of my chair and heaves his weight against it. "We haven't got all day."

"Aha . . . that's where I've got a secret," I say coyly.

"What are you talking about?"

"You'll see."

We arrive at the roller coaster and push through the thick lines snaking their way to the entrance of the ride. "Pardon me . . . excuse me please . . . watch your toes . . . sorry," I apologize as I inch through the crowd.

Ken, dumfounded, follows behind. After I nearly scrape

somebody's shins, he leans down to my ear and hoarsely whispers, "What do you think you're doing? We just can't cut in front like this."

"I'm not cutting in front," I whisper. "I'm cutting in back."

We arrive at the exit where a cute boy in an Alpine suit welcomes us and swings the gate wide to let us enter.

"See?" I say matter-of-factly.

"Be careful," the boy warns as he ushers us in. We flatten ourselves against a wall as a flow of people stream toward the exit. We are salmon swimming upstream.

Amid the noise of the crowd and the clank of gears, Ken and our guide in the Alpine suit lift me into the waiting bobsled. Hurriedly the boy buckles me in while Ken lowers himself behind me. A car slams into the back of our sled, and Ken grips me with his arms and straddled legs as our toboggan lurches forward.

"I'm not ready, I'm not ready," I yell.

Our car slides easily down the track. "Am I in?" I shout.

The sled jerks to a halt and then with a "click-click" engages onto the chain that pulls us up the steep incline. "Yes, you're in . . . what else do you want me to do?" Ken yells back.

"I don't know. I think . . . I think I'm going to die!"

The roller-coaster track climbs through a mountainous interior, an air-conditioned blast hits our faces, and darkness blankets our car just when we reach the top where our sled jerks again as the chain releases. We plunge off the crest. People scream into the downhill sweep, into the dark recesses of the mountain.

"Hold me . . . hold me!" I shriek in terror as my body slams from one side of the sled to the other, the car whipping and jolting down the track. "I don't have any balance!"

"What?" Ken hollers.

He releases his grip from his handholds and slips further down into the seat, pulling my body against his chest. With no way to hold on, both of us are at the mercy of the sled's racing twists and turns. Our bodies jam against the side as the sled snaps around a corner. He giggles hysterically.

After many long minutes, the sled begins to slow and then skids to a halt in front of the exit.

"How was it?" Our Alpine boy laughs as he sees us lying prone, exhausted, at the bottom of the sled. "Here, let me help." He offers a hand. "Oh, by the way, we occasionally let disabled people ride twice if they want . . . saves you the hassle of getting in and out again."

"You're kidding," I say with sarcasm. "You guys trying to get rid of us?"

"Hey, let's do it, Jon." Ken laughs with glee, scooting himself up behind me again. Another car slams into ours and jolts us forward.

"Wh–what? Hey, no," I say emphatically. "Not again. . . ." More cars hit us from behind and propel us down the track.

"Too late!" Ken laughs infectiously, squeezing my ribs.

Later, by the exit, we stop and catch our breath, puffing and wheezing. I fling my arm against him. "You jerk," I laugh, "I could have been killed. Seriously."

"Excuuuuuse me." He bows in jest. "I thought you were immortal."

"Youuuuu, you . . ." I power my wheels toward his toes.

As evening approaches, Disneyland becomes a sparkle of lights — truly a magic kingdom. A quartet sings under a glimmering streetlamp on the corner. Big Belgian horses plod along Main Street hauling old-fashioned streetcars. The strains of a Dixieland band playing Southern favorites drift our way. The aroma of hot buttered popcorn and roasted nuts fills the night air, and we head for a restaurant in the French Quarter.

For our dinner, Ken extravagantly orders every hors d'oeuvre on the menu.

"Being disabled has its advantages," Ken says, licking his fingers. "No standing in lines . . . going in the exits . . . getting on rides twice," he lists as he wipes his hands on his napkin. "Even your parking places are bigger."

He pushes away several dishes from between us and lightly

touches the delicate folds of the single carnation centerpiece. "Knowing you is a real plus . . . in more ways than one." He smiles warmly. He rubs his hands together as though pleased with himself, with us. "This is great, Joni. Don't you sense it?"

I do sense it. But I also sense that the day has caught us up in a fairy-tale world of make-believe, where real life takes a back seat to daydreams and fantasies. A place where nobody frowns. A place where you can wish upon a star.

I'm having as much fun as he is, I confess to myself. But I also know that my wheelchair batteries can't last much longer and that I'm keeping an eye on a new pressure sore. That it's getting late and that it takes two hours to drive home. And that, once there, it will take another two hours for Kerbe to get me ready for bed. Somehow these mundane things that are so crucial to my existence and so out of my control have a way of bolting me to the earth.

But Ken is on cloud nine. "Did I say something wrong?" He leans forward.

"Oh . . . no, not at all." I shake my head. "I hate to spoil things, but it is getting late," I suggest.

During the long walk through the emptying parking lot, Ken recounts the times we've shared recently. The party at Carol and Twila's. Our first date at the marina. Dinners at my house. Restaurants. Church. Young Life Club. Over three months have passed since we started dating. Through it all, I've watched Ken's affection for me deepen — every time we pray, every time we talk on the phone, every time we sit together at church or ride in the car.

And every time I sense his feelings increase, I double-check my own. What do I feel?

Our surreal day at Disneyland has frightened me in an odd way. The fantasy pushes me into a corner, makes me face what is happening in real life. Three months have passed and we have had no disagreements. No arguments. Nothing unpleasant. Everything is like the easy rides at Disneyland — no roller-coaster plunges. I yearn to probe deeper beneath the surface of what is going on between Ken and me. To find real substance, rock-bottom reality. *Where, oh where are we going?*

On the long drive home on the freeway I am quiet, and Ken asks me several times if I'm okay. I say, "Yes, I'm just thinking."

"About us?" he questions.

I turn to him and nod.

"I thought we had a great time."

"We did, Ken . . . Disneyland's always a good time."

"But it's more than that, Jon. We could have been anywhere today — the beach, a . . . a football game, a — "

It's clear his heart is ahead of mine. I feel guilty.

"You're right." I smile. "Just give me time to catch up with you."

He gives me a funny look. I can tell he doesn't know what I mean.

This is the first time I've seen Jack Fischer since he broke his neck. He sits across from Ken and me at the coffee shop and talks easily about his gymnastic buddies, smiling in honest pride for his friends who have gone on to National Championships or to the Olympics.

Ken likes Jack. That's understandable. They are both athletes. I lean on the armrest of my wheelchair and enjoy their conversation about sports and competition.

The parallel bars were Jack's favorite, and he describes his routines and his dismounts. He rambles on about his routine on the rings. The way he used to do an iron cross. Jack's year and a half of life as a quadriplegic hasn't rubbed away his spirit or the single-minded drive that made him a world-class gymnast. He is still world-class — even though he sits paralyzed in his wheelchair.

His boyish enthusiasm is charming. His eyes and smile flash like some clean-cut crystal — handsome, engaging. Although he can no longer snap his body into angular taut command, he is still muscular and sturdy; he adjusts himself, occasionally straightening his arms against his chair to shift his weight. Ken and I are impressed with his ability — *a super-quad*. I smile to myself.

Jack begins to ask me questions about adjusting and coping. I sense that he is not so much looking for answers as wanting to swap stepping-stone stories. We talk about courage and grace under pressure, about Christ and His gifts of endurance and patience, self-control and steadfastness. I can tell none of these gifts have been easily received. Instead of submitting with open palms, I picture Jack tightly clasping his weak and disabled hands around promises from the Bible, pulling down from heaven what he knows is his in Christ.

It's Ken's turn to lean on his elbow, smile, and listen.

Now, Jack tells us, he is looking for an apartment near our end of the valley and wants to enroll in Sam Britten's Center of Achievement at the university. He has plans to improve. Before we leave, we watch him manage a difficult transfer from his wheelchair to his car.

"You liked him, didn't you," I comment to Ken as we watch the car drive away.

"Yeah. He kind of reminds me of Vicky Olivas. You know . . . against all odds?" Ken pushes the toggle switch on the side of my van.

I shiver slightly in the night air, waiting for the mechanical lift to lower. "They're a lot alike in many ways, aren't they?" I propose as I power my chair toward the lift. "I mean . . ." I lodge my hand against the toggle switch that raises me to the van. "People like Vicky or Jack are easy . . . fun to be around. The models-of-inspiration type," I tease, swinging the lift into the van and ducking my head. Ken finishes clamping the spare seat in the driver's alcove.

"Don't you count yourself in the club?" Ken questions as he climbs into the seat and places his arm in my driving mechanism, preparing to take the controls for the long drive home. I position my chair behind him so I can see his face in the rear-view mirror.

"Do you think I'm an inspirational role model?"

"Sure you are." He tilts his head to catch my eye in the mirror. "Why? . . . Don't you like the idea?" Ken pokes buttons on the control box and starts the engine.

I smirk. "Well, I'm not even sure Jack or Vicky would relish the idea. I mean, it's neat to inspire others . . ." I pause to gather my words. "But I tend to think being typecast as an 'inspiration' puts you at a distance from people. You know, as though you were some plaster-of-Paris saint who doesn't live in the same world."

"Not so." He frowns. "Your example helps me to relate to a real world . . . to people like Jack."

"Ken," I say with emphasis, "Jack is the exception. Even Vicky, as tough as she has it, is an exception. Like I said earlier . . . they are easy, even fun to be around. You hardly notice their limitations. They make you feel good, they boost your — "

"I don't know what you're talking about," Ken interrupts, a bit miffed. Our discussion — almost our first healthy, solid disagreement — is cut short. Ken's words trail off, and he becomes preoccupied, or perhaps pretends to be, with the traffic as he steers onto the freeway. The topic is dropped.

The following Saturday Rana and I spend the afternoon at an aerobic Dance-A-Thon being sponsored by friends of Twila and Carol to raise money for a young man with severe cerebral palsy. In a wheelchair and unable to speak, Paul needs an expensive electronic communicator to replace his old wordboard. The funds from the Dance-A-Thon will be used to purchase the equipment through Joni and Friends.

Rana and I sit on the sidelines of the gymnasium watching the girls sweat through their jumping jacks, knee bends, and dance routines in pulsing time with the blaring cassette player. I look at my watch. They've been at it for hours, and hundreds of dollars have been raised. Besides that, I have a speaking engagement tonight at Los Angeles Baptist College.

"What time is Ken getting here with Paul?" Rana glances at her own watch and rubs the back of her neck. "I'm getting tired just looking at them." She motions toward the group.

I cast an anxious look toward the gymnasium entrance. "He should be here now." The dancers want to meet Paul and present the check to him in person.

While the music continues and the gymnasium resounds with bouncing, screaming girls, Sue, the aerobics leader, trots over to us, wiping her forehead with a towel. "We can't continue much longer, Joni," she sighs. "Do you know where your friend Paul might be?"

"No, but we'll find out," I resolve, putting my chair on high and speeding toward the gymnasium door. "Rana," I call, "telephone the nursing home, would you? And find out if anything's happened. I'll wait for Ken and Paul on the corner."

The clouds are darkening and the wind has picked up. I huddle in my coat and wheel up and down the sidewalk, watching for Ken's car. Finally, it skids to a halt at the curb.

"Where were you?" I challenge as soon as Ken opens the door.

"I'll explain later." He brushes off my question as he races to get Paul's wheelchair out of the trunk. "Are we too late?"

When the three of us get to the gym, the noise has diminished considerably. Most of the girls are sitting and talking in small groups or doing stretching exercises to cool down. They lightly applaud when they spot Paul being pushed by Ken.

Paul's hair is matted, shiny with grease in a few places. His shirt is stained and unevenly buttoned. Dried food is caked on his pants; smudges of the same are on his wheelchair. He sits with his legs drawn tightly in a stiff position and his gnarled and twisted hands clasp his wordboard. When he smiles, he shows yellowed teeth that need better care. I know the staff at his home are often overworked and underpaid, but I wish they would have made a better effort to get Paul ready today. Maybe Ken could have — should have — helped him.

After the presentation Paul grins at the girls and points to letters and words on his board. "Thank . . . you . . . very much . . . ," he communicates to them. His eyes glisten in gratitude.

By now I am late for my speaking engagement at the college. Outside, it is dark. A light drizzle begins to fall as Ken and Rana load Paul and me into my van.

I wait until we are on our way to ask, "Ken, what happened at Paul's place?" He doesn't answer me and I don't press it. Perhaps something happened that he doesn't want to mention in front of Paul.

"Good grief," Rana exclaims, leaning forward in the driver's seat. "It's really coming down. Do you know how far the college is up this road?" The windshield wipers slap away water, and through the window we can make out the smeary image of lights in the distance. "I see it!" She accelerates.

I'm late getting to the platform. I'm also wet and my wool sweater stinks. Even the notes I prepared have ink smears. I glance at Rana, sitting with Ken and Paul at the end of the front row of the field house. She shrugs her shoulders as if to say, "I wish I could help, but you're on your own." The place is packed; the weather hasn't put a damper on the students' enthusiasm. I wish I could say the same.

I'm relieved when the meeting is over, although it goes well. That in itself makes me ashamed of my irritation with Ken and Paul and the people at the nursing home. How can I harbor that attitude while talking about the grace of God?

On our way back to the nursing home, we stop at an all-night coffee shop for a snack. I hope it will dispel the difficulties of the day with a pleasant ending. Rana and Paul sit across from Ken and me. Paul points to a photo of a hamburger on the menu.

When our food arrives, I watch Paul grab at his hamburger with his spastic hands. He insists on feeding himself. His saliva mixes with the burger dressing and drools over his beard as he throws his head back and chews with his mouth open. He loses bits of his hamburger and bun this way, but I admire him for making the effort. Rana occasionally wipes his mouth. Ken is quiet and does not look up from his sandwich.

Before the meal ends, Paul motions toward the restroom. Rana and I look at Ken. No legbags this time. No trees, quick and convenient.

Ken shoots me a nervous glance before he pushes Paul into the men's room. He will have to lift Paul from his wheelchair, a man he only met today, and be his hands. "I hope they remember to use the wordboard . . . it's a first for Ken," I say to Rana with a weak smile.

It is later. Much later. Paul is home. Rana is gone. My wool sweater is drier. We close up the van and stand in my open garage. The storm has passed out of the valley and a slivered moon shines brighter than it should. Ken is still quiet, and I still want to end the evening on a nicer note.

"Did you . . . ah . . . manage okay with Paul?" I want to let him know that I understand his discomfort.

Ken shoves his hands in his pockets and shrugs his shoulders. "I suppose so. He explained how to, you know . . . do things . . . on his wordboard." He kicks an imaginary stone.

I picture the scene at the coffee shop: Paul's pride in feeding himself, refusing Rana's help, happily shaking his head no. The rest of us ignoring his mess. And Ken's absorption with his sandwich.

I imagine the scene in the bathroom. "It wasn't easy . . . was it?" I offer.

Ken doesn't respond.

"It . . . uh, wasn't any easier earlier at the nursing home. That's why you were so late. . . . Am I right?"

Ken slowly nods his head.

I continue, "I guess the place didn't —"

"The smell . . ." Ken looks up. "The place had this awful smell. I just didn't want to stay in there, Joni. They were getting Paul dressed, and I felt I couldn't help anyway. I waited outside, but they forgot to tell me when he was ready. That made us late." He waits for my reaction. "Joni, it was the smell. It was the drooling. It was . . . everything!"

I power my wheelchair toward the garage door, facing the night and the moon. "You know . . ." I breathe deeply. "Paul was in church the other week. He was watching me when you gave me that drink of water . . . remember, you held the cup to my mouth?" I look back at Ken. He nods.

"Well, you got involved in another conversation, but I noticed Paul motioning to me. I powered my wheelchair over to him, and he started pointing to his wordboard." Ken is looking directly at me now.

"You know what he said? He said, 'Joni, I am sorry you cannot use your hands.'"

We stand in the dark garage, our breath white and frosty in the moonlight flooding the concrete floor.

"Is what I'm saying making sense?" I feel a lump in my throat.

Ken still has his hands in his pockets, like a little boy caught in some mischief and about to be lectured — quiet, remorseful.

"Ken," I begin softly, "it's people like Paul, if anybody, who are the real inspirations. Not Jack. Not Vicky. Not me. It's like the last are the first, the foolish are the wise, and the weak are the strong." I stop to let my words sink in. "And . . . and I'm afraid you have me on some . . . some pedestal. Like one of those plaster-of-Paris saints." I turn my chair so I face Ken squarely, and in the moonlight I cast a long shadow over him. In the darkness I cannot see his face.

"I feel like I know the real you." He speaks, and his voice almost startles me.

"You don't know me," I chide. "You know a book. A movie. A record album. You take me to these speaking engagements. But there are things about me that would turn your stomach, just as surely as your stomach turned tonight at that coffee shop or in that bathroom," I insist. When he doesn't speak, I continue, "And I'm not just talking about bathrooms and legbags and being paralyzed. There are things about me . . . times when I'm not very nice to be around."

"So what are you saying?" Ken steps out of my shadow.

"I don't know . . . I don't know," I reply. "It's been months, and our friendship doesn't seem like it's going anywhere. Not forward. Not deeper. I haven't met your family . . . uh . . ." I grab at straws. "You're emotional about me . . . my feelings nowhere match yours. Why," I laugh, "this is the closest we've ever come to having a real disagreement." I shake my head in disbelief.

"So?"

"So I think we should end it. Here. Now. While it doesn't hurt."

Ken's eyes reflect the moonlight and I think I see tears. My heart knots and I look away.

"Oh. Oh, no, not again." The tone in Judy's voice alarms me.

"What? What's wrong?" I ask.

She removes the pillows stuffed behind me and slowly turns me from my side onto my back. "You know that red spot we've been watching? Well, it's open . . . your old pressure sore is open."

I wince and squirm my head into the pillow.

"I'm so sorry," she offers, placing her hands on my shoulders.

Judy scratches her head. "This time you'll be in bed for quite a while, I'm afraid."

"A week? A month? How bad is it?"

She presses her lips, afraid to prophesy. She rolls me on my side to examine the skin once more. "It's bad." Pulling up my covers, she adds, "Let's just take one week at a time."

In the silence of the next moments the implications begin to hit us: telling the office, bringing work home, arranging for different people to take care of me, canceling speaking engagements, curtailing painting, rearranging meals and bedroom furniture and housekeeping and . . .

"Onward and upward," Judy, the eternal optimist, sighs with a smile. "We'll do it."

"Yeah," I exhale. "We did it before. With God's grace I guess we'll do it again," I murmur, turning my head to the wall.

Drat it! Why didn't I watch this sore more closely. I remember my terrible times of depression last year when I spent three months in bed waiting for the same sore to heal. But this time I sense anger mounting.

222

Once again, I am not wrestling against the flesh and blood of a pressure sore, but against an unseen foe. It is a spiritual struggle with an enemy who uses my own attitudes and thoughts as weapons against me.

"Judy, call Rana and Vicky and Sam Britten and anybody else you can think of. Have them pray. . . . I need prayer." Even as I make the request, I feel my anger subside.

Judy scribbles names on a notepad by the television. "Do you want me to call Ken?"

Automatically I say, "Yes . . . please call Ken too." It's been days since I've seen him or talked to him. Yet deep inside, for some reason, I want . . . I long . . . for him to know. And to pray. At the same time I wonder if I am being fair to him and to his feelings.

Ken telephones the next day. He wants to come over after school. I say yes. Then I brood. What do we have to say to each other?

He arrives with flowers and a stuffed rabbit. I want to apologize for bothering him with my problems. I attempt to keep a friendly but obvious distance between us, weighing my words, playing the role of a casual friend.

"It's very nice of you to drive all the way out here," I say politely with a stiff smile.

Ken gives me a funny look and places the stuffed animal on my dresser. "What are you talking about? I've driven out here lots of times," he says, casually unwrapping the flowers. "Here. Let me put these in water. I'll be right back."

While he's gone, I decide I am being silly. I am the one who told Judy to call him. I am the one who told him it was fine to come over. So why am I playing this coy little game?

"So much for telling you we're through," I mumble when he walks back into my bedroom with the vase of flowers.

He stops midway between the door and my dresser. "Yeah, well . . . you never said we couldn't be friends."

His words remind me of the scene in front of the fireplace a few months earlier. *Most people either end up married or go their separate ways.* I was afraid then and I'm afraid now. Afraid I'll hurt him. Or myself. But perhaps he is afraid too, knowing it's a risk being with me. If so, he doesn't show it.

"Here." He pulls a bloom from the vase and extends it to me. "Smells nice, doesn't it?" I nod a little sheepishly. "How about if I do some shopping, then fix dinner for you and Judy? I'd be happy to feed you . . . maybe we'll read later." He reaches into his hip pocket and pulls out a paperback. "It's a book about friendship." He holds it up and grins.

Minutes later I hear the front door close behind him. When he returns with grocery bags, I listen to a mumbled conversation between him and Judy, to the cozy, comfortable sounds of clanging pots and running water. Familiar sounds, yet special.

Ken sets up a TV tray by my bedside. On it he arranges a placemat and linen napkin, a candle, and little salt-and-pepper shakers. He raises the head of my bed and straightens the collar on my flannel pajama top. Situating a chair between my bed and the tray table, he announces, "Dinner is served, madam."

I feel so vulnerable, so powerless, lying here as he spoons soup into my mouth and wipes my chin. Flat on my back, the world — other people — take on a different posture. I seem so weak and dependent; they seem so strong and capable. Like Ken. He takes control tonight as though a crisis has hit and he has assumed command. He cleans away the dishes, folds the tray table, and wipes the crumbs off my blanket. He decides on creative ways to make the evening meaningful, even enjoyable, in spite of my bedridden condition. We play backgammon. He reads to me from his friendship book and from the Bible. He is the one who suggests that we pray together, and he does the praying. He tells me not to worry and that he'll be back tomorrow.

"Tomorrow," I lament. "It's only been a couple of days, and I feel like I've been in this bed forever. Maybe I'll forget how to write . . . or paint. Maybe I've done serious damage to this sore and — "

"Stop . . . just stop it." Ken has a fatherly look about him. "Remember what we read out of Lamentations 3 earlier? His compassions never cease or fail. They are new every morning."

I nod my head, yes.

"God gave you grace for today. Sufficient . . . just for today and this day only. There's no grace available yet for tomorrow's problems." He places his hand on my forehead and presses slightly, as if to press his point. "So quit worrying."

He folds his hands behind his head and arches in a stretch, laughing. "Besides, didn't I hear you say that very thing at a speaking deal recently?"

Unlike my last stint in bed, this time the weeks seem to fly by. Ken paints the floorboards in the living room. He hikes my bedroom door off its hinges, scrapes it, seals it, and gives it a new coat. Occasionally, he helps Judy and Kerbe with chores around the house.

"What in the world . . . ?" I'm surprised one day when he lugs my big, clumsy wooden art easel into my bedroom. "What are you going to do with that thing?"

"It's not what I'm going to do," he pants and leans the heavy easel against a wall, "it's what you're going to do." He wipes his forehead with the sleeve of his sweat shirt.

"Paint? You expect me to paint while lying on my back?"

"Sure," Ken says, surveying the width of my mattress with his hands. "We can spread-eagle the tripod right over your bed. I think with a few pillows propped here and there you'll be able to reach your canvas."

He holds up one of my brushes as if to measure its length, starts to place it in my mouth, thinks twice, and then leans down to kiss me instead.

My heart races, and I tilt my head to invite his kiss. I don't have time to examine my feelings. All I know is his compassion and tenderness, his warmth and acceptance of me — with my dirty hair, greasy face, and bad breath. Strangely, a verse — "We love . . . because He first loved us"[1] — keeps ringing in my ears, and I wonder as this new compulsion, this desire to submit and let him lead the way, takes hold. I hold on to his kiss with my lips, inviting him to linger. The moment is warm and tender, casting off fears and misgivings. He presses his cheek to mine and strokes my hair off my forehead.

"Just friends . . . right?" He smiles with mischief.

Summer comes hot and dry. The Santa Ana winds blow over the north ridge, sweeping the scent of gardenia and roses through the open sliding glass door of my bedroom. Summer 1981. It's been three years since the movie, two years since my move to California, and one year since Ken came into my life.

And today marks the end of my two-month stay in bed with this pressure sore. It is completely healed now and I can get up.

To celebrate, my mother and father have come for a visit. They are also here to meet Ken, of course. Mom has been curious about him ever since Christmas.

All this calls for a complete change of scenery. Fresh air breezing through the bedroom is not enough to sweep away the stale sameness of a bed and four walls. On an impulse, we decide to go camping, and Ken, Rana, and Vicky agree to go with us. Ken and Judy, Mom and Dad throw tents, sleeping bags, and fishing gear into the van.

Ken steers, Judy navigates, and Vicky, Rana, and I sit in the back with my parents. Hearts full and happy, we sing. Camping songs. Oldies but goodies. We are singing hymns as we climb out of the valley onto the plateau of the north desert, past the little town of Mojave — up out of the hot plains and into the back side of the cool Sierra mountains.

Out of bed at last, surrounded by family and friends, and out in the grandness of God's creation, I no longer need the special grace He has given me during the last two months. Yet I sense it lingering near, bright and powerful, like a sweet scent of charged air after a lightning storm. Grace lifts my spirits as high as the lofty peaks we pass. Grace makes me smile with gratitude, humbly thanking the Father for giving me the chance to enjoy the beauty of ponderosa pines and sparkling lakes. Grace makes me feel as free as the wind that gusts through our open windows and ruffles my hair. *God, you are so good to me.* And I wonder at how powerful grace must be to overrule any residue of displeasure from pressure sores and months in bed.

It's joy, genuine joy, I feel. And yes, maybe Ken has something to do with it, I consider as I watch the wind toss his dark hair. Perhaps he too is a gift from God.

Tents are pitched and a fire is lit. My heart tugs a little, wishing I could help the others set up camp. But I'm not the only one who feels this way, I know. Vicky sits next to me in her wheelchair, and Daddy — the man who once pitched tents everywhere from Mexico to the Yukon — now stands and watches. But his arthritis and my disability don't deter our camping spirit. We decide to gather firewood, and my wheelchair makes a perfect truck for hauling the logs Daddy piles on my lap.

The sun settles behind the west side of the mountains, tinting the lake and trees a dusky mauve. The glow is eerie and golden, and for a moment we become almost as still as the surrounding rocks and trees as we watch the twilight phenomenon from our picnic table.

Ken and Rana set up the Coleman stove, and I turn to Vicky beside me. "What do you think of him?" I say out of the side of my mouth.

"He's a gift . . . a real gift," she says with a sly smile.

Despite my weariness with my confinement during the past months, I am happy when Judy and Mom tuck the heavy down comforter around me in my fold-out bed. How quickly I've forgotten the unpleasant nuisances linked with the idea of "bed." I fight off sleep to listen to the rushing wind in the tops of the ponderosas and watch the moonlight make dancing patterns on the sloping roof of the tent. Someone pumps hissing propane into a lantern, and I can hear Rana and Vicky murmuring in the tent next door. Ken slaps and punches the down of his sleeping bag outside by the fire. Snug, comforting sounds . . .

Ken takes my parents and me fishing on the high mountain lake while Rana and Vicky drive to Mammoth Mountain. He rents two boats — one for my parents and Judy, and one for us — and chains the two together. I'm comfortable in a beach chair wedged in the bow as we drift toward the shady lake edges where Ken tells us the fish are big and fat. We believe him.

He hooks and baits two rods and explains foreign words like "casting" and "reeling" to my mother and father. We laugh. Who cares if we catch anything — we're glad to be together.

Ken prepares a rod for me. "Here," he says, lodging it in my beach chair. "This is for your fish."

"But I didn't cast . . . you did," I protest lightly.

"Yeah, and you won't reel the fish in either. But you're still holding and watching and that makes it yours."

Our boats drift on the wind-rippled lake, and we chat idly and drink sodas. Mother shatters the silence of the lake with a sudden scream and turns her head away from the fighting fish on the end of her line. Ken tells her how to reel it in. She refuses to look but obediently cranks in the line. Ken nets the trout, and we try to conceal our excitement so that some distant fishermen who occasionally look our way will not think we are novices.

I'm designated the official "keeper of the fish." Ken strings the trout by their gills through a metal clothespin that he then snaps to my armsplint. I dangle my hand in the water and watch the captive fish squirm and swim alongside our drifting boat. I feel sorry for them and name each of them, hoping to persuade Ken to release our tribe.

Ken and I notice that my father, who says little and sits with his back turned to us, seems preoccupied. Occasionally, he mumbles and shakes his head. Finally, Ken gingerly steps into the other boat to investigate. In dismay he holds up a tangle of knots looped around the reel. My left-handed father has reeled in his line backward.

Our loud and spontaneous laughter rings across the mountain lake. Poor Ken! Fishing is such a science to him. But he teasingly shakes a finger at Daddy and then proceeds to untangle the mess while the rest of us enjoy the sun and scenery, nearly forgetting our lines in the water.

I keep watching him as nearly an hour passes. He works steadily and patiently, pulling a bit here and looping a line there. Mother insists that he stop and relax, but he is committed to his slow and meticulous task. I'm impressed. I think about the verse, "being found faithful in a few things," only to be given charge over "greater things."[2] . . . Would he show such patience sharing a lifetime with me in a wheelchair?

Later in the morning, after we've caught a "mess" of fish, Ken reaches over me and unhooks the chains linking the two boats. We drift apart, but my parents and Judy hardly notice. They are talking and casting and reeling and already recounting their fish stories.

Ken sits near the stern, slides a paddle from its sleeve, and dips it into the water. His head eclipses the sun, and the rays shine out around him like a golden crown. In the shadows cast by the glow, I can't see his handsome features — only his dark glasses and the white of his smile against his tanned skin. I can tell he is staring at me. I stare back. He cuts an appealing figure in his fishing vest and khaki shorts, the red bandana knotted around his neck echoing the red trim on his gray wool socks and the red laces of his hiking boots.

"I love you, Joni," he says suddenly. He lays the oar across his knees and lets the boat find its own way.

I smile back at him but say nothing.

"Ever since that Young Life banquet a year ago — "

I raise my arm out of the water, dragging the line of fish for him to see.

"Don't change the subject," he says.

I plop my weak arm back into the water. "Well, you know what? . . . I love you too."

Now it's his turn to smile at me and say nothing.

"But it's crazy," I say, looking off into space. "I mean, I love you with no strings attached. Clean. With no conditions." I clumsily swing my arm back and forth and the fish follow obediently, wriggling and flipping their tails. "That's new for me," I say quietly. "I haven't let my heart go many times . . . except for wild and crazy feelings I drummed up toward a friend during the movie. But that was so self-centered.

"But with you, I don't have to feel all consumed, like you are my life and breath. The love I have for you is freer than that." I breathe deeply. "I guess I love you for the right reasons."

As our boat turns through the water, a spectacular view of lofty crags with their shadows in snow looms behind Ken.

"It could work, you know," he says.

I question him with a look.

"I've been watching Judy and Kerbe. I know I can do the things they do for you . . . even the private things I've never seen them help you with."

"You're talking marriage?" I am a little surprised, even alarmed.

"Our life together could be a real ministry for the Lord, Joni." He leans forward and reaches for the toes of my moccasins.

I shake my head cautiously. "I don't know. I need some time."

"You just said you loved me."

"Yes, but marriage is a big step. I've got to be sure. There's my disability and . . . and Joni and Friends and . . . I've been in bed for two months. Maybe I'm not thinking straight — "

"Oh, I get it. Now that you're sitting up, the old 'I'm calling the shots' side of you is coming out. I liked you better when you were flat on your back — less in command, more responsive," he chides.

I'm confused. This is the sort of conversation you dream about having all your life, and suddenly when it's here you stumble as though you've never given marriage a thought. I'm afraid again —

that advice about either marrying or going separate ways. But I can't bear the idea of going separate ways. Must this happen so fast? Be so black and white?

"Look, there's no pressure." Ken reads my mind. "But I'll say this — I know the way you think, and I'm not about to be controlled. I love God and His Word. I can lead. I can make good decisions."

I find myself relaxing in his words. Perhaps it's because deep down I want him to be stronger than me. Maybe that is what irritated me months back — back when I wanted him to be more than just someone who admired me, looked up to me.

Over the next months we give ourselves time to think. I meet Ken's family — his parents, his sister, an aunt and uncle. They treat me a little cautiously at first, but that's understandable. They hardly know me — and I'm in a wheelchair and I'm not Japanese.

All the while I wonder how marriage would work. Our love now, I am finding, is restless by nature, continually searching and probing the depths of our relationship. And to be married would mean that we would not be taken off the front lines of love, but plunged further into the thick of things. Learning to become one. Sacrificing over and over again. Communicating, day in and day out. Not to mention housecleaning. Finding things we could really *do* together. Shopping. Menu planning and cooking. And we'd have to go to bed . . . sometime. And what about children.

Although these are good questions that need to be asked, I don't want a "yes" to Ken to be dependent on finding all the answers. In a way I want it to be a mystery. For how can our love prove to be sacrificial and committed unless it is separate, unattached from anything else that is like it or that has gone before? To have it any other way would be saying yes with strings attached.

Then, one rainy November afternoon he walks into my art studio. He admires the pot of red geraniums I am painting. Red is everywhere — tubes of it, stains on rags, tinted brushes, color tests tacked on the walls, the flowers on the canvas. And he asks me to marry him.

"Yes," I say, and the room glows, honestly glows, with the excitement and dazzle of red.

"Are you nervous?"

"Sure I'm nervous," Ken answers as he pulls the Scrabble game board out of its box. "The whole reason we've come East for Christmas is to get your parents' permission. They've probably been wondering what's been going on between us since summer."

"Isn't that funny?" I get sidetracked. "Here we are in our mid-thirties, asking our parents for permission."

"I hope it's easier with your folks than it was with mine," he says as he shakes the bag of letter tiles. I nod in agreement. "Don't worry though," Ken continues. "I can tell you already have a place in their hearts."

"If only I were Japanese," I joke and then grow serious. "But be prepared. My Mom and Dad think you're the greatest thing coming down the pike, but they're still going to have questions. I'm just glad we're doing this over Scrabble . . . believe me, it'll make the whole conversation, whatever turn it takes, go a lot smoother."

"I'll just let your mother win."

"Hah! You don't know my mother," I warn.

The four of us gather around the end of the dining-room table and draw our letter tiles. Mom goes first. She peers over her glasses, places her tiles on the board and scores high with a seven-letter word. I grin, wondering where in this competitive arena Ken will introduce his big question of the evening.

"Ah . . . Mr. and Mrs. E.," he begins when it's his turn. "Joni and I want to ask you something important."

"Now?" my mother asks. "Aren't you going to put down a word?"

"Well, yes ... eventually, but — "

"Good. Then let's keep it moving," she says, victory in sight. "I've got another good one here." Mother and Dad move their tiles in deep concentration. Ken and I just look at each other.

The evening passes quickly, and my mother, able to concentrate better than the rest, closes the game out easily with a win. But winning is not the only thing on her mind. Neither Mom nor Dad have forgotten the big question.

Ken tells them he would like to marry me. Just hearing him say those words again gives me butterflies. Mother says she knew all along. She can't wait to call Mrs. Tada. Dad has to lean forward and cup his ear, asking Ken to repeat his words.

"Wonderful, wonderful," my mother responds, folding her glasses into their case. "But how do you intend to ... uh ... manage?"

"It won't be easy." Ken and I step on each other's lines.

"I've been thinking about a budget," Ken begins. "Medical costs are up there, but my school gives me good insurance coverage, a dental plan, ah ..."

"Well, that's not what I really meant," Mom interrupts.

"Someone will help me keep house," I add hastily. "With my van, I can do a lot of my own food shopping ... you know, with the help of a clerk or bag boy, whatever. I can use other people's hands to help me prepare and set the table. I've trained ... let's see, four or five different girls to help me out with my morning routine — Ken leaves for work early. And he," I say, flopping my arm on top of Ken's shoulder, "can do my nighttime routine. Getting me undressed and washing my face, taking off legbags, stuff like that ... it only takes a short while."

"You, ah ... ," Mother says hesitantly to Ken, "understand how all that's done?"

Ken blushes. "Not all of it, obviously ... although I've washed Joni's face and brushed her teeth." He beams proudly. "She looks pretty good without make-up." He puts his arm around me and gives a playful squeeze.

My dad breaks in. "I can't speak for you, Ken, but I know that, ah, making, ah — " He nervously motions with his hands.

"Love? You mean making love?" I finish his sentence.

"Yes!" He raps the table. "That's the word."

"Daddy," I say with a wry grin, "you don't have trouble thinking of the word 'sex' when you need it in Scrabble."

"No, Mr. E.'s question is good." Ken gets to the point. "I know that Joni can't move. And she can't feel." He pats my knee. "But there's more to lovemaking than just an act. There's plenty of places that Joni can feel. We can be intimate, tender," he says as he reaches up and strokes the side of my neck with the back of his hand. I'm a little surprised that he's able to put it all into words so well. He's doing a better job than I could.

"I tell you, though ..." Ken shakes his head and rubs his hands on his knees. "There have been some people — really well-meaning — who've suggested that we should go away for a weekend. Give it a try. Experiment," he says with a wave of his hand.

Mother taps her fingers on the table. Daddy leans even further forward to be sure he hears every word.

"But we can't ... we wouldn't do that. Joni's disability doesn't give us an excuse to sin. Bend God's standards. Just because our circumstances are a little unusual doesn't mean we're the exception. God will only bless us if we obey Him, and we want — really want — that most of all."

This is the strength, the moral muscle that I've known all along was there in Ken. Upright in heart. Righteous and good. Wonderfully transparent. Clean clear through. Without guile. This is the depth, the intensity I've been looking for. It is a kind of magnetic power that is anything but animal and everything that is spiritual. And more than ever I realize how much I love him, really love him.

"I'm glad to hear that," Dad says softly.

"But Mr. E.," Ken teases and his eyes twinkle, "when honeymoon time comes, we won't have any trouble figuring out what to do. It's just going to take a little creativity," he says twirling his hand in the air, "a little ... inventiveness." He grins.

"I know who did it," I lean to the right and whisper in Judy's ear.

"I bet you don't," she whispers back.

"Yes I do. It was that guy's mistress," I say, my voice getting a little louder.

"Uh-uh. You're wrong. She was nowhere around when the murder took place —"

"Shh!" Ken frowns and leans away from me on his side of the theater seat.

"I'm sorry," I hoarsely whisper, holding back a chuckle. I turn back to Judy. "Keep it down. . . . Now what were you saying about the murder? I think that the mistress knew all along that . . ."

The Agatha Christie movie concludes, and Judy and I break into an excited discussion before the credits barely start rolling. Ken doesn't join in but silently gathers his sweat shirt and box of popcorn.

"Excuse me, please," he states formally as he steps over our legs to retrieve the wheelchair at the front of the movie theater.

Something's wrong.

After the two of them transfer me into my chair, Judy leaves for the restroom.

"What's the matter?" I keep my voice low as a few people file past us in the aisle. He doesn't say anything but looks down to adjust my feet on the footpedals.

"What's wrong?" I insist again after they pass.

Still he doesn't answer.

Okay. This is it. We're going to have an argument, our first. And here he is — the silent type. I feel myself getting angry.

Judy meets us as we leave the theater, waves good-by and heads for her own car. I'm relieved when she goes. Ken, I hope, is too. We need to get this resolved. We wheel toward the back lot where my van is parked.

I stop before we reach the lot. "I'm not going any further till you tell me what's wrong."

"Okay." Ken folds his arms across his chest. "You were talking during the movie . . . and you didn't stop even after I said something."

"Ken, first I wasn't talking, I was whispering," I say crisply. "Next, nobody could hear us."

"You were disturbing people," Ken accuses.

I look amazed. "That's ridiculous. Nobody could hear us 'cause nobody was around us. The place was nearly empty."

"Look, I had just gotten up to tell those teenagers down in front to put a lid on it, they were making so much noise. And then you and Judy . . ." He begins pacing. "You two go and do the same thing. How can I tell them to be quiet if you're not?"

"We weren't doing the same thing. We were whispering, not . . . not throwing popcorn and making a racket." My voice rises.

"Don't yell at me," Ken orders.

"Yelling? You think this is yelling?" I look at him wide-eyed. "You haven't heard anything yet — "

"Well, I don't yell."

"Well I do!" I wait and then add, "My whole family yells!"

"This is it," he mutters, pacing. "We get engaged and we become different people. I was afraid of this."

"Ken . . ." I try to control my voice. "I'm not a different person. This is who I am."

He stops and looks at me. "Haven't you ever heard of those verses about being angry and sinning not? Letting no unwholesome words come out of your mouth?"

Suddenly I feel trapped. Something ridiculously minor has become incredibly major, and he is pushing his expectations on me.

"Don't go throwing verses at me. Remember, love is supposed to cover a multitude of sins." My eyes narrow. "And I don't think I've even done anything 'multitudinous' here!"

I am ready to bare my fangs when a young couple gets out of their car at the edge of the parking lot.

"Excuse me," the young man says as they approach, smiling, hand-in-hand, "aren't you the lady who draws with her mouth . . . Joanie? We heard you speak at my mother's church once."

Shocked in midsentence, I glance at Ken, paste on a smile, and tell them yes. Before they can ask me questions, I introduce them to "Ken Tada, my fiancé." They look surprised and happy.

Ken weakly extends his hand, musters a smile, and mumbles a few words. His awkward, yet game way of handling the embarrassing encounter touches me. But at the same time I resent him for revealing my stubbornness, my lack of love. Suddenly it occurs to me that "wedded bliss" will be far more rigorous and demanding than I ever dreamed.

As Ken answers questions about our wedding, I meekly wonder if he is still all that excited.

The couple heads for the movie theater. Ken and I remain silent, watching them until they round the corner.

"So, Joni," he begins softly, "what *did* you talk about at his mother's church?"

"Huh?" I look directly at Ken. "Oh . . . yes . . . well, I probably talked about my paralysis helping me become Christlike. You know, being loving . . . self-controlled . . ." I lower my gaze. "Patient . . . without sin . . ."

"And?" he says, taking a step toward me.

"And I still want to get married," I say, smiling up at him, blinking back tears, ". . . if you do."

He gives me a big hug and we meander toward the van.

"You really thought the mistress did it? Want to know something? I thought she did it too," Ken says as he holds on to the armrest of my wheelchair.

I've sat in on bridal showers for so many others; it seems odd that it should be my turn. In my wheelchair, with its dusty gears and squeaky belts, I am slightly out-of-place among the delicately wrapped gifts, fancy paper doilies, and dainty finger sandwiches. But I'm glad that the room is decorated with crepe paper and ribbons, like any other shower.

The gifts are piled around my feet, and the daughters of two friends have the proud honor of opening each one for me. The ladies give me pots and pans, much needed since Kerbe and Judy will be taking so many of their kitchen items with them when they set up their own apartments. That makes me realize I will miss them — a lonely but brief thought in the middle of such joy.

A coffee grinder and mugs. Casserole dishes and an ironing board. Dishtowels and oven mitts.

My young friend struggles to lift a shiny steam iron out of its carton. She has to use two hands to hold it high for everyone to see. "How can you use this, Joni?" she asks honestly.

"The same way I will use those oven mitts."

"How's that?"

"By borrowing someone's hands. Just like I'm borrowing yours to open these gifts."

Her curiosity satisfied, she continues on to the next box wrapped in lacy paper with a huge white bow. Soon she is holding an exquisite, long black satin negligee. As everyone gasps in admiration, I quickly read the card, "With all my love, Vicky

Olivas." I share a knowing smile with Vicky who is sitting at the back of the room with several others in wheelchairs.

After punch and cookies, it is time to say thank you. I gather some thoughts to close our afternoon together.

"When I was a teenager, pulling together my life from a wheelchair, I dreaded the idea of marriage. In fact," I laugh, "I once said in *People* magazine that if I ever loved a man enough to marry him, I hope I'd love him enough to say no."

"A little late for that, Jon," Rana calls from her seat next to Vicky. More laughter.

"Yes . . . well, as you see, perfect love casts out fear,"[3] I respond, building a bridge from light to serious. "Really . . . I think one of my biggest fears back then — this is going to sound silly — was having a bridal shower. I was so afraid of sitting in front of a roomful of girls and not being able to open my own gifts. Unable even to untie the ribbons."

Friends have stopped collecting punch glasses, and several wander in from the kitchen. The room is quiet.

I stare at the carton of crumpled wrapping paper at the foot of my wheelchair. "I was scared if I got an iron, everyone would know that I couldn't use it, not with hands that were paralyzed.

"But perfect love does cast out fear, and I can honestly say I feel that love. From each and every one of you." I glance at Mrs. Tada and Carol, my future sister-in-law. I smile at Vicky. If anyone can understand what I am feeling now, she can.

"And," I add, glancing at the black negligee, "I can love myself. God has made it so . . . whether my hands hold an iron or not. . . . Oh, and by the way, my housekeeper is going to *love* using that iron."

In the weeks before our July wedding, I paint more to quiet my nerves than to meet a publisher's deadline. But the paint and the brushes don't want to do ordinary compositions, and I find myself, in an almost mystical way, designing paintings that are light and airy, with lots of space. My eye enjoys an off-center balance on canvas. It is painting that is distinctly oriental. Japanese.

Ken's parents welcome me warmly into their home. Though very American, they hold on to a few of their Japanese traditions, and we get to know each other better over sukiyaki and sunomono. They tell me childhood stories of Ken and Carol and show me funny photos of Ken — chubby-cheeked and smiling.

They ask questions about my family and are glad to learn that my sister Kathy is flying out early to help me with wedding preparations.

"You and Kathy will really enjoy Grandpa's birthday party next weekend," Mrs. Tada says, clasping her hands together. "In Japan, to be eighty-eight is an honored occasion."

A few days later when Kathy wheels me into Grandpa's home, I am struck by the similarities between him and my own father — his silver white hair, his glasses, and his smile. And they're both short. Grandpa even paints — Japanese birds perched on plum blossom branches, willow trees and chrysanthemums, misty mountains and lakes. He proudly hangs his work for everyone to enjoy, just as my dad does with his paintings. As I wheel through the rooms admiring his work, Grandpa explains his art in Japanese while Mr. Tada translates.

Ken, Kathy, and Carol wheel me down the steps into Grandpa's backyard oriental garden. He walks ahead of us on the neat gravel path that winds through carefully groomed shrubs and exotic plants. Occasionally he stops to describe a certain herb. Although I cannot understand his language, I can understand his pride and joy.

That afternoon I learn more about Grandpa's talents in both calligraphy and poetry as he shows us pages of his beautifully scripted haiku. I smile, thinking of the many poems Daddy has written. I can't wait for the two of them to meet.

During the party I also see the serious side of Ken's family as I hear about the loss of homes, businesses, and property during their confinement in Japanese internment camps during World War II. Ken's father was the mayor of such a camp. He talks about it easily, the past of pain and loss far behind him. We discuss his import-export trade and how he still travels to the Orient to negotiate for other companies. I promise him that next time I will bring copies of my books translated into Japanese.

Mrs. Tada — I'm learning to call her "Mom T" — is a smiling, outgoing lady with the same black hair and striking eyes as her son. She works as a bookkeeper for a large engineering firm but enjoys spending time in her kitchen and garden. I tell her I like to cook, and she promises to pick up some special Japanese staples and kitchen items the next time she drives to Little Tokyo in downtown Los Angeles. She wants to know how to give me a hug. I teach her, and when she embraces me, I realize that she is about the same height as I am in my wheelchair.

Carol, Ken's sister, is a college student, stylish and fun-loving like her brother, with the same dark, athletic good looks. During the party she flips through a fashion magazine, points out several photos of trendy dresses, and asks if we might go shopping together sometime. As she turns several more pages, I notice her glossy red nails against smooth tanned hands. I can tell I will enjoy having her as a sister-in-law.

At the close of the afternoon one of Ken's younger cousins performs a graceful dance dressed in a kimono and holding a fan. Grandpa makes a short speech in Japanese, thanking everyone for coming to celebrate this special traditional birthday. As we leave, I comment to Ken about how wonderfully different our backgrounds are.

That evening Kathy joins the two of us at a local sushi bar to outline last-minute plans for the wedding.

"H'm, tekkamaki . . . sashimi. Now *this* is a cultural experience for you two," Ken says as he rubs his chin, scanning the menu. "Ever tried raw fish, Kathy?"

"Ick! No. And I don't think I want to. . . . Let's see . . ." She examines the second page of her menu. "Aha! Oysters on the half shell. Now that's a Maryland dish for you. How about splitting a dozen with me, Joni?"

"Great. Ken," I say, nudging him, "want to share some?"

"Raw oysters?" He shakes his head in mock disgust. "You've got to be kidding!"

"And raw tuna is better?" I say as I sniff the air. "This place smells like whale breath."

"Maryland crab houses smell better?" Ken teases.

We laugh at the irony. Perhaps our two cultures are not that far apart after all.

"I can't wait for you to see my wedding dress, Kathy. It's so simple and elegant." I talk excitedly as I drive my sister and Kerbe to the bridal shop to help me with the final fitting. "And I'm going to have a wreath of hand-crocheted daisies with lace. It really looks Scandinavian, and I think I should wear my hair up."

July 3, 1982, the date Ken and I have set, is only days away and I am a typical bride-to-be. Excited. Anxious. Nervous.

"Well, you said you wanted this to be like any other wedding," Kathy sighs and smiles. "I'm glad you decided on wearing a long bridal gown. Only how are you going to keep a long dress from getting tangled in your wheels as you move down the aisle?"

"Greg Barshaw's got an answer for that," Kerbe says. "A soft wire netting all around the sides and back of Joni's wheelchair. No way she'll roll over her gown or train."

To get me into the dress, Kathy and Kerbe have to lay me down on the only couch in the shop, near the front entrance. They position a standing screen around the couch for privacy. Moments later, sitting back up in my wheelchair, facing a mirror, I marvel at how beautiful, how elegant I feel in such a gown. It does, however, need to be altered.

The fitting lady, a short woman who speaks unclear English, stands at a distance from me. She nervously winds a long yellow tape measure around her fingers. "I am so sorry. It is impossible." She shakes her head. "I am sorry."

I think she must mean that the gown just will not do. Perhaps, judging from her reaction, it is impossible to alter. Kerbe gathers material around the shoulder seam and asks if it can be taken in.

"No. I have never fitted someone like this." She flings out a hand in the same way one would cast off trash. "I am sorry," she says in a superior tone.

I am shocked and a little breathless. Kathy looks for our saleswoman. I can only stare at the fitting lady in stunned disbelief. The woman who sold me the dress approaches and asks if there is a problem.

"No, it is impossible," the fitting lady repeats. "I have never done anything like this before." She points in my direction, resolute, convinced, and immovable.

"Well, I've never done anything like this before either," I say in a desperate voice. "A wedding is a new thing for me, and you'll just have to try something new yourself," I insist, equally resolute and immovable.

This is not the way to handle the situation, I know. This is not the way we do it in those Joni and Friends workshops. *"For it is God's will that by doing good you should silence the ignorant talk of foolish men."*[4] The verse from 1 Peter flashes in my mind, and I know that I should be building a bridge rather than widening the gap. But this is my wedding, not a lecture in a seminar.

"Wait, please wait." The saleswoman steps in. Her voice is calm and soothing. "Let's work this out," she says gently. She quietly yet firmly addresses the fitting lady and then turns to me to apologize, placing her hand on my shoulder. With her fingers, she lightly lifts the lace on my headwreath and comments on how lovely I look. She kneels by my chair and gathers the extra material, folding the seam under.

"Where do you think we should pin it?" she looks up and asks the fitting lady.

The lady rubs her palms on the sides of her dress and reaches up to pull the tape measure from around her neck. Obediently, she kneels with the saleswoman and begins pulling pins from her wrist band. I watch in wonder as the fitting lady warms to the touch of the sweet, gentle spirit of the saleswoman. Within minutes the situation is defused and a confrontation avoided.

As I'm about to leave, the saleswoman places her hand on the armrest of my wheelchair. "You will look charming on your wedding day," she says. "I am a Christian, and I will be praying for you and your bridegroom that morning."

"Blessed are the peacemakers for they shall be called the children of God." [5]

Kathy and I lie in bed and watch the light of dawn shine on the splendid wedding gown that hangs in front of the bedroom window. Kathy holds my limp hand in hers, and together we softly sing to greet the day. My wedding day!

I have the "peace which passes all understanding." No doubts. No apprehensions. I feel . . . no, I am peacefully certain this is the right choice. Funny. I had the same conviction when I chose to do the movie. And move to California. And start a ministry to disabled people.

But love, pure and strong and deep, is far greater than convictions or decisions about a ministry or a move. Maybe this wonderful peace blooms from the assurance that our love has 20/20 vision. Our hearts haven't rushed ahead of reason.

"For marriage is the contemplation of the love of God in and through another human being" comes to mind — something I read recently, and I wonder what Ken is thinking this morning. I wonder how he slept. Is he nervous? No, probably not. I imagine he's enjoying this same glorious peace and quiet joy.

"Are you going to wear the necklace Ken gave you last night?" Kathy rolls over, leaning on her scrunched pillow, and fingers the delicate heart on the chain around my neck.

"Uh-huh . . . it'll look nice against the lace."

She smiles. "I don't get it. He gives you a dainty little necklace, and you give him a hunky Penn International 50-W fishing reel. Whatever possessed you to give him something so . . . so unromantic?"

I chuckle. "One of his friends in the wedding party gave me good advice: 'Encourage a husband to keep his dreams.' I guess the reel is a symbol of sorts that I want him to do just that." I pause and then make it a pronouncement: "May he always have plenty of time to enjoy fishing."

I am marrying a fisherman. A friend. A brother. A school-teacher. A racquetball player. I recall one of my earlier opinions of him: *A wonderfully ordinary guy.* But he is also extraordinary. And today he will be my husband.

"Yeah, some fishing reel. I hope you like cooking trout and tuna," Kathy laughs, throwing back her covers and jumping out of bed.

How odd to be discussing necklaces and fishing reels and tuna — such ordinary, unremarkable matters — on the morning of the biggest day in my life. But everything this morning seems at once ordinary and extraordinary. Breakfast with my parents, Jay and Rob, Kathy, and Kay, Jay's oldest daughter. Little Earecka, already in her long petticoat, bounds around the house. Jay washes my hair, helps me dress in casual clothes, hangs my gown in the back of the van, and sends me off with Judy while she oversees the rest of the family.

As I drive to the church amid the traffic on Ventura Freeway, I stay in my usual middle lane. But there's nothing usual about the day. "It's my wedding day," I happily shout to the cars speeding by. I wonder how the traffic is for Ken.

At the church my bridesmaids and friends help me dress. I watch in the mirror as they comb my hair and apply my make-up. I watch myself become a bride. I can't get over how calm I am. I don't chatter; I don't giggle. I sit and smile calmly, watching everyone else scurry around to get ready.

When my mother and sisters arrive, people begin taking photographs. Mother stands tall and proud by my chair as we pose for last-minute pictures. She is elegant with her blond hair swept back in a French roll. She lightly touches strands of hair at the back of my neck as she did when I was small.

I wonder how Ken's mom and dad are doing. I hope he's taking a lot of pictures too.

Then, an usher brings word that all the guests are seated and that it is time for us to line up. We move across the deserted grounds to the sanctuary entrance. I'm not wearing armsplints today so it's a little difficult to manage the bouquet of daisies on my lap and steer at the same time.

Jay and Kathy check the flowers in their hair in the reflection in the glass door at the entrance. They smooth their pale blue cotton gowns as they position themselves in line along with Kay and Carol and my friend Betsy.

"I love you, Jon," Jay whispers as she steps into line.

Earecka, my flower girl, twirls in her first long dress, watching the skirt bell. Vicky Olivas sits at one side entrance, in her wheelchair, greeting latecomers who sign the guest book at her side. At the other side entrance, Debbie Stone does the same.

The door cracks open and the majestic organ music stirs us. I catch a glimpse of Steve Estes — my longtime friend now helping officiate at our wedding — standing at the front next to John MacArthur. Still, I sense such extraordinary calm. I've been more nervous speaking in front of churches half this size.

Daddy looks resplendent in a gray morning suit and a Windsor cravat. Usually he's in suspendered Levis and a flannel shirt; I've never seen him dressed so formally. But he seems to be enjoying the look and fit of his suit. He beams proudly at me. His youngest daughter. His namesake. I lean toward his ear and, above the organ music, tell him that I will wheel slowly so he can keep up with me. He gives Rana one of his crutches and holds on to the armrest of my chair for support.

"Nervous?" he asks.

I smile and shake my head no. I feel exquisitely at peace, remarkably calm.

As my last bridesmaid begins her walk up the aisle, I inch my chair closer to the door and peer through the crack to catch a glimpse of Ken at the front. I see Diana. I see friends from the office.

Then, I see him. He waits at attention with hands clasped behind him, tall and stately in his morning suit. But he cranes his neck to look down the aisle. Looking for me.

My face grows hot and my heart pounds. Suddenly, everything is different. I have seen my beloved. The change is so dramatic I nearly step out of myself, wondering in amazement at my response. Joy. Anticipation. An overwhelming longing to be with him.

The music crescendos, and Daddy and I begin our arduous journey up the aisle, his cane clicking and my wheels turning slowly.

How we long for His appearing, I think, oblivious to the rows of family and friends. *When we see Him, we shall be like Him. . . .*[6] I have eyes only for Ken.

Marriage is the contemplation of God through another. . . .

This is how it will be when we see Jesus, I marvel, caught up in the music and the march, the candles, the flowers — all the symbols of two becoming one. There's no way — even with rehearsals and programs, even having attended scores of weddings — there's no way I could have prepared myself for this.

Nothing is like this moment.

Nothing will be like that moment.

Ken carries me over the threshold of the airplane door. The flight attendants direct us to the first row of seats, away from the view of the few other passengers in first class. Honeymooners. It's a silly word. And with all this special treatment — a surprise cake, Hawaiian leis, orange juice served in crystal glasses on a silver tray — everyone on board must know that this is our first full day as a married couple.

I love the privacy of our seats. We snuggle down into their high backs, rub noses, and snicker. Ken lifts the glass of juice to my mouth, sets it down, and twines my fingers in his. We share secrets and tell each other how wonderful last night was.

"We're about ready to begin the movie." A flight attendant bends over me and reaches for the window shade. Ken pushes our seats back, puts the earphones on me, stuffs a pillow between us, and we get ready for the film.

The cabin is darkened and the credits roll. *Whose Life Is It Anyway?* appears on the small screen directly in front of us. Immediately, I recognize it as the movie about a despondent quadriplegic who argues with his family and hospital to let him die. A depressing film, I've heard. Ken and I look at one another. What irony!

An embarrassed stewardess returns to apologize profusely. "And here it is your honeymoon!" she laments in a whisper, trying not to disturb the other passengers.

After she leaves, we grin at each other. Who's despondent

about being paralyzed? It doesn't make any difference to us. We can handle it.

The five-hour flight to Hawaii on the 747 passes quickly. As soon as we arrive at the gate, Rana and Judy come down from their seats in the cabin above to help us off the plane. This is a honeymoon with "extras," but someone needs to teach Ken how to do everything from giving me a bath to getting me dressed. Judy and Rana will stay at a hotel several blocks from ours and, when not serving as Ken's teachers, will enjoy their own vacation.

Outside the airport, we are hit with the heavy wet scent of jasmine and plumeria. The equatorial sun shines bright and hot, and we are glad for a fragrant breeze that lifts both the fronds of palms and our spirits.

Ken checks us into our hotel, tips the bellboy who will take care of our luggage, and immediately wheels me across the street to the white sandy beach. We'll worry about the room later.

What a breathtaking aquamarine the ocean is. The sun makes a highway of dazzling light on the water. Everything seems a collage of pink and aqua and green. Each wave curls perfectly in a crashing tube that stretches for miles down Waikiki Beach. An old pink terra-cotta hotel stands out from among the towering modern ones of steel and concrete. We decide we will eat dinner there.

Ken kicks off his thongs, runs his hands through his hair, clasps them behind his head, yawns and stretches. The tails of his Hawaiian-print shirt flutter in the breeze. Here, more than ever, he looks more Hawaiian than Japanese.

While he strolls out onto the sand, I notice a family of three approaching on the sidewalk. The son wears a South Carolina football jersey, and his parents tote straw hats and bags. As they whisper and disguise their glances, I can tell I've been recognized. Oh, well. No matter.

"I don't believe it. George, look who it is," the woman says, lifting her sunglasses.

"Well, I'll be," George responds, reaching for his camera in his tote bag. "Martha, stand with her, and I'll get a snapshot."

"Well, uh . . . I'd rather . . ." I smile and extend my arm for an introduction, but it seems niceties such as learning names and asking courteous questions are to be overlooked. They probably don't mean to be rude. And I'm used to the scenario. So I make an effort to introduce myself and ask their names. The boy in the football jersey sticks his hands in his pockets and looks away, embarrassed by the hoo-hah his parents are making.

"Oh, honey!" The woman in the brightly colored muumuu reaches around my shoulder and pulls me toward her, squeezing my cheek against hers. "We are just so . . . so thrilled to meet you. I read your book and saw your movie, and my neighbors just aren't going to believe me when we get home," she squeals.

"Hold still," George says as he looks through the viewfinder and waves his hand. "And Junior, get in there."

"Ah . . . please, if you don't mind . . . I, uh, would rather we not take pictures. I'm on my honeymoon," I whisper. "Besides, talking is much nicer than an old photo," I say to soothe the disappointment in their faces.

"You're married?" The lady straightens her arms to hold me at a proud distance. "Why, isn't that wonderful. Who's the lucky fellow?" She looks around for someone who might be my husband. She ignores the dark Asian man who approaches in his Hawaiian-print shirt, shorts, and thongs, and continues to look behind and around him. It occurs to me that they must take Ken for either a local from the beach or my tour guide.

The man and woman appear startled when Ken stops behind me and leans over the back of my wheelchair to give me a hug.

"This is my husband, Ken Tada," I proudly announce.

"Oh . . . yes, well, hello." The woman hikes her tote bag on her shoulder and extends a hand of greeting. Her husband does the same, telling "Mr. Eareckson" that it is nice to meet him.

I quickly steer the conversation back to the family, asking them questions about their home and church. After a few minutes they seem relaxed again. So does Ken. We smile and say good-by.

"Mr. Eareckson!" Ken mutters as he pushes me back across the street to our hotel. "Tell me, do I look Swedish?"

Underneath his wisecrack I sense more hurt than Ken is

willing to admit. As he pushes me to our room, I wonder how he will handle the other people who will say and do the same. As much as I'd like to deny it, I am a public person. And there will be others. Many others. Does Ken really understand that?

I feel protective, defensive of him. I know how people unintentionally put a spotlight on me that casts a long shadow over anyone who stands behind my wheelchair. Will the glare keep people from seeing reality, as it so often does? Will they know my husband has feelings? Will they care?

Like the lights on the movie set, that spotlight confuses the unreal with the real. And I want whatever becomes public about our life to be true and genuine. Yet more importantly, we need a life that is private and personal. Sane and balanced. I don't want Ken behind the chair. I want him next to me . . . out in front of me. And I want everyone to recognize him in that way too.

So the nagging question remains: How will we handle a life that is so public?

Ken unlocks our room and wedges a suitcase to hold the door open while he pushes me through. The bellboy has placed our hanging bags in the closet, our suitcases on the bed and dresser. A late afternoon breeze rustles the curtains by the open door to the balcony. Ken pushes me out on the balcony, and we silently watch the setting sun turn the aquamarine sea into pink glass. The fresh salty air pushes the disturbing thoughts out of my mind. We kiss and tell each other what a wonderful honeymoon this will be.

We go back into the room, and Ken checks out the bathroom, flicks the lights on and off, and sees if the television works. I sit in the middle of the room and watch. He takes off his shirt, throws it on the bed, unlocks his suitcase, and digs for a light sweater.

"Shall we unpack?" I ask after he finishes.

"Sure," Ken says, smacking his hands together. "Do you want your stuff put away?"

"Well . . . just take things out of the hanging bag so they won't wrinkle. I'll get Judy or Rana to unpack the rest when they come over."

Ken unzips the bag and lightly shakes the blouses on their hangers, smoothing any wrinkles. "Okay, I'm done," he says, folding the hanging bag and sticking it on the shelf of the closet. "What's next?"

"You mean . . . for me?"

He nods.

"Well, I'd rather help you unpack. Put things away. Decide what goes where," I say, shrugging my shoulders. "You know . . . like on the bathroom sink. You don't want my creams and cleansers all mixed up with your razor and aftershave."

He waves his hand flippantly. "Ah, I never unpack."

"You don't?" I say uneasily, eyeing the opened suitcase with socks and shorts half spilling out. "But I'd be glad to help . . . plan things out and all."

"Don't worry about it, Jon. It's not help I want," he says, stuffing his socks back in and clicking the suitcase shut. "I just prefer not to unpack when I travel."

Suddenly I want my hands. I want to unpack my husband's sweat shirts and shorts and push his suitcases under the bed and out of sight. I want to stand at the sink and neatly organize our bottles and jars. I want to hang up his shirts and line his shoes in a tidy row at the bottom of the closet.

I don't like the fact that he likes to live out of a suitcase while I like to unpack. And there's nothing I can do about it.

I conceal my frustration, but it bothers me. *Who's despondent about being paralyzed? It doesn't make any difference to us. We can handle it.*

And another nagging question remains: How will we handle our life that is private?

Ken and I lie on the mattress in front of the fireplace with our heads together, the sheets kicked back, and the blanket half on the carpet. Usually our bedroom is the sanctuary we retreat to for idle talk, but tonight, Friday night, we are camped out on the living-room floor to welcome the weekend and celebrate our first fire of winter. My wheelchair is parked in the corner with my sweater and Levis hanging sloppily on its handles, shoes on the footpedals, and corset on the seat cushion. Scruffy makes herself a nest on the crumpled sheet at the foot of our mattress. The television, sound muted, plays images in the background.

Ken holds, straight-armed, an open Bible above us. The track lighting casts a glow as we lie in the shadow of Ephesians.

This is one of those nice rituals we're getting used to after several months of marriage — reading the Bible together before we go to sleep. And the book of Ephesians is becoming something of a ritual too. When single, I used to quickly leaf over the fifth chapter about being married. Now, commands about husbands and wives are searched and studied with newlywed enthusiasm. We are overly zealous, perhaps, wanting to live this new life the right way, fearful of making too many mistakes. So we make each word in each verse a priceless gem to be examined thoroughly, turning it over and over, scrutinizing it from every angle.

"For this reason a man will leave his father and mother and be united to his wife, and the two will become one flesh," Ken reads slowly, emphasizing the part where two become one. "This is a profound mystery,"[7] he concludes.

He plops the open Bible on his chest to give his arms a rest, then reaches behind his head to wad the pillow. "Two will become one," he muses and stares at the ceiling. "Do you feel like one yet?"

"Yes . . . and no," I say cautiously, wondering if this is some sort of test. "If you mean, like it says, in the flesh . . . yes, I do," I say lovingly. But my heart jumps a little, wondering what he means. "Why? Is there a problem with the way we — "

"No. No, it's not that," he says, scrunching the pillow tighter.

"Well, if you mean two people becoming one spiritually, emotionally . . . all those marriage books say it takes time." I pause, listening to the fire crackle. "Maybe that's part of the profound mystery."

Ken scoots up on the mattress and leans his back against the sofa. He closes the Bible and lays it on the cushion behind his shoulder. Reaching down, he pulls the covers over his knees and crosses and uncrosses his feet, making funny little hills and valleys with the blanket.

"I wonder if the wheelchair is supposed to be a help . . . or a hindrance," he says softly.

Startled, I look up at him. "Well, it's supposed to be a help. At least, that's what we figured before we got married," I say. When he doesn't reply, I add, "You know . . . all that stuff about God's power showing up best in weakness?"

He nods. The light from above our heads makes deep shadows on his face, and I have to squint to see his eyes.

"You're finding it hard, aren't you?" I say tenderly.

He shrugs his shoulders, then reaches over and places his palm on my forehead. I move my head back and forth under his hand, enjoying his caress.

"No, everything's fine. It's just . . ." His voice trails off as he kicks the blanket again. "It's just things like waking up to turn you in the middle of the night . . . every night. It's okay now, but I can see that it could get to me in years to come. And even this . . ." He points to our mattress and the fireplace. "We try and do fun things that normal couples do, but none of this can be impromptu . . . totally spontaneous . . . like it would be for everyone else."

I turn away from his eyes and look into the glowing embers. Biting my lip, I try hard not to take his words personally, try to separate myself from the wheelchair sitting in the dark corner.

Ken goes on. "And your nighttime routine is easy enough, but it's hard to think that I will be cleaning out legbags every night for the rest of our lives." He shakes his head.

I'm tempted to snap back at him. This is exactly the sort of ground we covered before we married. Talking over the commitment, the sacrifice. "But, Ken," I say meekly, "consider all those husbands who have to help with three or four children. That's tough too."

"Yes, but kids grow up."

In a way he's right. Who could say before our wedding what our marriage would really be like. And I know all too well that nothing can really prepare a person for dealing with paralysis. I sympathize with his struggle. I'm glad he's honest about it. Even after all these years I'm not totally used to legs and hands that don't work.

"I know," I sigh and look into his eyes pleadingly. "I've lived with it for years now, and I still struggle every once in a while. I wish . . . I really wish I could make it easier for you." This is one of those times when I long to be able to move so I could sit up next to him with my back against the same sofa — facing our problems in life together. But I lie still and paralyzed underneath my half of the blanket.

"And it would be nice if God healed me. Life sure would be easier," I sigh with a smile.

"Healing? I thought you put that to rest long ago."

"Oh, I did. But it's still helpful to voice that down-deep desire to God every once in a while. Let Him know I'm looking for that new body . . . whether in this life or the next."

"I can just picture you folding the laundry," Ken chides.

"Yes, and I'd even stack the towels so only the folds would show," I say proudly.

"Oh, you would?" he says with a sly grin. "Well, maybe you'd also take the trash out for the garbage man."

"No siree. *There* I would draw the line."

We laugh and then I add quietly, "But I really wish I could make it easier, Ken."

He replaces his hand on my forehead. "I know you do. . . . I know." He smiles. We linger that way, listening to the fire, me resting under the warmth of his palm. "Thanks for being strong . . . strong when I'm weak. Maybe what we're experiencing here is two becoming one," he concludes, the burden lifted.

He doesn't need or want answers; he wants me to listen. To say I understand. Ken knows as well as I that, for the meantime, the problems linked to my disability aren't going to go away. But for me to say and really mean that I understand — that seems to divide the burden and multiply the bond.

And that's what I must cling to. Somehow, God will multiply the bond and make us one. *It will take faith — simple faith — to make it happen,* I think as Ken kicks off the blanket and gathers my pillows to turn me on my side for the night. He punches and stuffs the pillow behind my back, coils my drainage tubing, and positions my legs until I am comfortable.

I will not allow myself to believe that our marriage is weakened by the presence of a wheelchair. Even though I cannot toss and turn to settle myself snugly into bed for the night. Even though I can't rub my husband's back when he's tired. Even though what used to be a tidy linen cabinet now serves as a place to stack medicines and catheters, drainage tubes and corsets. Even though I must use other people's hands to prepare dinner and set the table, to fold my husband's underwear and put away his T-shirts . . . The list grows, but I cling tenaciously to promises of God's power showing up best in weakness — and of two becoming one; I dream as I close my eyes against the heat of the fire.

The next day is Saturday, a damp and breezy gray morning. A day for sweat shirts and working in the backyard. Ken offers to lend me his hands for several hours so I can garden. Borrowing other people's hands is not new for me, and I watch as Ken prunes and clips each rosebush, asking me exactly how it should be done.

I find myself mesmerized after a while, gazing in a transfixed way at his hands. I watch the way he turns his wrist for a better angle at the rose stem. His fingers squeeze the clippers and the stem snaps. His knuckles whiten, and little veins furrowing between muscles in his hands bulge with strain as he clips a thicker branch closer to the root. He runs his thumb over the tiny jagged edge of a leaf. He fondles the angry point of a thorn.

A chilly breeze sends the dampness through my sweat shirt. I shiver and circle my wheelchair to the other side of Ken for protection. He straightens to stretch his back. Resting, he reaches out to feel the velvet of a petal between his forefinger and thumb. He stoops and digs in the dirt, getting his nails filthy, and seems to take pleasure in rubbing the soil in his palms, breaking up any clumps.

An odd feeling begins to envelop me. I have the strangest impression that his hands are mine. I can almost feel the dirt. The rubber-handled clippers. The touch of a thorn and rose. I want to tell Ken what I am experiencing but am afraid to break the spell. This is so . . . so vicarious. His abilities, right now, at this moment, are mine, and I have the wonderful sensation that we truly are one at last.

How odd that God should use my weakness, my inability, to bring us a greater sense of unity. Of oneness. This must be what faith does.

It is a profound mystery.

Ken places his fork and knife on the plate and leans toward me to whisper,
"Do you want me to put the coffee on now?"

"It's all taken care of," I whisper back, glancing around the dining-room table at our guests. "I had Rana put the coffee maker on automatic."

This is new for me. I've never had to organize quite like this before. Planning menus. Choosing table linens. Timing everything to go in and out of the oven or on and off the stove, might seem simple to some, but I've used the hands of three different people at three different times today.

"Great lamb, Joni," Greg comments.

"Yeah, didn't she do a super job?" Ken says as he reaches for the meat platter. "My wife's a good cook." He takes another slice of lamb and then ladles a spoonful of mint sauce on top.

"Really? I'm glad you like it. It's a favorite recipe." My cheeks feel a little flushed. Not with embarrassment, but with pride. Although every person at the table knows that I didn't slice the garlic or rub the spices into the meat or place it on a rack in the oven, they all acknowledge that I cooked the meal.

And most importantly, Ken is proud. *"My wife's a good cook."* I savor the taste of his words.

After dinner our guests join in to clear the table and stack the dishes. I don't mind. In fact, I'm glad they feel comfortable enough to make themselves at home. And it gives Ken some help that I can't give.

Oh, I do so love being his wife. And this whole journey of two becoming one is what I enjoy most. It's an adventure. The path that we travel in a wheelchair, though, is sometimes covered with thin ice. But so far we haven't fallen flat. My disability hasn't made the journey arduous. I not only love Ken, I'm in love with him.

We sit around the table, lingering over custard pie, coffee, and small talk. Ken leans on his elbow and pokes his crust with a fork, telling Greg and Nancy some of his favorite stories about our new life together. Finally, though, Greg rises and stretches, saying that it's late and they should leave.

The front door clicks shut behind Ken as he walks out to the car with Greg and Nancy. I wheel to the kitchen to flick on the outside lights for them. Then I turn my wheelchair in a tight circle away from the wall switch and carefully bulldoze aside one of the dining-room chairs so I can reach the table. In a clumsy effort to help Ken with cleaning up, I lean forward, straining to wedge my arm behind several coffee cups and dessert plates. As I gingerly slide the dishes toward the edge of the table, my arm suddenly spasms. The dishes crash to the floor, and the forks clatter, the coffee and cream spilling on our oriental rug.

"Drat!" I grimace. My pants leg is soaked and a puddle of cream pools on my footpedal and drips on the rug. I cannot even wheel away from the mess for fear of picking up splinters and slivers of shattered china in my wheels and tracking the debris over the floor. So I sit. Frustrated and near tears, I make stupid wishes about being a paraplegic. Then, at least, I could use my hands.

I knew this evening was too good to be true, I bemoan. Our friends are barely out of the driveway and I've ruined everything. And poor Ken. He'll not only have to clean dishes, but me and this mess too. And I can't even help.

I will not allow myself to believe that our marriage is weakened by the presence of a wheelchair. My thoughts come back to haunt me. I know — I've reminded Ken — that God's power shows up best in weakness, but now I'm too weak to even pray for emotional strength.

The front door jars open. "Hey, wasn't this fun?" Ken calls

from the hallway. He enters the room and abruptly stops. "Wh–what?"

I wait, my stomach knotting.

He laughs. "What in the world . . . ?" He bends and picks up a broken dish. "Here," he says, rising, "let me get a dishcloth."

"I . . . I thought I'd be able to help," I stammer.

"Help?" he says, standing at the kitchen sink, waiting for the water to warm up. He adds, "It's not your job to clean up, Jon. You did enough making dinner."

I watch him in silence as he stoops to wipe the rug and floor. He refolds the cloth and swipes the crumbs off my pants leg, lifting my foot to dab the cream off the footpedal.

"It means a lot that you liked tonight . . . you know, the dinner and all," I say quietly.

He looks up. "Joni, I told you, it was great."

"No, I mean that I'm glad that you really thought . . . uh, thought that —"

" — that you actually made the meal?" he asks, his hand on my knee.

I smile.

He laughs again, and a wave of relief washes over me. I am weak but he is strong. He has lifted the burden, and I suddenly remember another time when I had done the same for him. With just a word, a smile . . . we bear each other's burdens and multiply more of those bonds.

Here I am, just like any other homemaker, I think to myself while watching the box boy load my groceries into the van. I move my wheelchair aside to allow a woman with a brimming supermarket cart to go to her car. She smiles as she passes. She carries a baby strapped to her chest in a kangaroo pouch. With one hand she handles the cart and with the other a toddler who insists on grabbing for grapes that spill over the bag. I smile. She and I have something in common: people might ask us both, "How do you ever manage?"

I notice a slogan on the license-plate holder of her station wagon. *Love is a daily decision.* I tell Ken about it when I get home.

He shrugs his shoulders and continues rummaging through the bags, asking if I got his favorite cookies.

I say no and ask if he brought in the mail. He mumbles and thumbs in the direction of the living room. I wheel to the sofa table, push a few letters around, and spot a third notice on a bill. I call back into the kitchen, asking if he's taken care of it yet.

"No," he says, as he walks to the living-room door with an opened box of crackers in his hands. He suddenly remembers that a letter came today from my mother. "It was a nice note," he says and walks over to the pile of mail and begins to sort through it one by one. No letter. He murmurs that it must be somewhere.

I wheel back into the kitchen to take a look at the casserole in the oven. No casserole. My voice has an edge when I ask why he didn't put dinner in the oven.

"What dinner?" he asks. There was no casserole thawing on

the kitchen sink when he came home. Oh, bother. I forgot to remind my attendant to take it out of the freezer this morning. I sound exasperated when I ask if he'd mind leftovers. He sighs, says that's fine, and grabs another handful of crackers from the box tucked under his arm. He opens the dry-goods cupboard and shuffles cans and jars around looking for peanuts.

He'll have to prepare dinner, I think to myself and decide that I better not push the point of crackers and peanuts.

He opens the refrigerator door and places several bowls of food on the counter. I suggest some ideas of warming up the leftovers, but he sends out a silent signal that he would rather do it himself. I leave him alone and head back toward the living room to look further for my mother's letter. As I pass, I spy it open on one of the kitchen chairs under the table.

"What's it doing *here?*" I mutter. I know Ken hears me.

"What's that?" he says with a hint of challenge.

"The mail. I wish we could decide on one place to put it."

The refrigerator door slams. "It's *always* on the sofa table, Joni."

"Well I *always* find it slopped on a chair or thrown on top of the medical cupboard or . . ." My words fade away. I've made my point.

"Are you in a bad mood or something?"

"No. Why, are you?" I snap.

Suddenly we are reading a bad script, speaking words that are poised, ready to strike and hurt. Why, he asks, don't I use my own razors. Why, I ask, does he use my good eyebrow tweezers to pick fleas off Scruffy. Each of us checks off a list of negatives, and the quarrel grows loud and grotesque, out of proportion and a little insane. I slam my wheelchair on fast forward and skim his toes as I pass him.

Dinner is forgotten, at least for a while. Fuming, I wish I could get out of the house and into my van, but I'd have to ask him to open the door to the garage. I don't want to ask him to do anything for me.

Instead, I park my wheelchair by the sliding glass door in the living room and stare blankly out at the backyard. Pots clunk on the counter and cupboard doors bang shut. Scruffy sits by the footpedal of my wheelchair, looking up at me with bewildered eyes. I feel my face losing the glowing red heat of the quarrel, and numb feelings of hopelessness fill the moments. I don't think. I just feel . . . despondent.

And paralyzed. I have never felt so paralyzed.

I drop my gaze to my motionless legs. I imagine myself stomping out the front door or standing up to him with an accusing finger for every pointed word I have to say. I picture myself gathering up the mail and throwing it defiantly in the waste can or banging pots and kicking cupboard doors shut, all in the name of leftovers.

But I cannot do any of these things — will never be able to do them.

I feel trapped. By Ken. And by God.

An hour passes, and the tactical satisfaction of sitting silently in front of the glass door also passes. I sense Ken enter the living room behind me. I decide that I shall speak soon if he doesn't, but he breaks the silence first.

"I think this is a lot more than we figured on."

"So what do you want to do about it?" When he doesn't answer, I turn my wheelchair around to face him. He sits slumped on the couch, arms folded, his gaze frozen on the empty fireplace as if wishing he were elsewhere too.

"I don't know. I don't know if it's me or you or your wheelchair. I just know I can't live like this. I can't stand it when you come on with that strong-willed tone of yours." I try to interrupt, but he continues. "And I know . . . I know," he says, holding his hand out like a cop stopping traffic, "it's because you're a survivor, a . . . a fighter. The wheelchair has made you that way." He pauses. "But I just can't handle you like that."

Since we're being honest, I peel back a layer of my heart and tell him the truth for the moment. "Well, I don't mean this to sound hurtful, but . . . I don't like you either. I feel like every time the slightest little conflict surfaces, you back off, and I'm the one who's supposed to walk on eggshells around the house. I can't live like that."

He looks up, not at all surprised with my confession. "Well, so we don't like each other," he says in a matter-of-fact way. We sit there in stubborn silence. I am out in deep and unknown waters, far beyond the shallows of my own security. We are in the dangerous and unpredictable depths of a real marital conflict.

"Maybe the only thing to do now is pray," he offers after a while.

I know he's right, but I don't want to pray for him. I'm ashamed I feel that way.

"I don't know what to pray for," he adds. "Let's pray about . . . oh, what the heck, I don't know . . . whatever." He lowers his voice as well as his head, sliding his hands through his hair.

He mumbles a few well-worn phrases, mechanically saying things about God and His greatness and goodness and holiness and mercy. But as I listen, I hear his heart begin to soften through his words. The pace of his prayer slows, and his quiet voice wrenches and pleads as he finishes.

My prayer begins just as hollow sounding as his — I'm reluctant to give way any more than is necessary, mouthing phrases I don't feel and pulling back from the full intensity of the moment. But I know prayer is the right way, and I have faith enough to doubt and yet still believe. After several moments, I too sense my heart beginning to melt. In a broken way I ask for mercy. Mercy for me, a sinner who jealously guards against the irresponsible use of my eyebrow tweezers. And mercy for Ken, who's just doing his best, just trying to make his way.

Ken prays again, and I find myself listening in as if hiding behind a confessional curtain, wondering at the way he exposes his heart, naked and bleeding, in prayer. Tears begin to well. It seems such a private, sacred moment. And as Ken continues to labor in his prayer, his hands tightly clasped, I have an overwhelming desire to quit praying and reach out to embrace him.

Within moments he abruptly stops, looks up and takes a deep breath with his hands on his chest. "I can't believe this. A load of concrete is off of me. I feel so . . . so light."

"That's amazing," I tell him. "And just seconds ago I felt the same peace. And contentment." I look at him with understanding eyes. Without thinking I utter those words, "I love you."

Ken rises and steps around the coffee table, his arms outstretched. He leans down and embraces me, burying his head into my shoulder. He holds me tightly. I'm nearly breathless.

We remember a verse: "No temptation has seized you except what is common to man. And God is faithful; he will not let you be tempted beyond what you can bear. But when you are tempted, he will also provide a way out so that you can stand up under it."[8] Our problems are not all that extraordinary, even with a severe disability. And our problems won't go away. But once again, grace and prayer — words that can sound so ethereal and esoteric — find substance and meaning through those very problems.

And we feel a sense of wonder at how strong Ken is when I am weak. At how weak Ken is when I am strong.

And how God, with His strength, keeps us both from falling from grace.

Jesus learned obedience from the things that He suffered. And Ken and I, servants no greater than our Master, learn to do the same. This is the gristmill of our marriage. And yet what peaceful fruit it yields. Ken and I are growing. Individually, yes. Together, so much more.

The heavy hand of heartache lays us low when we disobey. But we learn from suffering. My . . . that is, *our* wheelchair, this strange and oftentimes unwelcomed addition to our life together, makes us trust. Teaches us to obey. And we find joy, fresh and invigorating, each day.

We also find we have a message. Joni and Friends sends us to Poland where we speak before churches and give Christ's gospel to disabled people at rehabilitation centers. My books are read there. The film in Polish is shown there. But who am I . . . who are we . . . to inspire or encourage others who must suffer so much more than we do? Ken and I carefully study maps, learning the names of strange-sounding places like Katowice or Wroclaw. We also carefully study what we should say.

Behind a flimsy wooden screen that separates us from a noisy and packed church, Ken, with his strong and dark hands, grasps my lifeless fingers. We plead together in prayer that the Spirit will speak through us, empty vessels for His use.

I peek out from around the screen and peer into the faces of the people of Poland. Farmers with their families. Steelworkers and miners. Little boys who tug at each other and bump one another's shoulders. Young women with brightly colored kerchiefs, spots of blue and red and yellow dotted throughout a crowd dressed mostly in heavy dark coats and sweaters.

Two old women squeeze together on the front pew, their heads thinly framed in tight black scarves. Their faces are lined and tired, yet full rosy cheeks and blue eyes that sparkle tell us they enjoy their lives, hard though they may be. They look expectantly, yet subserviently, at their pastor as do so many others who are standing, crowded in the middle or side aisles. Everyone is listening to him make introductory remarks.

I can't understand why the church is so noisy, observing that no one is talking. Then it occurs to me that the din is from hundreds of coats and scarves and shoes and canes and crutches crowding and rustling against one another. The cold plaster walls of the church echo such sounds off the high wooden ceiling. It is a chilly night, yet the air is tight and hot and humid — and charged.

A young man, who I guess has multiple sclerosis, sits humped over in his pea jacket, his hands twisting a handkerchief. His wheelchair is old, the drab green leather torn. Its wheels are different sizes, as though he has pieced together mismatching parts, perhaps cannibalizing footpedals and armrests from other, older wheelchairs. My heart goes out to him, and I wonder if he will ask me about some rumors he has heard of wondrous medical cures in the West. Perhaps that's why he twists his scarf, anxious for hope and a chance to talk with someone who might hold some secret answers.

The bright scrubbed face of a young girl whose lips, full and naturally pink, are parted in a mild and gentle smile. Her eyes glow. I'm sure she knows Jesus. She sits in a molded orange plastic chair someone has provided at the end of the first pew and leans on a black cane. Spindly thin calves encased in old leg braces and 1940s shoes tell me she may have had polio.

I look down at my own wheelchair, each aluminum spoke of my wheels polished and clean. I look at my black seat cushion, a $250 price tag in the West. I have already met many disabled people in Poland who sit on couch cushions or doubled-up feather pillows. Or no cushions at all. I'm glad that I have worn a very plain wool sweater and that my hair is styled simply. I vigorously rub my cheek on my sweater sleeve to scrub off any trace of blusher. Ken guesses what I am thinking, reaches around my neck and tilts my head back and kisses me reassuringly.

He wheels me onto the platform and parks my chair next to the woman who will translate our message. The noise in the church increases as people slide forward in their seats or shoulder in front of one another to get a better view. Ken and I trade shy, nervous smiles with the congregation.

My message is about trusting and obeying. I had planned to share the story of the thoroughbred hunter I trained in show jumping as a teenager. Through my horse I have often drawn parallels between the absolute trust and confidence he showed me, his master, and the sort of unchallenged and abandoned trust and obedience God expects from us. But that story won't work here. The only horses I've seen in Poland are plowing fields or pulling carts. So I make up a story about their horses, obediently plowing the straight and narrow, plodding steadily under a heavy yoke. The farmers seem happy, surprised even, that I know the language of their earth. But I'm more happy that they so readily grasp the point — to trust and obey. The farmers, who handle harnesses and horses every day, also learn something new from a girl in a wheelchair.

"So then, those of you who suffer according to the will of God, commit yourself to your faithful Creator and continue to do good,"[9] I sum up. "Committing yourself to God is trusting Him ... continuing to do good is obeying Him," I say, my eyes making contact with the wizened old women who sit nodding in the front pew and with the black liquid eyes of the young handicapped girl who smiles back at me with confidence and hope. As I speak, I think about the struggles she must face here in Eastern Europe and how her faith, a gentle and fragrant offering to God, contrasts with the oppression all around her. In many ways she is a prisoner. Yet her confident gaze, her hopeful smile, even the way she leans forward on her cane tell me she is far more free than many I know in the West.

Ken comes back and joins me on the platform, and we talk about trusting and obeying in our marriage. We explain how the disability has become a weakness about which to boast, for then God's power rests on us.

Oh, but they mustn't think I am extraordinary or heroic. Me, this Westerner with wings on her wheelchair, able to smile and speak and write and paint and sing. We are by no means heroic, Ken and I. Marriage has made us face up to every hidden, disguised little weakness, and we know too well who we really are. We are sinners — thankfully, saved by grace. And that, appropriately, closes our message.

Nothing extraordinary or heroic happens this evening in church. But what does happen is a very ordinary, miraculous work of the Holy Spirit. The meeting ends, but people stay to pray and talk. The young man with multiple sclerosis seeks more of a cure for his despondency than his disability.

Ken kneels beside the wheelchair of a boy and draws him out with simple questions through the aid of a friend who speaks Polish. My strong husband touches the boy's fragile, thin arm, and he throws back his head and grins. This is so like Ken, taking time to open himself to another who hurts, sharing healing through his words and his smile.

The young girl with the cane hobbles up to me and says that she always knew, always felt that we were very much alike, very much one in the Spirit of Christ. I clumsily lift my arm in a welcoming gesture. She props her cane against my chair, and we embrace, two believers from different worlds.

As the girl holds me tightly in her arms, I watch Ken move to the next boy in a wheelchair. I picture moments when he and I have touched and embraced. I think about lavishing my life on him — pouring myself into him, just one other person. Yes, perhaps I would like to think of myself as having a great impact on the world, touching and influencing thousands of lives. But that thought is balanced by the realization that there are times when I do not even adequately touch Ken's life, the person closest to me. It is a humbling thought, and I feel tremendous gratitude for my husband as I watch him turn and greet some of the farmers.

The young girl straightens and dabs her eyes with her kerchief. She tells me how much my book has meant to her and then steps back to allow others to come forward. As her eyes continue to hold mine, I remember that it is not a movie or a ministry that makes my mark in eternity. It is not a book — or many books. It is not even the chance to travel so many thousands of miles from home to talk about Jesus. For this girl — living within limits I can hardly imagine, coming from a culture so strange and different — this girl and I approach God's throne in the same manner. Jesus asks the same of both of us.

Whether single or married, in plenty or in want, we must both trust. We must obey.

Everywhere we go in Poland people give us flowers — fresh, thick bouquets of friesians and sweet pea, tulips and gladiola in full bloom in our drab hotel rooms.

But how odd it is to see these same flowers swishing in the wind. Here. Here in Auschwitz. Even though the grounds of this death camp are so very tidy, delicate wisps of wildflowers crop up here and there, around the bases of brick buildings and trunks of trees. We wonder if the government, which operates a museum here, has sown wildflower seeds to brighten this horrible, depressing place.

I notice a row of lovely rose bushes planted just yards away from the gruesome gas chambers. I ask our guide about the roses, and he is quick to point out that where flowers are now was once hard, naked clay, every blade of grass picked clean by starving prisoners.

Bare bricks and barbed wire . . . storehouses of eyeglasses and hair and gold teeth, canes and crutches, shoes, hearing aids . . . stacks of yellowed and dusty record books, neatly tabulated numberless names . . . gallows and guard towers . . . even the ominous chimneys and the ovens — all these things I've always associated with Nazi death camps are here. And I shiver, not so much from the cold as from the thought that people handicapped like me were the first to be exterminated, labeled as "useless bread gobblers."

But even this thought is not entirely new.

It's the flowers. The flowers are something I didn't expect. And for that reason, their out-of-placeness touches me as nothing else.

We journey the short distance from Auschwitz to Birkenau. Here, trainloads of Jews and dissidents were emptied out into the freezing night to face the machine guns of powerful and insane men. Children were gun-butted one way; their mothers herded the other. Men were separated into groups of the old and young. But virtually all of them, millions of them, ended up in one place — the incinerator, now crumbled and overgrown at the end of the camp.

Nothing stands in this camp. Our guide explains that what appear to be orderly rows of heaps of brick were once the smoke stacks of wooden barracks. Nothing remains of the guard towers. Even the train tracks and railroad ties are rotted and uprooted.

But light, airy little field daisies carpet the acres, swaying in wave upon wave.

"What are you thinking?" Ken asks, stooping to pluck a wildflower.

"I was thinking of Tante Corrie . . . Corrie ten Boom," I finally answer. "She was in a place not unlike this." I nod toward the field of ghosts. "By all accounts, she should have died forty years ago in that concentration camp," I sigh.

Ken shakes his head in wonder. "Who would have thought she would leave that awful place. At fifty years of age," he marvels, his eyes fastened on the crumbled incinerators just yards away. "And then to start a whole new ministry."

I recall Tante Corrie's recent funeral at a small suburban cemetery a few miles south of Los Angeles. It was the flowers that impressed me that day too. No hothouse blooms stuck in styrofoam cut-out shapes of hearts or crosses or doves. No white satin banners with gold-sprinkled messages of sympathy. Instead, there were vases — tens of vases — of freshly cut tulips of yellow and red. Bouquets of dewy white carnations and bunches of heavy red roses someone had clipped from Corrie's backyard.

The casket was closed. The music was Bach. The eulogies were glowing but understated. The only extravagance was the profusion of flowers, and the little stone chapel was filled with a sweet fragrance.

Now I sit in silence in this vast field, memories of Corrie stirring my thoughts. The only things that move are the wind and the daisies. It is at once striking and poignant. For Corrie, who came out of the pit of this hell, would be the first to say that the suffering in this place confronted her with the reality of the love or hate in her own heart. The confinement of her lonely cell attacked her own vanity and lonely pride. The crushing needs of her fellow prisoners constantly exposed her own need to give and share. She could not blame. She could only forgive.

I drop my gaze to the daisies Ken has tucked into the straps of my arm splints. A knowing smile crosses my lips. I would be the first to say that my wheelchair confronts me daily with the love or hate in my own heart. It attacks my pride and constantly exposes my need to give to others who suffer. I have no one to blame for my circumstances.

I glance at Ken who sits beside me in the grass. God has placed us together to have and to hold. To build up. To encourage. To love. Our marriage tirelessly exposes my need . . . our need to give and share and to cast aside blame.

I recall another memory of Corrie and flowers: the evening at that convention when, amid the applause of thousands, she lifted her bouquet of roses toward heaven. She would be the first to say that books on a bestseller list mean nothing — except that lives are changed through them. She would say that a first-run major motion picture of her life was not worth the accolades — except that people were helped through it. Even a ministry that took her all over the world with opportunities to speak and meet headlining names in evangelical circles — even that, she would say, only counts in the Kingdom as far as it serves Christ.

And I would say the same. In both my public ministry and my private life with Ken, God constantly asks me to uncover my face. But that is my joyous choice: to ask Him to chasten and purify and melt any resistance to change I might secretly hold on to.

I smile. In fact, I throw my head back and laugh out loud. And

I tell Ken of the time I first met that remarkable woman years ago when we were both attending a convention where our new books were being presented. Corrie approached from down the long red-carpeted hallway of a hotel. People were all about and many sought her attention. But she strode directly toward me, hiked her cane on her elbow, reached for my hand with those strong hands that all survivors have, and announced in her thick Dutch accent, "One day, my friend, we will be dancing together in heaven because of the Lord Jesus."

And today I can laugh and rejoice because Corrie is dancing now. Over the Devil and over this place.

And once changed, we shall join her.

Epilogue

"Whoever tries to keep his life will lose it, and whoever loses his life will preserve it."

Luke 17:33

It is another month, another year. Ten years since the movie. If asked, I would say that I have found who I am. A prisoner of Christ. Free in Christ. I know where I'm going.

The changes in my journey keep unfolding like the petals of one of those huge pink roses from the bush near our bedroom window. Every once in a while that line from the song in the movie rings true for me: "Each mile I put between the past and the future in Your hand, I learn more of Your providence and I find out who I am."

Who I am — really am — keeps changing. But in a nice sort of way. A movie and a marriage, not to mention a ministry to disabled people, have taught me that in losing my life — trusting, obeying, submitting — I am finding it. Like that rose, I am a bud being "transformed from glory to glory."

It hits me especially this evening how much everything has changed. We sit in the back of a crowded school auditorium in Montreal, Canada. My mother has joined Judy and me on this trip, and the three of us watch, without the benefit of a translator, a French version of the movie *Joni*.

The movie. I have nearly forgotten those wrenching times of fits and starts in my walk with Christ. Putting on masks and painfully ripping them off as though they were stuck to me with adhesive. My discontent and restlessness during that film taught me never to be surprised by my sin. And there will always be new and painful adjustments, even though by the grace of God I have fully accepted my wheelchair.

The movie went on to grow in its own way. We still hear — years later — reports on showings around the world and how through its message tens of thousands of people have stepped into the Kingdom of Christ. I feel humbled and warmed at that. This strip of celluloid with its transparent images has a life of its own.

As I watch, I hear the familiar actors and actresses saying words that make no sense to my American ears. But the images are intimate, and I study the pretty actress in the blue bathing suit as her brown hands grasp the edge of the raft, and in one graceful motion she fluidly lifts her body out of the water. Her knees bend, and she pitches forward in an awkward dive, her body slicing into the surface of the water. She is under.

But I have come up and out. I can tell. Nothing about this scene jars me. It is, after all, a movie about a seventeen-year-old girl who long ago and far away fell into the water. And fell into a whole new life.

I look at my mother who still is gripped by these scenes. Yet she has changed. Tears no longer stain her face when she thinks of my wheelchair. My dear dad, too old and frail to make this special trip to Montreal with us, has changed also. We will telephone him in Maryland tonight from our motel-room phone, but I know how bad his hearing has gotten — he will barely understand us. Mom and I will call Jay and Rob and talk to Earecka — she is learning so many new grown-up words. Then we will call Ken back in California. Oh, how I miss him when he is not able to travel with me.

"Each mile I put between the past and the . . . future . . ."

The future. Nothing about the future jars me either. I used to have this idea that God was leading me to some particular end in this life, some desired goal. I'd get so excited, so anxious, I would barely pay attention to the present moment.

But I'm finding out more and more that reaching a particular earthly goal is merely incidental. It is trusting and obeying the Lord Jesus Christ in the mile of the journey right now that counts.

I close my eyes and think about this moment around me. There is a girl in a wheelchair at the end of the row in front of us.

There is a teenager sitting directly ahead, her boyfriend sensuously rubbing her back and neck as she squirms. I must make certain to talk with them. An elderly couple sits in folded chairs at the other end of our row. I hope they don't rush away. This is the moment — and perhaps these are the people who, by the Spirit of Christ, will be changed tonight.

I keep my eyes closed and listen to the movie in French. If I were to open them I could tell, line for line, what the characters are saying. They represent a family and a small group of friends just trying, with God's grace, to get on with their lives. To find out who they are and where they fit in the Kingdom.

It is just an old, old story of people losing their lives only to find them. New characters have been added — Ken and the Tada family, Vicky and Rana, Judy and Sam, and many others. There are some different locations besides the Maryland farm — places like California and Poland and Montreal.

But the journey continues. And it is still a drama of choices and changes for us all.

NOTES

The Movie

1. 1 Corinthians 10:12 NASB.
2. Ephesians 4:17–19.
3. Romans 12:3.
4. "Journey's End" by Rob Tregenza. Used by permission.
5. Isaiah 40:31 KJV.
6. The quotes are from Dr. Martyn Lloyd-Jones, *Studies in the Sermon on the Mount* (Grand Rapids, Mich.: Wm. B. Eerdmans, 1971), 62.
7. 1 Corinthians 15:39–40, 48, 50.
8. James 4:8–10.
9. Arthur Bennet, *Valley of Vision* (Glasgow: Banner of Truth, 1983), 187.

The Ministry

1. John 19:28, paraphrased.
2. Matthew 25:35, 40.
3. 2 Corinthians 1:9.
4. James 2:15.
5. Mark 2:3–5.
6. Matthew 16:17 RSV.
7. 1 Corinthians 1:27.
8. Ephesians 6:13.
9. Ephesians 6:13, 16.
10. Ephesians 6:12.

11. "When Pretty Things Get Broken" by Joni Eareckson Tada. Used by permission.

12. Colossians 2:6–7.

13. "Joni's Waltz" by Nancy Honeytree. Used by permission.

14. 2 Corinthians 10:5.

Our Marriage

1. 1 John 4:19.
2. Matthew 25:21, paraphrased.
3. 1 John 4:18 RSV.
4. 1 Peter 2:15.
5. Matthew 5:9 KJV.
.6. 2 Timothy 4:8 and 1 John 3:2, paraphrased.
7. Ephesians 3:31–32.
8. 1 Corinthians 10:13.
9. 1 Peter 4:19, paraphrased.